Seducing the French

Seducing the French

The Dilemma of Americanization

Richard F. Kuisel

UNIVERSITY OF CALIFORNIA PRESS

Berkeley / Los Angeles / London

Contents

Preface

"Great Britain is an island, France the cape of a continent, America another world," Charles de Gaulle once observed.[1] The nation's most celebrated modern statesman aptly voiced the common Gallic opinion that America was more than different. It was something new and momentous, but not necessarily admirable.

Among Western European nations France has been known for its anti-Americanism. Recently, in contrast, it has drawn equal notice for its fascination with America and American material and cultural products. Now the American way has apparently seduced the French. Curiosity as to why the French once perceived America so harshly and later seemed to succumb to the American way of life is a natural response for an American historian who has studied and lived in France. Attempting to answer the question led me to realize that profound historical issues are involved. For the answer depends on a particular French understanding of America. The French response to America in the twentieth century derives, in large measure, from an assumption that the New World is a social model of the future. Thus investigating Gallic attitudes toward America and discovering the layers of meaning and how they have changed led me to understand how French people think and feel about themselves, their identity, and the process of modernization. Examining the Gallic response to America gave me a way to comprehend French perceptions of how modernity endangered "Frenchness." It also revealed ways to explain the fundamental socioeconomic and cultural changes of the postwar years or what has been called the "new French Revolution."

My aim is not a comprehensive examination of all the ways America touched postwar France. I make no effort to investigate how America may, or may not have, influenced such fields as education, science, music, or film. Such a study, for the present, is an impossible task, a project too vast and diffuse. While a comprehensive survey might give us more to think about, it would only marginally advance our conception of French struggles with modernity. For we need to understand not only how the French assessed the American social model, but also why they perceived America as they did and how they actually reacted to what came to be called the "American challenge." Answering the "why" means learning about what, according to the French, were the stakes of the game. Equally important is deciphering the various ways the French responded—resistance, selective imitation, adaptation, and acceptance—and how these responses changed during the postwar period. Knowing how and why they reacted to America helps us understand how France became modern or "Americanized" and yet remained French. Or, put differently, understanding the French response tells us how and why France moved along a path parallel to, yet different from, that taken by the United States.

My approach to the problem is to abandon any pretense of comprehensiveness and to select several encounters between the two societies in which the issue of modernity was paramount. Each encounter raises a different aspect of Americanization, for example, in the arrival of American consumer products like Coca-Cola, dollar investments, or mass culture; and each encounter elicits the response of different strata of French society. In some instances the protagonists will be politicians and government officials. In other instances they will be businessmen and trade unionists. In still other encounters they are the denizens of St-Germain-des-Prés, the Parisian intelligentsia. And in some cases we hear from ordinary citizens. The voices available to us at present are essentially elite voices, but whenever the evidence permits, we also hear the grass-roots response toward America and Americans. Taken as a whole these encounters and their different audiences explain how the French perceived America and how they responded to Americanization. They also tell us why responses in France were what they were. If my method succeeds, this study will provide an accurate picture and an explanation. Like an impressionist painting my text will convey the whole without covering the entire canvas.

This project began with my determination to avoid the superficial and inconclusive commentary that has often passed for interpretation of

French views of America. I hoped to move analysis beyond the jottings of transient French visitors and Parisian literati who knew us only at a distance. To this end I looked to direct, intensive encounters between the two peoples, especially those of a socioeconomic and political character where the American way was best displayed. Thus I chose the Marshall Plan, economic missions, foreign investment, and American consumer products as arenas where the French met us, our ways, our policies, and our institutions, so to speak, face-to-face. These encounters, I assumed, would provide real tests of how the French viewed the American way.

Yet as I pursued my historical research for "hard" evidence, I realized that the Gallic reaction to America included the attitudes and preconceptions that the French brought with them to such meetings. The American way was what the French thought it was. There was a cultural dimension even to encounters of a basically economic or political character. Industrial experts, for example, touring factories in the United States under the aegis of the Marshall Plan, responded to American prosperity as a challenge to the French way of life. These hardheaded industrialists and trade unionists, it became clear, were projecting on America their fears for France and, to a lesser extent, their hopes as well. Believing that French national identity was at risk, they expressed their reaction most generally and abstractly as the defense of *civilisation*. In consequence my study of economics and politics also required a serious examination of cultural preconceptions. I was led by my search into the realm of culturally conditioned constructions of an American reality.

My voyage of intellectual discovery took me into the choppy waters and cross-currents where politics, economics, and culture meet. Such a broadening of my research, however, did not lead me to subordinate economics and politics to culture. I did not conclude that the French response to America was purely imagined: America was not simply Gallic invention, not mere cultural construction. If we were a mirror before which the French saw themselves, we were also a tangible social landscape that the French experienced. If anti- (and pro-) Americanism was, at one level, a reflection of French thought about personal identity and the future, it was also a confrontation with the content of postwar America. America and Americanization were realities that the French—politicians, visitors, or those surveyed by opinion polls—had to face after 1945. The United States was a superpower that provided security and exerted enormous influence on postwar Western Europe. Americanization was a process of economic modernization, and America was the first consumer society and possibly a harbinger of Europe's future.

What this study explores is the interconnectedness of economics, politics, and culture in postwar Franco-American relations. These dimensions are juxtaposed rather than ordered in some hierarchical fashion that assigns priority of either explanatory power or meaning to one element or another. The phenomenon of anti-Americanism, or for that matter of philo-Americanism, is multidimensional in its causes and its meanings. It derives from French encounters with an American reality as well as from Gallic preconceptions, anxieties, aspirations, and sense of self-identity. Anti-Americanism, in short, was (and is) about both America and France.

My voyage led me to one other discovery. The French generations that I studied, those of the middle to late twentieth century, carried with them in their response to America a keen sense of national identity—an identity they were quick to defend. They believed in such categories as "the French" and "Frenchness" and "the French way of life." We need not debate whether such social and cultural abstractions were real or invented. What is certain is that such assumptions determined how our Gallic cousins viewed us. It was this "Frenchness" that they perceived to be at risk because of the emerging power, prosperity, and prestige of the New World. Thus I refer to a category like "the French," often without nuance of class, religion, region, generation, gender, or any other such qualifier, not as a handy rhetorical device but because I accept these generations' strong subjective sense of national identity. Since, with rare exception, the French of these years, be it labor organizer or businessman, diplomat or intellectual, responded to America as representatives of a *civilisation* at risk, I employ their collective categories and refer to "the French." What follows is my attempt at understanding what, in all its variety, "Frenchness" was and why it was seemingly put at risk by America.

This project has benefited greatly from fellowships granted by the German Marshall Fund of the United States, the Woodrow Wilson International Center for Scholars, and the John Simon Guggenheim Memorial Foundation. These fellowships, along with support from the State University of New York, provided the time and assistance for the research and writing of this book in Paris, Washington, D.C., and Stony Brook.

In Paris, thanks to Louis Bergeron, Pierre Nora, and Patrick Fridenson, the Ecole des hautes études en sciences sociales hosted several seminars at which my work-in-progress was presented. In Washington, D.C., thanks to Samuel Wells and Michael Haltzel of the Woodrow Wilson International Center, and to David Calleo of the School for Advanced International Study, these institutions sponsored sessions at which my work was discussed. Victoria de Grazia organized a similar session in Florence sponsored by the European University Institute.

I wish to express my special appreciation to Pierre Nora, Stanley Hoffmann, Patrick Fridenson, Herman Lebovics, William Keylor, Chiarella Esposito, and Jacqueline deWeulf who have read all or parts of this book and contributed important suggestions for its improvement. Whatever deficiencies remain are my responsibility.

I am also in the debt of numerous archivists and librarians—especially Hélène Volat of the Stony Brook University library, Mme Bonazzi of the Archives nationales, Mme Dijoux of the Service des archives économiques et financières, Mme Genès at the Commissariat général du plan, Philip Mooney at the archives of the Coca-Cola Company, John Butler at the Economic Cooperation Administration archives in Suitland, Md., Claudia Anderson at the Lyndon Johnson library, and Sally Marks (now my wife) at the National Archives, to whom this book is dedicated. The publishers Denoël allowed me to use their private archives for research.

I also wish to acknowledge the various forms of assistance given me by Bernard Cazes, Jean-Marie Domenach, Pierre Grémion, Jean-Noël Jeanneney, Denis Lacorne, Edgar Morin, Michel Margairaz, Marc Meuleau, Diana Pinto, Anton DePorte, William Friend, Jacqueline Grapin, Simon Serfaty, Nicholas Wahl, Lenard Berlanstein, Charlotte Thompson, Irwin Wall, and Henry Rousso. William Becker and the History Department at George Washington University generously provided a place to work for a visiting scholar. Sheila Levine, Dore Brown, and Edith Gladstone, at the University of California Press, by their careful attention to my manuscript made important contributions. I wish to express, however belatedly, my special debt to the late Jean Bouvier, who encouraged me to believe an American could write French history. Finally, I want to thank the mentor who has served as my model for historian and teacher, Gordon Wright.

Versions of several chapters of this study have appeared in *French Historical Studies, French Politics and Society, The Tocqueville Review,* and *L'Histoire.*

CHAPTER 1

Anti-Americanism
and National Identity

The worry that America constitutes a challenge to France is a rather recent phenomenon. For over a century after the American colonies declared their independence, the two nations lived in separate worlds on the same globe. The war for independence had generated a brief, but later often celebrated, Franco-American alliance. There was a long early history of intermittent encounter and mutual observation that inspired some acute cross-national studies such as Alexis de Tocqueville's admirable *Democracy in America*. Yet aside from these few connections, some "carriage trade" tourists, and formal diplomatic relations, the two nations had little in common. There was limited trade between them, scant French emigration across the Atlantic, and no diplomatic alignment. For the longest time the French had no need to take the new nation seriously. The two nations' trajectories did not intersect.

All this began to change in the midst of the First World War when France needed to tap America's financial and economic resources. Once the United States intervened militarily in the war it became a major actor in European affairs and briefly, after 1918, participated in the postwar reconstruction of the Old World. Yet by the early 1920s Americans had been chastened by involvement in European affairs, irritated over such issues as the Allies' reluctance to pay war debts, and determined to free themselves of "European entanglements." Nevertheless, even as America in its governmental role retreated across the Atlantic, other links such as foreign investment developed, and curiosity about each other's society grew. French visitors began to treat America as a lesson in precocious, but deviant, behavior.

By end of the 1920s American economic and technological prowess was beginning to make an impression, though largely a negative one, on French observers. According to the title of one of the most popular (and also one of the most hostile) French commentaries of the interwar years, America represented scenes of a possible European future.[1] If France's future was in the making across the Atlantic, was it a matter for rejoicing or despair? Interwar observers like Georges Duhamel and André Siegfried announced the major themes that succeeding generations of America-watchers elaborated. They contrasted French civilization with the wasteland of American mass culture and Gallic individualism with American conformism. Americans, from this perspective, might be wealthy and powerful, but they were dominated by businessmen like Henry Ford who trained their fellow Americans to be mass producers and consumers—creating a society of comfortable conformists and cultural philistines.

In the 1930s whatever appeal America had as a paragon of prosperity collapsed under the upheaval of the depression. Those French writers who had warned of the "American cancer" seemed vindicated. The American economic model was not only spiritually sick, it also failed to satisfy material needs. American isolationism and French protectionism attenuated relations even further. Now F. Scott Fitzgerald would write of Paris as "Babylon Revisited" and complain that with the disappearance of the tourists and expatriates, the Ritz bar had gone back to the French. When war again seemed imminent, in 1938–39, Washington stood on the sidelines while the French hoped that, at best, one day the United States would become an ally in the defense of democracy and French independence.

It was the Second World War that brought America and Americans into the French landscape. Up to then, the New World had been of marginal interest except to the writers who sketched its negative stereotype. But in the postwar world the French could no longer ignore America because the United States began to exercise a certain hegemony over France. This hegemony has had social, economic, and cultural, as well as political-strategic, features. It is the former dimensions that I wish to examine. Formal state-to-state relations form a background to my investigation and on occasion will occupy the foreground, but they are not at issue here. My focus rather is the French perception of and response to America as a social model.

In general how did this American model appear to the Old World? Postwar America represented prosperity, especially in its elevated standard of living, and technological prowess. Or as the model was commonly conceptualized, America represented the coming "consumer society." This term suggested not just the mass purchase of standardized products of American origin or design such as Kodak cameras or jeans; it also denoted a style of life that encompassed new patterns of spending, higher wage levels, and greater social mobility. It featured new forms of economic organization including different kinds of industrial relations, business management, and markets. And the new consumerism depended on different cultural values. Consumer society suggested a life oriented around acts of purchase and a materialistic philosophy. It valued the productive and the technical and was accompanied by the products of the new mass culture, from Hollywood films and comic strips to home appliances and fast food.

Postwar America was a model France could not ignore. The future was across the Atlantic. America was a challenge. As the French came to understand the challenge, the question they asked themselves was how to attain American prosperity and power and yet keep what they believed was French. In particular, how could the French accept American economic aid and guidance; borrow American technology and economic practice; buy American products; imitate American social policy; even dress, speak, and (perhaps worst of all) eat like Americans and yet not lose their Frenchness? Would the pursuit of American consumerism come at the expense of French national identity and independence? As one journalist plainly put the question, was a bistro any longer French when it served Coca-Cola rather than red wine?

In short, postwar America appeared as both a model and a menace. The issue for the French was to find the way to possess American prosperity and economic power and yet to avoid what appeared to be the accompanying social and cultural costs. The challenge was to become economically and socially "modern" without such American sins as social conformity, economic savagery, and cultural sterility. Cast in its grandest terms the issue was, how could France follow the American lead and yet preserve a French way of life?

France has not been the only country to face the dilemma of the American example. The issues raised by this study bear on a global phenomenon of basic economic, social, and cultural changes that has unfolded during the second half of the twentieth century. Asia, Africa, Latin America, and both Eastern and Western Europe have been transformed along the lines of some vaguely American model. This process of global change should not be trivialized by such curiosities as teenagers in Bangkok sporting blue jeans and listening to rock music. There is a kind of global imperative that goes by the name Americanization. Although the phenomenon is still described as Americanization, it has become increasingly disconnected from America. Perhaps it would be better described as the coming of consumer society. Whatever the case, the phenomenon to be observed in postwar France has parallels all over the world in recent decades.

••••••••••

Reflecting on the French response to Americanization is especially pertinent today when Gallic self-consciousness, always acute, is unusually intense. The 1990s are likely to keep the question of national identity before the French public. As new, mainly Arab, immigrants refuse assimilation and challenge dominant cultural models, as waves of outside influences wash over the cultural landscape, as an increasingly integrated Europe deprives France of autonomy, and as French political, economic, and social structures come to resemble those of other Western nations, French exceptionalism seems at risk. France seems in danger of losing its uniqueness. The sociologist Alain Touraine, for example, asks, "Does a French society still exist?" And Fernand Braudel, after a lifetime of writing history that avoided national frontiers, at the end of his career wrote wistfully about *The Identity of France*.[2]

The process of modernization that has swept across postwar France threatens to homogenize the nation and forces the French to try to discover, preserve, or invent what has been, and is, unique about their national community. Understandably the French have become preoccupied with the question of who they are. One scholar, noting the French public's current passion for reading history and nostalgia about the national *patrimoine,* concludes: "What we are currently witnessing is a crisis of national identity."[3] Historians, among others, have joined the search for a definition of Frenchness. The last decade has seen a flood of books about French nationalism. These include studies of the origins of the French nation; the formation of historical memory; the assimilation of immigrants; the intercourse between France and its colonial empire; and the development, decline, and diffusion of French culture.[4]

What such studies demonstrate is the fabricated or artificial quality of the notion of a national community. What has defined, and continues to define, Frenchness (fig. 1) is complex, changing, subtle, contested, and arbitrary rather than simple, fixed, distinct, consensual, and given. It is

1. An image of Frenchness. (Courtesy Agency Magnum/Henri Cartier-Bresson)

not a matter of geographical space, history, language, the state, or even culture, though all of these contribute. None of these criteria provide precise, impermeable, or permanent boundaries for the French nation because much of what defines its identity is imagined. France is an invention, a conceptualization. Like other nations, it is to a large extent a collective subjective perception.[5]

Recent research has also established that a sense of nationalism is usually constructed by a kind of dialectic with "others," with those outside the collectivity whose difference helps define the singularity of one's own community or nation. National identity is formed through negation, by establishing a counteridentity, by constructing a "we"/ "them" dichotomy.

Examining French responses to America, or more precisely to Americanization, points up how the French conceived of their uniqueness during the middle and late twentieth century. For America functioned as a foil that forced the French, especially after the Second World War, to assert what was distinctively French. Beginning in the interwar years and reaching a climax in the first postwar decades, America served as the other that helped the French to imagine, construct, and refine their collective sense of self.

Defining national identity, however, is a continuous process. It evolves rather than being natural or sustained as a fixed conceptualization. Thus what worked to define collective identity prior to 1970 functioned less well afterwards. Once Americanization became a global process rather than a foreign invasion and once other cultural and economic dangers or alternatives arose—for example, Arab immigration, Japanese products, or the European community—the dialectic of forming identity by negating Americans no longer articulated French uniqueness. As this American other began to fade, the American way lost its power to oppose and formulate Frenchness. Thus before 1970 Frenchness, as measured by the American other, had featured attributes like individualism, *la douceur de vivre*, and humanistic *civilisation*. Once a certain level of Americanization occurred, however, the French found more and more reason to look elsewhere than across the Atlantic for contrast to the French "we." This shift in focus helps to explain why during the 1980s the French turned inward, examining their past, to define what the French nation was and is.

··········

The phenomenon of French anti-Americanism has long filled the editorial pages of newspapers, inspired vituperation and humor, and formed the subject matter for scholarly treatises. Even when commentary transcends the character of banter, it rarely extends beyond intellectual curiosity about contrasting national images. Compendiums of what French visitors said about their travels in the New World or of what the literati trumpeted from the Left Bank about America can be intriguing. But they can advance our understanding of the phenomenon only if we view them as historical problems. We must do more than find pithy observations, catalog cohorts, or detect shifts of how America was perceived if we wish to explain either the causes or the significance of perceptions concerning the new continent. For behind the flow of words and emotive outbursts about America lay the most serious issues confronting contemporary France.

At the outset we must attend to some definitional problems and provide some background to French thinking about America. Measuring the potency of French anti-Americanism depends on its definition. If mere criticism of America or Americans qualifies as anti-American, then the net is so wide that we might catch an unexpected fish. Who, for example, wrote: "I don't know any country where, in general, there is less spirit of independence and true freedom than in America"? Answer: Alexis de Tocqueville.[6] Perhaps we should be more restrictive in applying the label if the Frenchman most closely associated with America is guilty of such an observation. But we could go to the other extreme in narrowing the definition. As one scholar observes, if anti-American means "a full-blown contempt for anything American or a systematic and permanent opposition to everything American," then anti-Americanism does not exist![7] Even Jean-Paul Sartre, who in the wake of the Rosenberg trial likened America to a mad dog suffering from rabies and urged Europeans to sever relations, also admired American literature, films, and jazz. According to this restrictive definition, one of the most celebrated "anti-Americans" escapes the label, which Sartre himself did not think he deserved. He wrote in 1946: "I am not at all anti-American, neither do I understand what 'anti-American' means."[8] Another scholar argues that Charles de Gaulle should not be classified as anti-American because he did not base his policy toward the United States on a rejection of American values. De Gaulle was merely a realist in international affairs. If Sartre and de Gaulle do not fit the category, then either Gallic anti-Americanism is a mirage or we need a better definition of anti-Americanism.

Classification in this instance is not an exercise in the scientific method. Most discourse about America is difficult to classify as either "for" or "against," and extreme stances are extremely rare—though they exist. Affirmative and critical postures are not rigid categories and often overlap or merge into one another. And the same person may express conflicting attitudes or even alter his or her views—this shift is invariably from negative to positive rather than vice versa. Perhaps most perplexing is that admirers and adversaries often use the same images but attribute opposing values to them. The historian can be conceptually precise and consistent if not rigorously scientific.

First, anti- and pro- (or philo-) Americanism are descriptive categories signifying sets of attitudes that are predominantly, if not systematically or permanently, admiring or critical. Second, the nature or significance of the indictment or praise and the intensity and range of an individual's feelings or attitudes about America are the determining features. Third, the phenomenon is mixed in a normative sense. Individuals frequently express contradictory attitudes. And when the sample is a social group, discord is the rule. The mix of normative attitudes must be conceived as a duality (pro- and anti-) and dealt with as an analytical unit. Fourth, neither broad nor narrow definitions are useful. A single critical comment does not make the speaker "anti-American." Or, in an opposing vein, the individual does not need to challenge basic American values to qualify. Fifth, the transitory nature of attitudes is irrelevant. Once expressed, no matter how fleetingly, they can be categorized. A lifelong commitment to contempt is not required in order to merit the label "anti-American." Finally, for historical analysis the significance of such attitudes does not depend on whether or not the speaker was well informed about America. No matter how irrational, emotional, self-serving, or "false" the images may be, they form part of the phenomenon.

Disapproval of another country and its people sometimes amounts to nothing more than a compilation of petty complaints. In that case the category of anti- is inappropriate. In the 1950s the journalist Art Buchwald decided to "investigate" the sources of rising British antagonism toward the United States. He solicited responses by running an ad in the London *Times* asking the public to tell him why they disliked Americans. His "analysis" of the replies led Buchwald to conclude that "if Americans would stop spending money, talking loudly in public places, telling the British who won the war, adopt a pro-colonial policy, back future British expeditions to Suez . . . stop chewing gum, dress properly, throw away their cameras, move their air bases out of England . . . turn over the hydrogen bomb to Great Britain . . . not export Rock'n Roll, and speak correct English," why then the two peoples might like each other again.[9]

What is essential in determining anti-Americanism is the nature and range of grievances and the intensity of feeling. Distaste for chewing gum or Hollywood does not qualify. Contempt for Americans or American foreign policy or consumer society as "the American way of life" does. Anti-Americanism, despite its lack of intellectual rigor, can illuminate trends and issues in social, economic, political, diplomatic, and cultural affairs—making it a phenomenon of considerable historical importance.

The Gallic response to America, as discussed earlier, was heavily marked by the French thinking about themselves, their identity, and their future. To a degree, their construction of the American way came from a common belief in a French way. But there is another distinction that we must make as we analyze attitudes about America. At one level responses were determined by national stereotypes. At a second level the French were reacting to circumstances.

French perceptions of America have been and continue to be highly patterned. There is a certain repetition associated with stereotypes even if the same images are evaluated in contradictory ways. America is a "young" country. This may mean either that Americans are open, curious, and lively or else that Americans are immature and naive. In general Americans are supposed to be youthful, dynamic, wealthy, pragmatic, optimistic, and friendly, but they are also seen as materialistic, puritanical, vulgar, and even racist and violent. They are *les grands enfants*. Such Gallic perceptions were already evident during the late nineteenth century and seem virtually unchanged today as contemporary opinion polls verify a consistent sociocultural image of Americans.[10]

At this level the historian is faced with fixed or perhaps slowly evolving attitudes. This kind of thinking about America is both cognitive and emotive and tends toward simplification to the point of caricature. It also seems immune to contrary information or experience. When Harvard students made a comprehensive sociological study of a village in Anjou in the 1960s, they encountered the familiar stereotype: Americans were rich, materialistic, and rather undisciplined. Despite intensive intercourse between the students and villagers who became familiar and friendly with them, the older disagreeable image of "other" Americans endured.[11] The sources of such stereotypes are complex and even a bit mysterious, but they probably arise from a combination of conventional wisdom about Americans; certain written sources, especially the press and those influential best-sellers that capture a generation's imagination (like Georges Duhamel's caustic *America the Menace* during the 1930s); the mass media, increasingly the cinema, television, and music; formal education (for example, the image of America conveyed in textbooks); and travel and contact with Americans (soldiers, tourists, students) or those who claim to know Americans.[12]

In contrast to the substratum of virtually fixed stereotypes that pass from generation to generation are what might be termed contingent attitudes—more temporal, even ephemeral, attitudes that derive from specific historical circumstances, often from foreign policy and trade relations. A historian might, in this vein, explain the anti-Americanism of the early postwar period as a result of Cold War politics. In this instance militant anticommunism made Washington champion the cause of European defense and German rearmament, which in turn incited the Communists to accuse the United States of warmongering and write "Yankee Go Home" on the walls of French towns. But political circumstances, as we shall see, are insufficient explanations for a phenomenon that had far deeper roots. Situational factors, moreover, can sharpen or blunt stereotypical attitudes but they seldom transform them.

....

Before we investigate postwar encounters, it is important to introduce evidence from a rich body of writing about America from the 1920s and 1930s that drew the lines for the postwar discussion. In many ways the image of America as a society suffering from standardization and materialism is a legacy of the interwar years.

Interwar literature about America—largely impressions drawn from cross-Atlantic visits and from the works of America's own critics such as Sinclair Lewis, Faulkner, Dreiser, Dos Passos, and Steinbeck—praised the New World for its vigor and wealth yet, taken as a whole, conveyed a negative impression of American civilization. The American people rarely appeared as more than a caricature. French travelers described America as an urbanized and mechanized society whose principal cultural attraction was Hollywood.[13] This literature conjured images of a New York City teeming with people and adorned with skyscrapers. It described in graphic detail the mechanized slaughter of livestock in the Chicago stockyards. *Américanisme*, defined as the quest for abundance through standardized mass production and consumption, evoked Henry Ford's assembly line, ubiquitous billboards, rows of simple wood houses, packaged foods, and tractors plying vast farms. In a play of 1924 entitled *Les Américains chez nous*, Parisians learned how mechanized American farming threatened the pastoral idyll of the French countryside.[14] Food was subjected to ridicule. A celebrated French chef found American food "doctored, thermochemical, and dreadful" and surmised that jazz bands played loudly in restaurants in order to stifle "the cries of despair emitted by the unfortunate diners."[15] Even admirers of the New World, like André Maurois and André Siegfried, whose books translated America to the French between the wars, were anxious about the rigidities of standardization. Maurois expressed his annoyance at his inability to order black coffee in a New York restaurant because the norm was coffee with cream.[16] And Siegfried worried that Americans were becoming "Fordized."

Hollywood appeared to be the quintessential expression of American culture. The French tended to attack American film-making as an "industry" that produced meters of banal celluloid escapism for profit. Gallic reservations about mass culture were already apparent: Hollywood threatened true culture because it subordinated quality to box office receipts. And the cinema was but one of many forces that "standardized" people. Just look, these French visitors noted, at how women in Los Angeles imitated the appearance of movie stars.

A smug tone of French cultural superiority marked this reporting about the New World. In its most extreme form America was denied a civilization of its own.

There is no American civilization . . . there is still no American civilization. . . . The only civilization in America is the old civilization of Europe which is still the theoretical basis of institutions and customs. But for the rest . . . the box-like skyscrapers, the vile speakeasies, the over-sized cities spoiled by racketeering, the government of gangsters . . . the hundred-page newspapers full of inanities higher than the Chrysler building . . . the splendid laboratories without scientists, the to and fro of divorces, the king-cinema, the empty churches? Civilization?[17]

Or as one commentator noted, whereas Americans showed tourists the Chicago stockyards, the French instinctively escorted visitors to the Louvre and Notre Dame.

The classic summary of this Gallic indictment, which for many years tickled the palates of the Parisian literati and informed provincial school-children about the New World, was Duhamel's *America the Menace* (its original title, *Scènes de la vie future,* was far more discreet). For Duhamel the machine set the rhythm of American life, whose goals were production and profit. As one historian notes, Duhamel saw future citizens becoming "happy slaves, comfortable brutes, ignorant manipulators of an antiseptic, technicized horror of inhuman efficiency." In exchange for their comfortable bondage Americans received new appetites, wrote Duhamel:

They yearn desperately for phonographs, radios, illustrated magazines, "movies," elevators, electric refrigerators, and automobiles, automobiles, and, once again, automobiles. They want to own at the earliest possible moment all the articles mentioned, which are so wonderfully convenient, and of which, by an odd reversal of things, they immediately become the anxious slaves.[18]

American culture, in Duhamel's corrosive prose, was vapid escapism: Sunday drives in the new car, mindless Hollywood movies, and mass spectator sports. He observed:

What strikes the European traveler is the progressive approximation of human life to what we know of the way of life of insects—the same effacement of the individual, the same progressive reduction and unification of social types . . . the same submission of every one to those obscure exigencies . . . of the hive or of the anthill.[19]

Ridiculing Americans' penchant for conformity, he sarcastically proposed a League for the Creation of Public Scandals whose members would breach social norms with such modest infractions as refusing to ride the elevator, attend the cinema, or buy a highly advertised soap. Or these nonconformists would smile, sing, or promenade aimlessly.[20]

America the Menace may have gone too far in its anti-Americanism for many French critics, but it conveyed the nature of the indictment. Even a far more friendly, and much better traveled, visitor to the New World like André Siegfried, who admired Yankee idealism, still noted that Americans believed that the dignity of human beings resides in their standard of living.[21] The source of Duhamel's and Siegfried's reservations was a humanistic and aesthetic revulsion at a mechanized and monotonous society. Other intellectuals in the 1930s, following in Duhamel's footsteps, were to add a philosophical and moral dimension to his visceral attack.

These intellectuals, most of whom were young, issued an unequivocal antimodernist critique that portrayed America as a negative model for France. They were indignant about reducing human beings to the function of producer-consumers and saw in mass society, materialism, and standardization the end of *civilisation*. They were also expressing an internal French debate about the merits of advancing capitalist production. The late 1920s, after all, had seen a great surge forward in France of what was then termed industrial *rationalisation*, which seemed to threaten old ways.

Emmanuel Mounier, the founder-editor of the review *Esprit*, identified industrial capitalism and economic liberalism with bourgeois decadence and denounced the notion that human progress should be measured by the accumulation of material goods. Possessions and comfort—the ideals of the bourgeoisie—destroyed the will for sacrifice and effort. Money was economically sterile and led to avarice. Machines and factories degraded work and the worker. The economy should be in the service of human beings, not the other way round. American society—materialistic, impersonal, and dehumanized—was this bourgeois "utopia" made real. Mounier feared that France would lose its soul by imitating the United States.[22] His alternative was a philosophy called "personalism" that mixed humanist, Christian, and communitarian ideals. *Esprit* proposed a Christian precapitalist rejection of the modern.

On the right, other young intellectuals such as Robert Aron and Arnaud Dandieu published essays like *Le Cancer américain* that also denounced the American way for France. The pursuit of production and the use of reason as an adjunct to technology placed France on a material and quantitative terrain where it could not compete. The "American conquest" of the globe represented adoration of the gods of credit, production, and technical intelligence. For Aron and Dandieu the alternative to the modernists' equation of human progress with materialism and dessicated Cartesianism was a vague "spiritual revolution" that reasserted the moral essence of human beings. Other intellectuals of this generation, some of whom flirted with fascism, joined the chorus of anti-Americans. Thierry Maulnier, who many years later became a member of the Académie française, construed America as the "new barbarism" reducing human beings to animalistic needs, enslaving them to an economic monster, and defining them by their functions. It was the writer's duty, according to Maulnier, to denounce this barbarism and renounce making the intellectual a hawker of happiness. And Robert Brasillach equated modernization with the victory of the masses and their base instincts. He too preferred a premodern economy and exhorted the French to buy artisanal products in preference to manufactured ones.

All these young theorists of the 1930s rejected an Americanized version of modernity. To the functional anthill of the New World they preferred the small pleasures of mischief, exuberance, uniqueness, and spontaneity as well as the sterner values of frugality, camaraderie, and heroism. Their opposition was distinctly premodern, its roots in Christian asceticism and fellowship as well as traditional humanism; they combined aesthetic and intellectual elitism with a strong sense of regret about the nation's decadence. All agreed that modernity, as embodied by America, was the wrong path for France. Echoes of this interwar anti-Americanism, sounded first by the right, reverberated during the Cold War among the left.

The post-1945 stereotype had been established by 1930. Americans were adolescents, materialists, conformists, and puritans. And perhaps racists to boot. But America was still a remote threat in the 1930s. Trouble loomed in the East, not in the West. As one traveler observed: "The immediate danger for us is not being Americanized, but being Germanized."[23]

....

With this background and these distinctions in mind we can now turn to Franco-American relations during the early years of the Cold War and the political-ideological debate.

CHAPTER 2

The New American Hegemony

The French and the Cold War

What was said or thought about America in a political and ideological sense during the early days of the Cold War opens this study. High politics accompanied by an analysis of public opinion are the initial topics. We begin with the political elements of anti-Americanism because they colored the other encounters and in a sense informed them all. Geopolitical and ideological issues form not only the substance of this chapter and part of the next, but they also suffused the atmosphere of the early Cold War and deeply penetrated French consciousness. This does not suggest the primacy of politics, however, for French social and cultural perceptions of America were highly developed during the interwar years before the emergence of the United States as a global power.

From this geopolitical perspective the key issue was how France should align itself in a Europe being partitioned between East and West. Should France welcome American protection and hegemony, maintain a more independent stance, or look to the East? And how much accompanying American influence was desirable? It must be noted that during the Cold War French attitudes toward America were functionally related to the reputation and behavior of the Soviet Union and for many, especially on the left, anti-Americanism was a consequence of the attraction of Soviet policy or of communism.

In this opening chapter we shall hear principally public voices—those of government officials, both French and American, and of party leaders—as well as those, less distinct but equally important, of private French men and women expressing their feelings about America. The views and efforts of the left-wing or *progressiste* intelligentsia and the Communists will be addressed in the following chapter. The common dilemma that faced the French and unites these initial chapters was how to assess the new American power and its policies toward Europe and France.

· · · · · · · · · ·

Anti-Americanism during the Cold War, in my interpretation, did not represent the French and was in its most polemical form essentially the product of leftist Parisian, especially *marxisant* and Christian, literati and of the Communist party (Parti communiste français, or PCF). These strident anti-Americans (who will be closely examined in the next chapter) expressed their contempt in political or ideological terms. The United States was a capitalist behemoth threatening French political, social, economic, and cultural independence. Americans were, from this perspective, guilty of economic imperialism, warmongering, racism, incipient fascism, and cultural debasement. Attacks from the left distressed American officials and reporters in Paris and, at times, even the American public.[1] Some of this critique resonated among the wider French intellectual community, the political class of the Fourth Republic, and the French people, but it did not represent them.

In contrast there were many other commentators who offered either equally emotional panegyrics or calm, nuanced appraisals. These pro-Americans were more appreciative of America's virtues than they were critical of its vices. But these early Atlanticists—academics like Raymond Aron who wrote for *Le Figaro,* or literati like André Maurois who wrote popular books about America—may have enjoyed wide audiences, but they received far less attention in the sanctum of St-Germain-des-Prés than did newspapers or reviews like *Le Monde, Esprit, Les Temps modernes,* or *Les Lettres françaises,* which all expressed an aversion for America.

The less articulate mass of French men and women shared some of their anxieties. When the intelligentsia and Communist militants addressed certain issues—those that made America appear as a dominating influence—they also captured the attention of a wider public. Anti-Americanism was not purely a Left Bank or Communist property. Anti-Americans spoke for a large audience when they addressed three concerns. Injured national pride was one root of popular, but not necessarily visceral, anti-Americanism. It appeared that the United States had exchanged prewar isolationism for a new global reach and, at the very moment when France had ostensibly sunk to the rank of a secondary power, had emerged as a superpower, stirring up the potent emotions of envy and pride. Second, American economic success inevitably attracted jealousy and resistance. Americans proselytized for consumer society as an alternative to French conceptions of a balanced economy and traditional ways of production, selling, saving, and spending. Third, at least for the elite, was the danger that America would export its mass culture, threatening the French conception of humanistic and high culture with adulteration by the technical values and products of mass culture. In other words the productivity mania, Coca-Cola, and the *Reader's Digest* were a danger. Advertising, in its brash, loud, and vulgar way of hawking products and in its artistic pretensions, represented both consumerism and popular culture. Even the most ardent philo-Americans such as André Maurois or André Siegfried expressed this cultural anxiety. Such popular perceptions of an American menace did not mean that the French were anti-American at this time, but it did mean that polemicists could count on a certain unexpressed sympathy for their attacks.

Inside the hexagon, as the French usually refer to their country, most members of the public seldom thought or cared much about America. They may have harbored the stereotype of "les Américains" and undoubtedly felt twinges of anxiety about America's new power in international affairs, its economic weight, and its cultural presence compared to their nation's relative decline. But they liked America and Americans, consumed most of America's exports, and ignored Sartre's attacks (if they even knew of them) and the signs calling for the Yankees to "Go Home." The French man or woman in the street or in the fields ignored, disagreed with, or, at most, took a little silent pride in the attacks on Yankee hubris.

In short, a substantial and influential part of the intellectual community and the powerful Communist party were anti-American at this time. While the French people shared some of the same apprehensions, they should not be designated as anti-American.

· · · · · · · · · ·

The decade following 1947, the year that nominally signifies the beginning of the Cold War, marked the peak of the politico-ideological debate about America. This was the moment when being for or against America, to some partisans, represented taking a stand for or against peace and *civilisation*.

The Cold War debate about America emerged from tense wartime relations between the two nations. If the fall of France in 1940 marked the nation's loss of status as a great power, the war years and the experience of foreign occupation and collaboration only deepened the humiliation of defeat. Liberation from the Germans required a massive invasion of Anglo-American forces that earned the liberators enormous goodwill but had little effect on restoring damaged self-esteem. Moreover, and rather hidden from the public, was the stormy story of Franco-American relations during the early 1940s. Neither the collaborationist wartime officials in the Vichy government nor their rivals in the Resistance enjoyed amicable relations with the Americans.[2] Washington maintained diplomatic relations with Marshal Philippe Pétain's government until 1942 because it assumed Vichy would be of more use in defeating Germany than was the Resistance. But both Vichy's diplomatic alignment (increasingly accommodating to the Germans) and the direction of its internal policies ran afoul of Washington, and in the end actual fighting between American and Vichy troops broke out during the invasion of North Africa. Indeed Vichy was the first French government to struggle openly against American cultural penetration.[3] And by 1944 with Allied bombs raining down, Vichy propaganda attacked "Jewish" America for its atrocities. Paradoxically, rapport was scarcely better between the United States and the pro-Allied Resistance. Washington's dalliance with Vichy and President Franklin Roosevelt's stubborn opposition to Charles de Gaulle's leadership as head of the provisional government stirred rancor and distrust. And the powerful leftist elements in the resistance movement in metropolitan France harbored reservations about what the future would hold should France be liberated by the Americans and become dependent on the citadel of world capitalism.

Newsreels have captured for posterity the image of joyous crowds celebrating with GIs as Allied troops marched across the country in the summer of 1944. But liberation by outsiders only verified France's fall from grace. France had lost and America had gained in rank. This was the key political-psychological "fact" of the early postwar era. Injured national pride, unacknowledged but real, filled the underground spring that fed anti-Americanism. A France already torn by internal division, humiliated by defeat, occupation, and collaboration, and slightly embarrassed by its liberation faced a crisis of national identity. The cultural revulsion against America, as one historian argues, may have been a kind of "compensatory defense reflex" by which the liberated excommunicated the liberators.[4]

After the war the United States and France gradually became diplomatically aligned. In time the Fourth Republic relinquished its hope of balancing between the two superpowers and sought a formal alliance with the United States and a position within the Atlantic bloc. Interim aid began under the Blum-Byrnes agreement of 1946; the following year came the announcement that led to the arrival of massive Marshall Plan aid in 1948. In 1949 France and America signed a military alliance, the North Atlantic Treaty Organization (NATO), and were soon fighting a joint war in Indochina. Military assistance at first supplemented economic aid and, once the Korean War began, virtually replaced it. But continuous feuding marred the alliance in the late 1940s and early 1950s.[5] Most of this tension was confined to official circles, but at times the public perceived the quarrels. First came friction over trade and economic policy. The United States refused to relax its obstacles to imports from France, yet it counseled and pressured Paris to remove its trade barriers. When the Fourth Republic, for example, tried to protect the French film industry from an influx of Hollywood movies, the American government, as a condition of the Blum-Byrnes loan, insisted that the French keep their market open to Hollywood imports.[6] Recriminations followed. Politicians and the press in France complained that Hollywood studios had forced quotas of American productions on an industry grievously injured by the war. French movie houses were soon inundated with American films, more because of problems with the French movie industry than because of imports, but the domestic outcry led to scrapping the Blum-Byrnes agreement.

There were also disappointments over the amount and the allocation of economic aid. Blum-Byrnes awarded the French far less than they wanted and much less than the British had received.[7] When Marshall Plan aid began, troubles only escalated. While the United States sought a balanced approach to French recovery, one that expedited economic renovation but maintained financial stability, the Fourth Republic pursued massive modernization at the risk of rampant inflation. The use of counterpart funds, that is, matching funds accumulated by the recipients of aid and controlled by America, was a continuous source of friction between Washington and Paris. In 1949 Economic Cooperation Administration (ECA) officials, who administered the Marshall Plan, were so dissatisfied with French financial and economic policies that they threatened to block the release of counterpart funds. In this instance they reported that the French minister of finance made a "moving appeal" to American officials to avert the interruption of aid.[8]

American administration of aid, which often seemed patronizing and tactless, fueled rumors about the French Republic's dependence on Uncle Sam. There was good cause for French irritation when an ECA official in Washington took the French minister of agriculture to task about discourteous treatment of American tourists in French stores and hotels.[9] American officials justified their behavior by arguing that they acted only to monitor the use of aid and to protect American interests. Yet their demands and threats caused uneasiness about the submissiveness of the Fourth Republic.

Complicating Franco-American relations was the example of Britain. Viewed from Paris, London always seemed to receive preferential treatment whether it was a matter of strategic planning or of economic or military aid. France's repeated efforts to attain equal status with Britain as part of a three-power Western directorate were rebuffed. An equal irritant was Washington's anticolonial sentiments, especially with respect to North Africa and Indochina. As Paris perceived it, the United States in its rigid anticolonialism had dislocated the British and Dutch empires and now seemed to be cheering on independence movements in overseas French territories. Although Washington eventually came round and provided military assistance to help fight the war in Indochina, Franco-American military operations in Southeast Asia from 1950 to 1954 seemed to antagonize both sides.

Worst of all, from a French perspective, was the widening policy divergence in the treatment of Germany. From the early disputes over releasing controls on German industry to the bitter quarrels over economic and political recovery and later over rearmament, the German problem drove the Allies apart. In fact during 1945–46 Paris proved at least as big an obstacle as Moscow in discussions over joint Allied occupation policies toward Germany. In order to strengthen Western Europe against possible Soviet aggression, the United States in 1950 adopted the cause of German rearmament. Needless to say, the French were not eager to see their recent occupiers back in uniform. A confidential State Department opinion survey of that year showed that half of the French public thought American treatment of Germany was too lenient. A typical attitude was, "I'm afraid the Americans will help the Germans make a rapid recovery. They should be allowed to suffer a little. Then they would understand."[10] Later, when the Fourth Republic voted down the proposed European Defense Community (EDC), which the United States viewed as the best path to German rearmament and Europe's defense, American rancor made newspaper headlines in France. This pattern of mutual recrimination provoked anti-Americanism in official circles and had repercussions on public opinion as well.

Ideological zealotry accompanied America's new hegemonic position in Western Europe as America went on crusade against communism.

Senator Joseph McCarthy sought out Communists in high places throughout the United States and stirred the nation into a frenzy. Washington found security abroad in the division of Europe, including Germany, between the superpowers and expanded its reach on a global scale to halt the Communist danger. An expansionist and ideological American foreign policy made the French anxious. After the signing of the NATO accord in 1949, American troops returned to France. The United States built a large military infrastructure on French territory, and American military staff and GIs became a common sight. Some thought this buildup was a prelude to an American military offensive against the Soviet Union. An overwhelming advantage in atomic weapons made the American military presence even more ominous.

Within France the United States tried to use its political and economic leverage to strengthen centrist and leftist non-Communist parties and to curb the influence of the French Communist party, especially on the labor movement.[11] As early as 1946–47 the United States government, with the active assistance of American labor unions and the Central Intelligence Agency (CIA), worked to divide the Communist-dominated labor federation, the Confédération générale du travail (CGT). When schism occurred, however, it derived more from internal French labor discord than from American intervention. At the governmental level the non-Communist parties of the ruling coalition in 1947 acted on their own to eject the Communists. Washington was pleased. A year later the State Department mounted a massive cultural offensive as part of the Marshall Plan to neutralize Communist propaganda. America was fighting the Cold War on French territory.

Given wounded national pride, it is no surprise that French patriots of all stripes were prompted to shake their fists at Uncle Sam.[12] Washington's aggressiveness and clumsiness, as it seemed to some, threatened to plunge France into another war. And, one American journalist noted, the French were "tired of being occupied."[13] There were thousands of Americans working for agencies like the ECA in Paris and thousands more serving in the military elsewhere in France. Communists, neutralists, and colonialists were only some of those who actively resisted what many observers crudely labeled "American imperialism."

This political and ideological antagonism is not sufficient, however, to explain the outburst of postwar anti-Americanism. It had other causes and dimensions. The debate about America during the Cold War also echoed prewar charges about "America the menace." It should be remembered that postwar France inherited a critical assessment of *américanisme* from the interwar years. If the literature written about the New World before the war often admired American dynamism, affluence, power, and even certain cultural achievements, on balance the collective judgment had been negative—especially when observers conceived of America as an economic-social-cultural model. Most of these critics, commentators like Georges Duhamel and Robert Aron, attacked from the political right or center. The postwar generation did so from the left—some from a faith in communism.

....

The pattern of friendly quarreling of the late 1940s led to serious confrontations at the diplomatic level during the early and mid-1950s. The American ambassador cabled home in 1952: "Franco-American relations are cooler than at any time since Gen[eral] de Gaulle resigned in 1946."[14] In part this chill reflected the accumulated acrimony from negotiations over military assistance for the war in Indochina and the release of counterpart funds. In part it resulted from French recalcitrance over ratifying the EDC treaty that Washington sought. In addition, the United States frowned on the continued French presence in Tunisia and Morocco. Finally, there was annoyance over American unwillingness to treat its Atlantic allies as true partners. The ambassador confessed, "Some of our actions and sometimes the way we do things, give ammo [ammunition] and tend to give plausibility to Commie charges that we dominate Eur[opean] 'satellites.' "[15]

In 1952 Vincent Auriol, the president of the Republic, after learning of remarks made by American officials about giving priority in aid to Germany, sent a scathing confidential letter to his ambassador:

The French are weary of being called beggars. . . . They are tired of the favours conceded to Germany and they don't understand the betrayal in the African question. They are wondering whether we are in the Atlantic Pact only to be humiliated.[16]

The United States embassy in Paris reported that the French were coming to believe that the American government and Congress considered them "fumbling and incompetent" and wanted to "start telling the French what to do in all fields, foreign and domestic."[17] In late 1952 when the French government perceived that Washington was trying to force it to redo its military budget, raise taxes, and permit close outside supervision of its rearmament program, the conservative premier, Antoine Pinay, was stung into action. None of what Washington was doing was new, though it may have been more heavy-handed, but the French now took exception. Pinay and his ministers rebuked the Americans for unjustified prying into matters that were internal French affairs.[18] The Pinay government could take advantage of growing resentment within and outside parliament over the popular perception that France was being pushed about in sensitive matters like German rearmament and North Africa.[19]

Relations between the Allies deteriorated further in 1953 and 1954. Paris lacked confidence in American leadership because the Eisenhower administration seemed at first uncertain of its direction and unwilling to curb Senator McCarthy.[20] There was apprehension in Paris that growing American military strength might lead the United States on an anti-Communist offensive. And there were mutual recriminations over responsibility for the defeat in Indochina and the Geneva settlement in 1954.

But worst of all was the National Assembly's refusal to approve the EDC in the same year. In order to pressure the assembly into ratification, Secretary of State John Foster Dulles issued his famous threat of undertaking an "agonizing reappraisal" of American policy toward France.[21] French legislators still voted against the treaty. The United States felt betrayed and used by the Fourth Republic, which had dragged out negotiations and had promised ratification but in the end reneged. Dulles in turn snubbed the French on his visit to Europe. By 1954 the intimacy that had characterized relations was over. Pierre Mendès France, who became premier in that year, asked the American under secretary of state to curtail propaganda in France and to cease subsidizing French publications.[22] Shortly thereafter Washington began to phase out its aid programs. American influence over French policy had peaked and thereafter waned.

After 1954 and before de Gaulle's return in 1958 there were further outbursts of anti-Americanism caused by troubles in the NATO alliance. Colonial struggles continued to promote anti-Americanism among the French public, which tended to blame the United States for the predicament in North Africa. Washington allegedly withheld its full support for France's effort to accommodate the independence movements in Tunisia, Morocco, and Algeria.[23] American policy toward the Algerian war, which began in 1954, did not improve the rapport. Washington, hoping to keep North Africa anchored to the West, tried quietly to move France toward a negotiated and liberal solution. But the American government was perceived as providing inadequate support and sometimes even aiding the nationalist Algerian revolt at the expense of its ally: the United

States refused to allow the transfer of American-built military equipment from Indochina to the French army in Algeria yet supplied arms to Tunisia from fear that the latter would turn to the Soviet bloc for weapons. Some of these American weapons, to the dismay of Paris, ended up in the hands of the Algerian rebels. At worst, French opinion viewed America as appeasing the Arab world out of economic interest or as preparing to step in and replace the French in North Africa.[24]

The Suez Canal crisis of 1956 momentarily undermined the alliance. After the United States had intervened against the Franco-British-Israeli invasion of Egypt, a poll indicated that as many as half the French people had either "no confidence" in the United States or "not much."[25] The press viewed the United States as duplicitous and guilty of betraying its ally in time of need.[26] Jacques Soustelle, a prominent Gaullist politician, compared the United States to a mythical beast that was so absent-minded and myopic that it devoured its own feet without even realizing it. Soustelle complained that France was caught between "two colossi, one of which has no heart and the other has no head."[27] The American ambassador, Douglas Dillon, warned Washington of the "bitter flood of anti-American feeling now seething through France." Dillon noted the "deep emotional conviction" that in the Suez affair the United States was "callously indifferent" to the vital interests of its principal allies and was ready also to "humiliate them unnecessarily" in the United Nations in order to retain its own position in the Arab world. And the United States' refusal to alleviate the oil crisis in order to bring its allies to heel angered many bystanders: "The little people of France are being touched and they are stubbornly convinced [the] U.S. is to blame."[28] This flood of anti-Americanism was to recede quickly, typifying the rapid changes in attitude over American foreign policy.

··········

Soon after the war ended, officials in Washington became concerned about the image of the United States in France, a country where the strategic and political stakes were extremely high. A State Department memorandum of 1946 stated, "The world drama of Russian expansion is being played in miniature on the stage of France."[29] Anti-Americanism was attributed to prewar and wartime distortions of America, to sensitivity and jealousy about France's recent humiliation, to the misbehavior of GIs, to fears of and ignorance about the United States' foreign policy, and to pro-Soviet and chauvinist attacks. As a result, the French falsely regarded the American way of life as "essentially materialistic and hedonistic," suspected that Washington's motives were "selfish and predatory," deprecated America's cultural achievements, and distorted its moral and social values. Ambassador Caffery bombarded Washington with feverish dispatches about Communist-inspired anti-Americanism.[30] Officials recommended an informational campaign to combat French anti-Americanism. But it was not till 1948 that the United States government acted.

In tandem with the Marshall Plan, the State Department mounted a massive cultural and informational campaign to redress America's image. The aim was to negate Communist polemics and persuade the French that America wanted only peace and freedom and respected French independence. Presenting American artistic and scientific achievements as well as the benefits of the American way of life, it was assumed, would help create a more attractive image. Slowly at first, but then with gathering momentum that reached a climax in 1952, the United States inundated France with press releases, radio programs, and documentary films. It established informational libraries, cultural exchange programs, and elite organizations like the Association France-Etats-Unis. Marshall Plan agencies contributed a mass-circulation, glossy monthly entitled *Rapports France-Etats-Unis,* which paraded the comforts of consumer society and published articles like "American Painters at Giverny." In 1949 some 15 percent of the population, according to the State Department, heard Voice of America programs such as "Ici New York."[31] During the last six months of 1950 an estimated five million people viewed American documentaries. Some ten thousand leaders received publications such as *Ce que dit la presse américaine.* American academics like Gilbert Chinard lectured in Paris and approximately five hundred Fulbright awards per year facilitated Franco-American scholarly exchange. At the peak of this cultural offensive, the United States Information and Education Agency in France printed twenty thousand copies of a biweekly bulletin describing different aspects of American life; subsidized newspapers and reviews, for example, *Franc-Tireur* and *Preuves;* and aided European intellectual activities like the Congress for Cultural Freedom.

One outspoken American information officer in Paris observed:

As of October 1952, some 70 Americans and several hundred French employees are engaged in cultural and informational work on behalf of the U.S. government in France. We are providing maps of our country to school children and corn-husking demonstrations to farmers. We are publishing a monthly magazine with circulation of more than one million copies. We are making American music available to French radio listeners and showing French engineers how to reduce the costs of cutting and bending steel pipe. We are distributing films on American surgery and manuals of trade union organization.[32]

At the same time, he noted, the American media, which were largely outside government control, overwhelmed the French with American fiction, films, and magazines; their activity led him to warn: "There is a great psychological danger inherent in an excessive American presence in this country." The problem, as he saw it, was there was little relation between creating a favorable view of life in America and ensuring political commitment. A poll of workers around St-Etienne, he observed, revealed no correlation between attitudes toward the United States or the Soviet Union and political preferences. Many Communist workers were contemptuous of Russia, for example. As a contribution to Washington's political aims, the cultural offensive, according to this skeptical official, was "largely a waste of time and money when not actually harmful."

The Fourth Republic, encouraged by American officials and CIA dollars, contributed to this anti-Communist campaign of cultural propaganda.[33] Centrist governments of the period, who were as militantly anti-Communist as the Americans, provided information and funds to a counterattack mounted by a moderate deputy, Jean-Paul David. Aroused

LA COLOMBE QUI FAIT BOUM

2. Picasso's peace dove (*opposite*) and the anti-Communist version, "the dove that goes boom," with its creator, Jean-Paul David (*above*). (Pablo Picasso, *Peace Dove*, © 1992 ARS, New York/SPADEM, Paris; courtesy Bettmann)

by the Communist-inspired peace movement and in the wake of the Korean War, David launched his own movement called Paix et Liberté in order to spread "the truth" about the PCF, the Soviet Union, and communism. Employing a variety of modern communication techniques, Paix et Liberté sponsored radio programs and published a history of the Communist party in the form of a comic strip. One of David's most celebrated efforts was a poster of a dove (a transparent allusion to Picasso's symbol of peace) transformed into a tank—the bird's head a turret and its beak a cannon brandishing an olive branch—that carried the caption "The dove that goes boom" (fig. 2) and thus revealed that the Communists were preparing for war while proclaiming peace. Paix et Liberté was discreet about the United States and NATO and carefully portrayed the global confrontation as a contest between the free world and the Soviet bloc. While Washington openly supported Paix et Liberté, the latter avoided references to the United States and never appealed, as Dulles did, for a rollback of communism in Eastern Europe. Naturally the PCF charged that David was in the pay of the American embassy.

The propaganda contest over America became a quarrel over high culture in the spring of 1952. Paris in May was the site of an international art festival entitled "L'Oeuvre du XXe Siècle" sponsored by the Congress for Cultural Freedom—an organization that received subsidies from the CIA. The purpose of the festival was to show Europeans, especially Parisians, that the West was culturally vigorous and to disprove Communist accusations of decadence. Orchestras from Boston, Vienna, and Berlin, the New York City ballet, and Covent Garden Opera, among others, performed for the city. There was an exhibition of twentieth-century artistic masterpieces, many of which were French, and literary discussions by such illuminati as W. H. Auden, William Faulkner, and André Malraux—the last the only internationally prominent French intellectual who participated.

While most Parisians were impressed by the display of the West's artistic brilliance, the festival also provoked nasty nationalist sniping.[34] One leftist newspaper, *Combat,* carried an editorial on "NATO's Festival" with snide remarks about the provincials from Alabama and Idaho, and freedom in a nation that lynched blacks and hounded anyone accused of "un-American" activities. The Communist daily unmasked the event as a way of spreading bellicose and fascist ideas and enrolling French intellectuals in a "cultural army." A conservative paper called the festival magnificent and contrasted its vitality with artistic conformity in the Soviet bloc. This same daily welcomed the Boston Symphony yet noted, "The Americans have landed, but under the command of a Frenchman" (Charles Munch). And the director of the Paris Opera ballet, affronted by exclusion from the festival while George Balanchine's New York company performed, declared haughtily: "Gentlemen, with respect to *esprit,* civilization, and culture, France doesn't take advice from anyone; it gives it!"[35] This outburst of cultural arrogance was exceptional. But some intellectuals used the event to register their cultural disdain for the United States. "Paris has been—and still is—the only creative center in the world," one newspaper asserted.[36] Of course these judgments were not purely aesthetic since the propaganda function of the event was transparent. It must have seemed that praising the festival meant, at least indirectly, also approving NATO and German rearmament. The organizer of the festival, Nicolas Nabokov, wrote privately: "Despite what it may have looked like to people reading the French press, the festival was a psychological success in the complex and depressingly morbid intellectual climate of France. Of course, in any other country we would have had both more sympathy and more support."[37]

....

If the historian leaves Paris and its political and cultural battles in order to view France as a whole, what attitudes toward America can he uncover? How did "the French," defined here in the sense of public opinion, view America and Americans in the early 1950s? Speaking definitively about this subject is virtually impossible. Such attitudes were too diverse, volatile, and contradictory and the documentation is too thin to write with any precision or confidence. In principle, public opinion is difficult to chart because it mixes memory and anticipation, unity and multiplicity, stability and plasticity. Moreover, it is both expressed and latent.[38] And in this case it was probably also suffused with massive indifference. Despite these problems we have sufficient material from public opinion polls, newspapers, embassy and consular reports, and other sources to sketch a profile of French views. The basic source is an extensive opinion survey about America carried out in 1953 at the height of Cold War anxiety.[39]

How did the French people in the early 1950s learn about the United States and Americans? Newspapers, according to the opinion survey, were the principal source of information, supplemented by radio programs, films, books, personal conversations, and American periodicals like the *Sélection du Reader's Digest* and the *Rapports France-Etats-Unis*. Both periodicals unabashedly propagandized for the American way of life. *Sélection du Reader's Digest*, which published over a million copies, praised American scientific, technical, social, and economic achievements with articles like "The Cold Finally Conquered," "Here Come the Modern Harvesters," or "Hurrah for the Suburbs" (as well as rhapsodies about America's contribution to Europe's liberation, reconstruction, and protection). Only 2 percent of the 1953 sample had been to the United States though half knew someone who had visited; travelers' impressions were strongly favorable. Throughout France, the most visible signs of America were U.S. military bases, American tourists, a growing number of American consumer products, and, especially, cultural exports such as Hollywood films. Yet the French admitted that they did not know much about the United States—a situation that has changed little to the present. During the Cold War very few French citizens knew who Joseph McCarthy was. (This is not to suggest American superiority in knowledge of the French. When J. Edgar Hoover was informed in 1964 that Sartre had joined an anti-American organization, Hoover supposedly scribbled a memo: "Find out who this Sartre is.")[40] But the majority did not believe crude misrepresentations such as tales that most Americans lived in skyscrapers or that divorce had destroyed the American family.

The image of Americans was a familiar composite. Americans were rich, youthful, dynamic, practical, and modern. To an extent this was the mirror image of the French, who commonly viewed themselves as poor, old, and traditional. Americans were admired for their high standard of living, their open society, their comforts, and their technological prowess. Local newspapers reported speed records set by American transcontinental planes and carried news of the latest gadgets, such as portable radios and plastic auto bodies.[41] In the late 1940s, when the French still suffered from severe housing shortages, dailies carried photographs of new American luxury apartment houses; visitors to the United States marveled at the extravagance of American hotels, stores, trains, and restaurants. This new world was associated with economic expansion and money—"Dieu dollar." To a lesser extent it was also hailed as the liberator of France, a close ally, and a democracy. American culture was different—it recalled Hollywood, cowboys, and jazz. Above all Americans lived in a modern society: they were "modern people always taking the lead toward progress."[42] This stereotype was quite stable from 1945 through the 1950s and long after that as well.

If Americans were modern, they also made the French uneasy. Their image cast a shadow. The French in their assessment of America tended, more than other nationalities, to perceive Americans as *dominateurs*.[43] The most common image evoked when the French spoke about the United States was power.[44] In 1952 American domination appeared to them more in political, military, and economic guises than as a cultural menace. But American hegemony haunted the French.

If the stereotype of Americans was stable, foreign policy acted as a volatile variable that caused abrupt swings in popular appreciation of the United States while raising the specter of foreign domination. It is not surprising that approval of American foreign policy waned after the enthusiasm of the liberation. Erosion set in as the French perceived a hardening of American policy into an anti-Communist mold, as East-West tensions grew, as substantive differences between the Allies emerged, and as Washington seemed to interfere in French affairs both at home and abroad. French grievances centered on Washington's advocacy of German recovery, especially rearmament, and its lack of support for the French position in North Africa and Indochina.[45] Washington also drew reproach for its military bases in France, for the conduct of the Korean War, for its irritating way of treating the French as poor relations, and for its lack of understanding of European affairs.[46] These developments stirred uneasiness about America as a *dominateur*. The danger of American hegemony, however, appeared to be at least as much economic as it was political-military.[47] There were vague misgivings about the expansion of American capitalism.

From a sample of Frenchmen in 1953 who voiced their feelings about the United States, approximately three-quarters expressed positive attitudes: especially sympathy, gratitude, and, somewhat less, admiration. Yet a quarter of the sample (which corresponded rather closely to the Communist vote) also expressed negative feelings that ranged from apprehension or irritation to antipathy and dislike.[48]

It must be emphasized that eruptions of popular resentment occurred within a context of Gallic friendliness toward the United States, a preference for alliance with the West rather than the East, and a positive appreciation of Americans. Of those, for example, who perceived that the superpowers were bent on global domination, almost twice as many attributed this aggressive stance to the Soviets as did to the United States.[49] The greater fear lay to the East.

Fear of Yankee ambitions appeared, however, even in assessments of what the French liked most about Washington's policy—its economic and military aid and its sponsorship of European unification. In the case of the Marshall Plan, which opinion welcomed (without knowing much about it), Gallic skepticism refused to ascribe altruism to the giver. In 1947 almost two-thirds of a polling sample attributed the program either to American need for foreign markets or to American desires to intervene in European affairs.[50] Three years later, according to a confidential American survey, only one out of four French citizens thought the plan was working completely to France's advantage.[51] And once the Marshall Plan ended, though American financial aid was widely appreciated, it was still perceived as motivated by anticommunism or by a desire to dominate others especially for commercial purposes.[52]

French opinion perceived the United States not only as driven to acquire world markets but also as obsessed with fighting communism (and ready, a minority thought, to launch a preventive strike against the Soviet Union). Far fewer attributed to American policy a true desire for freedom, peace, or democracy. What was most unnerving about Washington's policy was that it seemed to endanger peace. It is difficult to overestimate the anxiety about war, especially atomic war, that permeated French consciousness during the Korean War from 1950 to 1953. The United States, in French eyes, shared responsibility for this tension with the Soviet Union. A down-to-earth response came from a farmer in the Vaucluse in 1950 when agronomists recommended that he plant fruit trees because these were best suited to the soil and climate: "Plant orchards so that the Americans and Russians can use them for a battlefield? Thanks, not so dumb!"[53] The farmer felt so insecure about the future that he refused to plant trees that would require years in order to produce income. At the same time a potential subscriber to *Rapports France-Etats-Unis*, the mouthpiece for the Marshall Plan, asked the periodical for a public promise to "burn all the subscription lists, letters, and other compromising papers in case the Russians come."[54] A year after the signature of the Atlantic pact, only a third of the non-Communists supported it while the Communists considered it a step toward war.[55] Irrespective of political affiliation French voters in 1952 overwhelmingly opted for neutrality in the event of war. Only Communist voters believed, however, that the United States was preparing a war of aggression. All other voters believed that if any nation were making such preparations, it was the Soviet Union.[56]

When the French expressed themselves about their nation's place in the postwar world they blended a passion for independence with realism. A pragmatic assessment of France's position dictated that alliance was the only plausible route to security. The French strongly preferred reliance on the United States over either neutrality or alliance with the Soviet Union. The optimal stance was a Western alliance that gave more support to French interests (in North Africa, for example) and also allowed more independence for France.[57] Still, some 30 percent opted for "absolute neutrality" (though only half of them thought it was actually possible), and others expressed a strong desire for increased independence. The longing for independence and for nonalignment persisted through the 1950s. At the end of the decade, when asked about preferred "allegiance," only 4 percent of those surveyed looked East and 24 percent looked West while almost 50 percent wanted France to favor neither East nor West.[58] Those intellectuals who espoused a third way, or independence during the depths of the Cold War, touched the hearts, if not the heads, of their fellow citizens.

American military bases, like the Atlantic alliance, also aroused mixed feelings. If almost half of those surveyed disapproved of the bases, there was also doubt that their removal would improve national security.[59] Over half the respondents expressed willingness to receive American soldiers in their homes and most would speak with them in the street. If a majority said the French should adopt a friendly attitude toward the

GIs, over a third preferred a more reserved stance. At the air force base at Châteauroux (Berry) the military lived separately from the French in a kind of colonial setting.[60] The troops used the town as an escape from military discipline, engaging there in antisocial behavior that did not endear them to the local inhabitants. The town's Communist newspaper publicized the misbehavior of the "occupiers," including the accidents caused by speeding in big cars. Despite the divisions and tensions between the two communities, the natives who were interviewed twenty years later remembered the American base and the soldiers warmly. The experience of the 1950s also served to sustain the illusion of Americans as happy, young, practical, attractive, and generous. This stereotype was nearly the opposite of the local inhabitants' self-image. They tended to see themselves as old, tired, poor, unattractive, and grasping. In this case we see French perceptions of Americans functioning as an ideal, rather than as a menace, in the internal debate about national identity.

Ambivalence, according to the 1953 survey, also marked general attitudes about American influence as it did feelings toward NATO and military bases. On the whole the French viewed the United States as a constructive force—but there were risks. The American presence aided peace, freedom, and socioeconomic progress yet also threatened national independence. America was tolerated. Almost no one wanted American influence increased, and two out of three respondents wanted it diminished.[61] Of those who had seen "U.S. Go Home" graffiti 40 percent disapproved (and wanted it removed), 13 percent approved, and 26 percent were indifferent (21 percent had no opinion).[62]

To those who perceived America as a menace it appeared multidimensional, brandishing economic, political, and military weapons. But almost none (only 4 percent) of the participants in this poll perceived America as a cultural threat.[63] There is evidence that the perception of cultural danger was more an elite, than it was a popular, concern. Moreover, the average French person welcomed most American consumer products such as kitchen appliances, periodicals like the *Sélection du Reader's Digest,* cigarettes, and even canned food (though chewing gum and Coca-Cola appealed only to a tiny minority). Opinion was sharply divided over American films and jazz.[64] With respect to consumer products and mass culture, public and elite opinion diverged.

This same survey reveals some social and political distinctions among the populace. Rural or urban residence and occupational categories, except for the working class, made little difference. With respect to age groups it was the oldest generation of men and women (over 65) who displayed the greatest sympathy and gratitude. Those in the youngest category (ages 20 to 34), who found America progressive and more eagerly adopted some American ways such as dress, also showed more apprehension, irritation, and antipathy. The youngest disliked America's domineering ways and its foreign policy. But youth corresponded strongly with left-wing politics. And by far the most important determinant of attitude was political affiliation.

The Communist electorate with its working-class base was distinctive in answering questions related to the Soviet Union and to the possibility of war between the superpowers. Only those who identified themselves as Communist voters registered systematic hostility to the United States.[65] Here was the mass base of militant anti-Americanism. Nevertheless, on certain issues such as the perils of Americanization, the Communists only amplified what others thought. Voters for the moderate MRP (Mouvement républicain populaire) were consistently the most favorable to America. And Gaullist voters, who along with MRP voters displayed the most sympathy and gratitude toward the United States, viewed American influence in Europe as pacific, saw the Marshall Plan as indispensable, and approved American rearmament of France. Gaullist anti-Americanism was scarcely visible in 1953 except for opposition to Washington's sponsorship of European unification. On colonial issues and German rearmament, Gaullists were no more critical of the United States than the moderate parties.

Most revealing were the distinctive attitudes of the elite or what the 1953 survey called *personnalités dirigeantes*—meaning parliamentarians, high civil servants, academics, business managers, and other professionals. They were better informed about the United States and far more favorable toward it than was the general public. Almost a third had visited America and recalled Fifth Avenue or sunny Florida beaches; they relied on more direct sources of information, such as conversations with Americans. These leaders, unlike the general public, displayed real enthusiasm for borrowing American production techniques. They were also more willing to grant Washington selfless and humane motives. They were more positive about certain aspects of American policy, such as military and economic aid and European unification, while they objected more strenuously than the general public to Washington's policy toward North Africa. Elites and the public shared the same worry about American hegemony, but the upper stratum expressed even more hostility to any extension of American presence, especially American cultural influence. These *personnalités dirigeantes*, more than the average

French men or women, criticized Americans for being immature and uncivilized and disliked the American way of life, for example, its tension and pace. A typical complaint was, "American influence in Europe endangers good taste."[66] Elites, more than others, harbored cultural anti-Americanism.

At the end of the 1950s the general assessment of the United States was favorable. Approximately 40 percent of those polled held a "very good" or "good" view, 40 percent held "neither a good nor bad" attitude, and some 11 percent professed a "poor" opinion. The Soviet Union fared much less well. Yet the French continued to divide over allegiance in the Cold War with a handful preferring the Soviets, a quarter the United States, and half wanting to stand outside the blocs.[67] The French liked or tolerated most things about America—with certain strong reservations about American influence on their soil. They also opined that in the future the United States would continue to have the highest standard of living but that France was the best place to live. Despite the appeal of the American way, the French way was unsurpassed.

··········

The most distinctive feature of French attitudes during the early 1950s was the uneasiness about American domination. More than other Europeans, the French harbored misgivings about American political, economic, and cultural ambitions—and at the same time welcomed the Western alliance and United States aid. Popular opinion (Communist voters apart as a special case) shared elite concerns about national independence, disapproved of some of Washington's policies, for example, toward Germany and North Africa, and expressed skepticism about American altruism. There was a widespread desire for a recovery, if not of prewar status, at least of national independence. A majority nursed the hope of non-alignment between the superpowers and balanced this hope against the reality of need for American protection. Yet another salient feature of opinion was the difference between elite and popular opinion over Americanization. While almost no one wanted American influence increased, the average French men and women made far less than the upper classes did of the danger from either popular culture or consumer products.

The stereotype of Americans and America remained fixed throughout the decade and heavily marked attitudes. Like most collective wisdom about others, the label that identified *les grands enfants* was pejorative, although it contained strong positive attributes as well. And the Gallic caricature of Americans was in certain respects the mirror image of the

French people's self-image. If Americans were conformists and youthful, then implicitly the French were individualists and mature. Here French identity was defining itself by negatively stereotyping Americans.

But the volatile nature of feelings about America arose from the evolving conjuncture of international relations. In the foreground were the disappointments and quarrels among the Allies and the intermittent explosions of resentment over issues like decolonization. In the background were dependence on the Yankee superpower and the fear of war raised by the Cold War, especially by American anticommunism.

American aid, products, and propaganda did not cap this deep reservoir of political dissatisfaction. In fact, the presence of United States military bases led to as many unpleasant encounters as to friendships. American economic aid did not earn much gratitude because many saw it as an act of self-interest rather than one of generosity and because it was often invisible. A French worker laboring on a construction project that had been funded and supplied by the Marshall Plan perceived no American gift—only wages for hard work. American exports to France were not always the finest expressions of American industry and culture. Chewing gum, Hollywood films, and comics did not convey the noblest images of the United States. Furthermore, the entry of American corporations, along with the influx of products, aroused concern about "economic imperialism." Finally, the American cultural offensive that peaked in 1952, at least as the socialist-inclined coterie of St-Germain-des-Prés saw it, antagonized as much as it converted—though in the long run certain programs, like that of cultural exchange, may have had benefit. American propaganda could not loosen the roots of the left's aversion. It is this source of anti-Americanism that we must take up next.

CHAPTER 3

Yankee Go Home

The Left, Coca-Cola, and the Cold War

In the early years of the Cold War America became the subject of heated political and ideological controversy that escalated rhetoric into action and even violence. There was pushing and shoving among deputies in the National Assembly, dock strikes against the transport of American military equipment, a mass demonstration against an American general appointed to head NATO, an effort to oust the editor of *Le Monde* for his anti-Americanism, and collective pleas from the Parisian intelligentsia to Washington on behalf of Julius and Ethel Rosenberg. Even that most American of consumer products, Coca-Cola, was drawn into the fray.

The strident complaints and accusations voiced in this chapter will be those of Communist party members as well as leftist journalists and intellectuals. Ideology and politics form the basis of this encounter with America. Here are the defiant shouts of Communist militants and the confident pronouncements of Parisian mandarins assessing in philosophical and ideological language the meaning of American policy and hegemony in the early 1950s.

The political and intellectual universe of Paris should not, however, be construed simply as anti-American. It was contested territory. The governing coalitions of the Fourth Republic had tied their fortunes to the Atlantic alliance; the French, as we have seen, wanted American protection and liked Americans and much of what America exported. Most visitors to the United States praised the New World's vigor and prosperity, avoided politics, waxed eloquent about "Americanism," or

refused to make simplistic generalizations about the "American character."[1] A pro-American element also flourished among the intelligentsia.
Raymond Aron and François Mauriac, for example, championed the
Atlantic alliance and André Maurois lauded the American way; there
were pro-American reviews like *Preuves*. But on the left it was the
anti-Americans who predominated and who captured the most attention.

· · · · · · · · · ·

A "civilization of bathtubs and Frigidaires" is how the Communist
poet Louis Aragon described the United States in 1951.[2] Aragon was
one of many writers and journalists who, along with Communist party
officials, led the postwar attack on America. The party had been forced
out of the governing coalition in 1947 yet remained the largest party in
the National Assembly and commanded roughly 25 percent of the
electorate. Beginning in 1947 Communist propaganda savaged every
feature of the American presence in France.[3] The Communists coined
such phrases as *marshallisation* and *coca-colonisation* to suggest the
United States was trying to colonize France. Washington had supposedly
ordered the ouster of the Communists from government in order to
make France safe for "Yankee trusts." From the Communists' patriotic
perspective the Fourth Republic was a servile regime unwilling to defend
French independence.

The NATO pact, which faced ratification in 1949, raised Communist
anti-Americanism to a fever pitch. In an effort to block American military
aid, Communist-led dockers in Marseilles, Bordeaux, and other ports
prevented the unloading of American war matériel. "Yankee Go Home"
defaced walls (fig. 3). In 1949 the party launched a peace movement to
mobilize support against the United States. Utilizing the Stockholm
appeal of 1950 to ban atomic weapons and appealing to the widespread
fear of war between the superpowers, the Mouvement des partisans de
la paix organized peace marches and a "peace vote." Fifteen million
French citizens signed the Stockholm appeal.[4] And when the government of Georges Bidault in March 1950 attempted to end Communist
obstruction of the war in Indochina by passing a bill against "sabotage,"
Communist deputies in the National Assembly turned violent. One MRP
deputy was beaten and the premier's desk was nearly overturned on him.

The heavy polemical barrage that accompanied these actions was
crude to the point of being ludicrous. Nevertheless, most of the charges
had some basis. The Communists merely distorted programs and motives. A few examples convey the character of this polemic. According to

3. Communist magazine cover. (*Démocratie nouvelle* 12 [1951];
Bibliothèque nationale)

the Communists, the Marshall Plan aimed at opening France to American products and investments. Writing about such aid, one columnist
asked: "Why do they prefer to feed wheat to the pigs and send us corn?"
Because, he answered, if the United States has to choose between

animals—including pigs—and Europeans, it prefers animals.[5] And NATO was preparing Western Europe to resume "Hitler's war" against a peace-loving Soviet Union. When war came, American planes would drop atomic bombs on the Soviet Union while French troops would fight as infantry alongside a resurrected "Nazi army." The presence of GIs was another foreign "occupation" and the "Amerloques" (a popular pejorative term for Americans) were likened to the Nazis. With the Korean conflict Communist propaganda reached new heights, or depths, denouncing the United States government and military as "monsters" and "war criminals" and charging the United States army with the use of germ warfare.

Addressing life in the United States, the Communists accused American schools of ignoring European culture and of fearing science because they suspected it of atheism.[6] The prominent physicist and Communist, Irène Joliot-Curie, after being held overnight by immigration officials on Ellis Island, said her detention was a sign of weakness. The daughter of the discoverers of radium remarked that Americans preferred fascism to communism because they thought "fascism has more respect for money."[7] Even the much publicized American standard of living was a fraud. L'Humanité, the party's daily, ran a series of articles in 1948 with such titles as: "One could starve with a telephone"; and "Not everyone has a bathroom." The Frigidaire, militants were informed, was a useless gadget most of the year, except for making ice cubes for whiskey cocktails. It was usually cool enough in France so that a traditional garde-manger "placed on the window keeps the leftovers of Sunday's lamb until Wednesday."[8]

Among the Left Bank literary and artistic elite, prominent figures like Aragon, Pablo Picasso, and Paul Eluard worked actively with the Communists. So many intellectuals aligned themselves with the Communists in the early postwar years that the PCF liked to think of itself as the "parti de l'intelligence."[9] The reasons for alignment were numerous and the relations with the PCF ranged from those of party intellectuals like Aragon to others of independence and a certain distance. Such engagé intellectuals were dubbed compagnons de route (fellow travelers) or philo-Communists. The circles of friendly writers, scientists, academics, actors, and artists included Claude Roy, Daniel Guerin, Emmanuel d'Astier de la Vigerie, René Etiemble, Yves Montand, Vercors, Edgar Morin, and Frédéric Joliot-Curie; at the outer fringe were Maurice Merleau-Ponty and the staff around Emmanuel Mounier at the review Esprit who disapproved of Stalinism but refused to be anti-Communist.

For these *compagnons de route* the Soviets had proven themselves to be antifascists, and 1917 and 1789 were twin landmarks in the march of human progress. Such intellectuals looked with favor at the PCF not because they were captivated by the party's doctrinal eminence but because of its record in the Resistance and its strategic political position. Even if its program was a hodgepodge of Soviet-inspired homilies, the Communist party was the most powerful party on the left.

Anti-Americanism appeared in much of their writing. Daniel Guerin, for example, concluded after visiting the United States that the promise of a new mass society had been betrayed by American labor and checked by the domination of gigantic trusts.[10] Claude Roy contributed a far more sympathetic and apolitical account of his visit but remained convinced of American bellicosity.[11] Aragon, angered by the temporary substitution of a new Ford automobile for a missing sculpture from a Parisian square that honored Victor Hugo, wrote:

A Ford automobile, the civilization of Detroit, the assembly line . . . the atomic danger, encircled by napalm . . . here is the symbol of this subjugation to the dollar applauded even in the land of Molière; here is the white lacquered god of foreign industry, the Atlantic totem that chases away French glories with Marshall Plan stocks. . . . The Yankee, more arrogant than the Nazi iconoclast, substitutes the machine for the poet, Coca-Cola for poetry, American advertising for *La Légende des siècles*, the mass-manufactured car for the genius, the Ford for Victor Hugo![12]

Aragon's poetic diatribe revived prewar fears of America as a cultural menace. And by 1950, unlike 1930, the United States was a present danger. Party speakers railed against the American cultural invasion— sadistic comics and pulp literature. Edgar Morin, a member of the party who later became a prominent sociologist, called the *Reader's Digest* "a pocket-sized stupefier." According to Morin the magazine propagated the myths of American capitalist civilization. With its innocent optimism ("You're timid? Cheer up. Here are 148 ways to overcome timidity") *Reader's Digest* served as a "drug for little minds."[13] The novels of Hemingway and Faulkner, it was said, showed a society charged with violence, racism, injustice, despair, and misery. War, according to Hollywood, was an adventure; American soldiers were invincible. And English expressions like "toothpaste" and "surplus" were corrupting the integrity of the national language. This cultural colonization was particularly annoying since the United States was "intellectually in the cradle."[14] For a moment Marx was on the side of Racine, Rabelais, and the Académie française.

What was the purpose of the Communists' polemic? Preventing the integration of France into the Western bloc was its general aim. More specifically, it hoped to subvert the Marshall Plan by arousing resistance, among the working class in particular, and by dampening the generosity of the American Congress. It also sought to damage the reputation of domestic political rivals and prevent them from becoming too cozy with the Americans. Thus it called virtually every non-Communist party or leader in the Fourth Republic from the Socialists to de Gaulle an agent of the United States. In addition, it mobilized party militants and aroused the electorate. Without question Communist voters most consistently voiced anti-American sentiments. Almost 60 percent of PCF voters thought the United States was readying for an aggressive war and 95 percent disapproved of the presence of American bases in France.[15] Here was the most formidable and intractable bloc of French anti-Americanism.

But anti-Americanism was not confined to the Communist party or even fellow travelers during the Cold War. It found adherents among left-wing Christian *progressistes* and so-called neutralists.[16] For these intellectuals, relations with the PCF were fragile and attitudes toward the Soviet Union were checkered, but they judged the United States, or at least its policy, harshly. And they were often more forgiving and less afraid of the Russians than of the Americans.

The overriding issue was to avoid war and define the place of France in the emerging bipolar world. In particular what strategy best guaranteed peace and gave France security and independence? While the Communists seized the Soviet option, Christian *progressistes* and neutralists tended toward nonalignment in the struggle between East and West. They hoped to build an independent, unified, and socialist Europe. For these intellectuals Americans were the intruders. The American presence was palpable compared to that of the Russians, whereas the United States itself was remote and virtually unknown in these circles.[17]

Some rallied to the Communist-sponsored peace movement, as did, for example, progressive Catholics who wrote for *La Quinzaine,* a review launched in 1950 by the Dominicans that aimed at reviving French Catholicism, especially among the working class. *La Quinzaine* oscillated between neutralism and an unqualified pro-Soviet stance.[18]

Other, more influential, *progressiste* Christians, like Emmanuel Mounier and Jean-Marie Domenach at the review *Esprit,* also refused to oppose communism; they denounced the Marshall Plan and NATO for incorporating Western Europe into an American protectorate and destroying hope for an autonomous and pacific Europe. Emmanuel Mounier, who had expressed his distaste for America in the 1930s, wrote to an American friend in 1948:

The Russians, the Russians for sure. But the Russians are still a long way away. And what we know, what we see are the tons of American paper and American ideas and American propaganda in our bookstores. . . . Our prime ministers must visit the American embassy before making their most important decisions; there is an American shadow over us just as there is a Russian shadow over the other part of Europe.[19]

The *Esprit* circle found some virtue in the PCF but maintained its autonomy.

The brilliant young writer Albert Camus also tried to find a third way between the superpowers even as his outspoken anti-Stalinism earned him notoriety among the community of fellow travelers. Yet Camus, who had been pleased with his visit to the United States in 1946, criticized Americans for their "worship of technology" and the enervating character of American radio and movies.[20] Still other neutralist intellectuals, most notably Jean-Paul Sartre and his celebrated team at the review *Les Temps modernes,* attacked American policy but came to the side of the Communist party only when the Fourth Republic seemed poised to ban the party in 1952.

When *Le Monde,* which was obligatory reading for the Parisian intelligentsia, adopted a neutralist position on the Cold War, the United States acquired its most formidable critic.[21] The daily's founder-editor was Hubert Beuve-Méry, who harbored deep misgivings about America. The newspaper's position was most succinctly put by one of its columnists, Maurice Duverger:

Between a sovietized Europe and the Atlantic empire, the second solution is clearly preferable because in the first instance slavery would be certain, whereas in the second case war would only become probable. Should circumstance dictate this dilemma we would choose the least terrible alternative. But since we are not conclusively locked in, a third solution remains: that of a neutralized Europe.[22]

Beuve-Méry and his staff ascribed to the United States an overweening desire to dominate Western Europe and yet no determination to defend it should a crisis arise. He retained the image of American troops retiring from Czechoslovakia in 1945, and leaving Central Europe to the Red Army. But above all, Beuve-Méry argued, if Western Europeans sided with the United States, they would only make war between the superpowers more, rather than less, likely. He refused to choose between capitalism and communism. Nevertheless, he did not equate the competing ideologies: "It is not a question, whatever one thinks of the dollar, of mass production, and the *Reader's Digest,* of placing the United States and the Soviet Union on the same footing."[23] For free men would not choose a Soviet-dominated Europe.

Neutralism was most forcefully spelled out in *Le Monde* by Etienne Gilson, the eminent Thomist philosopher who had been Beuve-Méry's teacher before the war. Gilson doubted that Washington would automatically protect France and chose armed neutrality over NATO; it was America's turn to host the next world war. The Catholic philosopher enflamed the debate when, in 1949, he accused Washington of wanting to dump its responsibilities onto Europe.[24] Gilson accused the United States of using dollars to buy off Europeans so that the continent would be the site of the coming American-Soviet conflict.

A debate that was ostensibly over neutralist foreign policy escalated into a nasty attack on America when *Le Monde* published a series of articles on "Imperial America" by Pierre Emmanuel, poet, journalist, and contributor to *Esprit.* Emmanuel was one of many leftists to whom American immigration authorities had refused a visa. He ridiculed President Truman as a "former suspenders' salesman" and derided American anticommunism as a sign of panic.[25] Afraid of its own emptiness—because it had nothing but a temporary advantage in industrial prowess—the United States adopted anticommunism as a pretext to expand its power. According to Emmanuel, Americans searched in vain for a raison d'être that would survive the astonishing power that history had capriciously awarded them. He noted that almost every European who had been to the United States was appalled by its social conformity and by the sight of humanity reduced to producers and consumers. A lack of political maturity predisposed Americans to fascism. The FBI might one day rival the Gestapo. To him, both the United States and the Soviet Union were totalitarian—"the one in power, the other in deed." He rejected the Communist solution but could find no consolation in the American way. In the end he could counsel Europeans only to defend their Christian values as the ultimate protection against both totalitarianisms. Europeans would outlast the Americans because they retained an "idea"; "should the new Holy Roman Empire take Washington for its capital, its heart and brains will remain in Europe."

Emmanuel's evocation of Christianity corresponded with Beuve-Méry's sensibility. Behind the editor's neutralism was a stern Jansenist temperament that was offended by the materialism that America embodied. Before the war Beuve-Méry, trained by the Dominicans, had voiced his aversion for capitalist values. At heart the incorruptible editor was a Christian moralist who had a phobia about the corrupting powers of money; he was immune to the charms of America. A visit to the United States in 1945 failed to assuage his misgivings about the American way and only reinforced his worry about America's political ambitions.[26] *Le Monde*'s repugnance for *américanisme* was expressed by Maurice Duverger:

The American threat remains for the moment less urgent, less serious, and less dangerous than the Soviet menace. . . . Between the invasion of *Gletkins* and the invasion of *Digests,* we certainly prefer the latter; however, in the long run the civilization of *Digests* will kill the European spirit just as surely as the civilization of *Gletkins.*[27]

Beuve-Méry's aversion for American society surfaced, as we shall see, in *Le Monde*'s treatment of the Coca-Cola affair.

Opponents, especially convinced Atlanticists like Raymond Aron, François Mauriac, and Paul Claudel, attacked the paper's neutralism as an illusion. French freedoms and independence, they argued, depended on American protection. Aron refused any equivalence between the United States and the Soviet Union drawn by some neutralists and chided them for their leftist dogmatism. He pointed out the American socioeconomic system was far more democratic than that of most European countries.[28] And Paul Claudel, the noted Catholic author and head of the Association France-Etats-Unis, took exception to Pierre Emmanuel's labeling the United States an imperialist nation. America was, if anything, generous, according to Claudel. If Europeans should take pride in their past, as Emmanuel urged, Claudel suggested they also recognize that Americans had turned toward the future.[29]

Gilson's and Emmanuel's columns nearly led to Beuve-Méry's removal as editor. From inside the paper René Courtin, a co-director, was outraged by Emmanuel's articles and found the neutralist line dangerous and unfair to the United States. Courtin tried without success to force Beuve-Méry's resignation.[30] Others, from the right, debunked neutralism by pointing out it required an unprecedented rearmament drive. The most extreme opponents called *Le Monde* crypto-Communist and suggested that Beuve-Méry deserved the Stalin prize.

Beuve-Méry's response to the "realists" who embraced NATO was to advocate nonalignment and moral resistance to the superpowers.

"The task before us, as they used to say, is a labor of the Capetians. It offers more difficulty, more interest, and certainly demands no less virility than appeals to hatred and recourse to the atomic bomb or napalm."[31] Beuve-Méry later observed that the term "nonalignment" would have served *Le Monde*'s cause better, because "neutrality" wrongly suggested passivity or defeatism whereas he and Gilson proposed a strong independent position for France between the superpowers. Beuve-Méry abandoned strict neutrality when he endorsed NATO in 1949 and unmasked the Communist-sponsored peace movement as a political gambit. But the newspaper's director sparked controversy by also declaring that the NATO pact would inevitably lead to German rearmament.[32] After 1950 *Le Monde* continued to try to escape the logic of submission to the United States and German rearmament by seeking an independent way to defend France.

Le Monde's neutralism had the support of many of its readers and its position was shared by other left-wing journals like *Esprit, Les Temps modernes, Franc-Tireur,* and *France-Observateur.* The latter's formula was "Neither Washington Nor Moscow." Claude Bourdet, who edited *France-Observateur,* maintained his neutralist position long after others had surrendered one. In 1952 he wrote to an American review advising Americans to "leave us alone."[33] For a brief moment in 1948–49 the campaign for a third way, a European strategy within the Cold War, crystallized into a new political movement, the Rassemblement démocratique révolutionnaire, led by such intellectual stars as Bourdet, Sartre, Georges Altman, and David Rousset. But the movement failed to find its following and quickly dispersed—in part because of disputes over relations with the United States. Nonalignment might have been a preferred stance for these mandarins but it attracted little support from the public who, while sympathizing with neutralism, preferred the security they had within the Atlantic alliance.

The leftist intelligentsia represented by *Le Monde* scorned pro-American dissenters. Among the Parisian literati, *Preuves* was the principal advocate of the United States; the "American review" was what *Le Monde* dubbed it.[34] Communists and *compagnons de route* ostracized those who contributed to it as reactionaries or American hirelings (in fact, *Preuves* did receive subsidies from the Congress for Cultural Freedom). Among its contributors were such celebrated anti-Communists as Raymond Aron, Thierry Maulnier, Denis de Rougemont, Arthur Koestler, Herbert Luethy, and Ignazio Silone. And it received support from the Socialist and the MRP parties. The purpose of *Preuves* was to detach the intelligentsia from its neutralism and its fascination with the Soviet bloc. It engaged in ideological warfare with journals like *Esprit* and *France-Observateur* and tried to nullify pressure from the PCF for intellectuals to join the peace movement. While *Preuves* unmasked Stalinism as a totalitarianism, systematically defended Washington's foreign policy, and praised American institutions, it was not uncritical of the United States. The review, for example, distinguished its anticommunism from that of Senator McCarthy, and it argued that if the Rosenbergs were guilty they should not be executed. Despite the eminence of its contributors *Preuves* achieved intellectual respectability only in the late 1950s after the passing of the harshest phase of the Cold War. Its American connection was a handicap. Reading *Preuves* openly, at an institution like the Ecole normale supérieure in the early 1950s, was generally considered to be an act of defiance.

Aversion to the American way, which was acute on the left of the political spectrum, also appeared (though to a far lesser extent) on the right—even among proponents of Atlanticism. Raymond Aron, who wrote warmly of NATO, had, as we shall see, his reservations about America. The Gaullists, who had organized themselves into a new political movement, the RPF (Rassemblement du peuple français), in 1947, were Atlanticists yet included those who disapproved of America. This complex stance is not unfamiliar within the tradition of anti-Americanism among French conservatives. André Malraux, the eminent novelist and arbiter of artistic taste, was the principal spokesman on cultural affairs for the RPF. In his appeal to the intellectual community in 1948 Malraux denied America's cultural claims:

There is no culture in America that claims to be American. That's an invention of Europeans. . . . And American culture, once its European element is removed, is a field of technical knowledge more than it is an organic culture. Besides America now sets the tone in popular culture, in radio, film, and the press.[35]

But the Soviets, unlike the Americans, according to Malraux, wanted to do away with European culture altogether. Menaced both by Americans and by Russians, the Gaullists preferred the protection of the United States, as most of their compatriots did. Thus the Gaullists were not a major source of anti-Americanism in these years. Malraux, for example, participated in the 1952 cultural festival sponsored by the Congress for Cultural Freedom. And de Gaulle might criticize the Fourth Republic for failing to guard French independence vis-à-vis the United States, and he might disapprove the structure of NATO and denounce the EDC, but need for American protection and militant anticommunism kept the RPF within the NATO camp. Only after the Korean War did de Gaulle and the RPF move away from Atlanticism.[36] In the depths of the Cold War, the major attack on America came from the left.

• • • • • • • • • •

In 1952 the Communist party treated the capital to a violent celebration of anti-Americanism. The occasion was the arrival in Paris of General Matthew Ridgway to take command of NATO forces. The American general, according to the Communist press, was a "war criminal" and a "microbe general" because of the allegation that he had ordered the use of bacteriological weapons in the Korean War.[37]

He comes dripping with the blood of martyred Korean and Chinese women, children, and old people against whom he has committed crimes of the most unspeakable savagery. He is the war criminal whom history will always call "Ridgway the plague." He comes with the curses of the people ringing in his ears for having been the first to execute the hellish plans of the dollar princes: to kill human beings with bacteria carrying cholera, plague, and other contagious diseases.[38]

The Communists intensifed their effort to block the expansion of American "militarism" not only because of the wars in Indochina and Korea, but also because they wanted to obstruct the restoration of sovereignty to the German Federal Republic. The formula "U.S. equals SS" and comparisons between Hitler's Germany and Truman's America linked Germanophobia with the United States.

Confrontation with the Communists over General Ridgway grew likely once Antoine Pinay became premier in the spring of 1952. Pinay was the most conservative premier the Republic had had since 1946 and he was tainted by collaboration with the Vichy regime. *L'Humanité* charged Pinay with leading France toward a third world war that would make France an "atomic desert."[39] In the face of the government's prohibition of a demonstration organized by the peace movement for 28 May, the PCF decided to test Pinay's repressive intentions. As many as twenty thousand demonstrators paraded with placards reading "Ridgway Murderer," "Go Home!," "Americans belong in America," and "We Want Peace!" (fig. 4). Clashes with the security police left one demonstrator dead, two hundred wounded, and several hundred arrested, including party secretary Jacques Duclos. Those arrested and beaten by the police included two "worker-priests"; these were idealistic young priests who lived and worked among the proletariat in order to bear

4. Ridgway riots: police and civilians battle in Paris, May 1952. (Courtesy AP/Wide World Photos)

witness to their faith and ended up associating with such Communist-sponsored causes as the peace movement.

At this point the Pinay government became overzealous in its drive to isolate or break the Communist party.[40] Some officials were looking for an opportunity, and the May demonstration seemed to deliver the Communists right into their hands. As well as violence, ideological hysteria made for comedy—in this case the story of Duclos's pigeons. On the night of 28 May the police stopped Duclos's car near one of the demonstrations and discovered two pigeons in the back seat. According to the police report, the birds were rolled in a blanket, smothered but still warm. The police concluded they were carrier pigeons that Duclos had used for communications during an illegal demonstration. They arrested the party secretary. Duclos spent a month in jail, though he claimed the fowl were meant for a casserole; others speculated they were part of a flight of "peace doves." But the government had to back down when an autopsy revealed the birds in question were simple domestic pigeons. The pursuit of Duclos had exceeded Pinay's intentions.

Wanting only to discredit the party, the premier intervened to dampen the zeal of the fanatics who had arrested the party leader.

The anti-Communist mania of the Pinay government had unintended consequences. It aroused Jean-Paul Sartre. Up to then Sartre had opposed the Marshall Plan and NATO, blamed the Korean War on the West, and espoused neutralism, but had not been an outspoken opponent of America. If forced to choose sides in the Cold War, he preferred the Soviet Union, which he believed represented progress toward human liberation, over the United States, which he deemed a reactionary force. But he was at odds with the PCF. And his views of American society and civilization were nuanced.[41]

Sartre was fascinated with American jazz, film, and literature. He had toured the country twice in 1945–46 trying to fathom its contradictions. He was delighted with America's vigor and the easy relations among social classes. He admired American devotion to freedom and human dignity. Sartre mused on how Americans reconciled conformity with individualism. New York symbolized this reconciliation—the streets were monotonous and uniform but the skyscrapers bold and unique. But he disapproved of the ugly racism, the harsh treatment of the underprivileged, and the effects of mechanization on labor. And he analyzed *américanisme* as a new form of social control. Writing to the *New York Herald Tribune* in 1946, Sartre stated that he was not anti-American because one could not be for or against such a complex society in the same way that one could be "antifascist."[42] But when the Fourth Republic began to hound Communists, as Senator McCarthy was doing in the United States, Sartre counterattacked.

In 1952 the celebrated leader of existentialism denounced America and became a *compagnon de route* of the PCF. His notorious attack on the United States as a country suffering from rabies was a response to what he called the "legal lynching" of the Rosenbergs in 1953.

Decidedly there is something rotten in America. . . . You are collectively responsible for the death of the Rosenbergs, some for having provoked this murder, others for having let it be carried out; you have allowed the United States to be the cradle of a new fascism. . . . One day, maybe, all this goodwill will heal you of your fear; we hope so because we have loved you. Meanwhile, don't be surprised if, from one end of Europe to the other, we scream: Watch out, America has rabies! We must cut all ties with it or else we shall be bitten and infected next.[43]

Sartre was expressing a visceral anger at American politics and policy. He saw himself fulfilling the intellectual's mission as he had defined it in

1946 to a New York newspaper—"to denounce injustice wherever it is to be found, and this all the more when he loves the country which allows this injustice to be committed."[44]

Sartre's companion, Simone de Beauvoir, who had been ambivalent about the United States during her visits there in 1947—she praised American dynamism and freedom but found it suffering from conformism, consumerism, anti-intellectualism, racism, and psychological ennui—joined Sartre in his new aggressive anti-Americanism. Seeing two American soldiers enter a hotel, she reflected how in 1944 these men in khaki had represented freedom but now defended a nation that supported dictatorship and corruption all over the globe—the regimes of Franco, Syngman Rhee, Batista, Salazar. Even though Sartre abandoned his alignment with the PCF in 1956, he and de Beauvoir continued to view the United States as the source of international political reaction and the Americans as a "people of sheep." Their interest in America subsided, yet Sartre and de Beauvoir continued to denounce American imperialism as responsible for the ills of the world.

During 1952–53 the Rosenberg trial, like General Ridgway's appointment, fueled anti-Americanism to the point that some took to the streets of the French capital. Most of the Parisian press argued for leniency for the convicted spies. *Esprit* said the Rosenbergs represented possible innocence crushed by patriotic passion, fear, and pride. Jean-Marie Domenach noted the resemblance between the spy trials simultaneously under way in New York and Prague (the Slansky trial). In both instances justice had submitted to political passion. In both instances fanatics had once again made the Jew the target.[45] Seeking a pardon for the condemned, Domenach and many other French intellectuals, including Sartre and de Beauvoir, sent telegrams to Washington and to Prague—to no avail. *Le Monde* noted that legal forms had been followed but that the judge's references to the Communist loyalties of the Rosenbergs had prejudiced the jury. The paper suggested that Judge Kaufman was unduly severe in sentencing the couple to death because he was trying to disassociate the Jewish community from the spies and thus had acted out of reverse anti-Semitism.[46] When President Eisenhower refused a pardon and the Rosenbergs were executed, *Le Monde* accused the president of succumbing to mass hysteria aroused by Senator McCarthy's witch hunt and to the frustrations of the Korean War. Beuve-Méry wrote that justice was done but that the execution was a serious defeat for all the countries of the Western alliance because in it the cause of truth and humanity lost ground. Free peoples, he wrote, were "frightened of seeing a growing shadow of gigantic idols fed by lies, terror, and denunciations. They fear the time, perhaps close at hand, when the choice will only be between the role of executioner or martyr . . . "[47]

To the Communists, the Rosenbergs had been declared guilty because they were pacifists, democrats, Jews, and partisans of Soviet-American friendship. When President Eisenhower decided against clemency, the Communist party, which almost alone believed in the Rosenbergs' innocence, turned out its militants to demonstrate before the United States embassy. There followed over eight hundred arrests and one shooting.

· · · · · · · · · ·

All the elements assembled so far in this analysis of Cold War anti-Americanism converge in a single episode—the strange affair of Coca-Cola. Here an American corporation unwittingly set off a furor that involved the Communist party, the Parisian intelligentsia, certain interest groups, the parliament, and the cabinet of the Fourth Republic as well as the American government.

Perhaps no commercial product is more thoroughly identified with America than Coca-Cola. One company official called it "the most American thing in America." Another wrote approvingly of this confusion: "Apparently some of our friends overseas have difficulty distinguishing between the United States and Coca-Cola."[48] When a magazine wanted three objects for a photograph that were peculiarly American it selected a baseball, a hot dog, and a bottle of Coke. This soft drink originated in Atlanta during the 1880s as a quasimedicinal, yet refreshing, nonalcoholic beverage. From the beginning the drink was associated with mass advertising, a high consumption society, and free enterprise. Since the soft drink satisfied no essential need, the Coca-Cola Company utilized extensive advertising: signs, special delivery trucks, articles like calendars and lamps that carried the distinctive trademark, radio commercials, and slogans such as "The Pause that Refreshes." The company carefully cultivated an image for its product: Coke was wholesome and pleasant. And the company's history exemplified the virtues of free enterprise. Robert Woodruff, the company's longtime president, once remarked that within every bottle was "the essence of capitalism." The founders of Coca-Cola became rich, powerful, and famous. Top company executives claimed presidents of the United States as friends. Up to the 1920s, however, the company confined its sales largely to North America. Only then did it begin to reach out for opportunities abroad.

The richest new markets lay in Europe, Latin America, and the Pacific. The Coca-Cola Export Corporation began in 1930 to handle overseas business and was soon operating in some twenty-eight countries. Technological advance (such as finding a way to concentrate the syrup that was the basis of the drink) facilitated exports. The export corporation normally employed a franchise system that allowed foreign nationals to own and operate bottling subsidiaries. Local interests provided capital, materials, and staff—almost everything except the concentrate—when they signed a contract to become a Coca-Cola bottler. The mother company helped the new bottling franchise get started and supervised product quality and advertising while non-Americans operated the franchise and earned the bulk of the profits. It was an ingenious system that minimized the Atlanta company's participation and furthered the product's rapid expansion.

In Europe this early multinational had made only a modest start by 1939, but the Second World War proved to be a boon. Woodruff stated the company's wartime policy: "We will see that every man in uniform gets a bottle of Coca-Cola for five cents wherever he is and whatever it costs."[49] The distinctive Coke bottle accompanied the GI into war. Company employees were assigned as "technical observers" to the military in order to take charge of new bottling plants set up close to the front lines. Coca-Cola, to some GIs, became identified with American war aims. One soldier wrote home: "To my mind, I am in this damn mess as much to help keep the custom of drinking Cokes as I am to help preserve the million other benefits our country blesses its citizens with."[50] As a result of the war, two-thirds of the veterans drank Coke and sixty-four bottling plants had been ferried abroad, most at government expense. The next step was to mount a systematic campaign for the European market.

The late 1940s saw Coca-Cola expand rapidly on the continent. Bottling operations began in the Netherlands, Belgium, and Luxembourg in 1947; then came Switzerland and Italy, and France followed in 1949. The Olympic games in Helsinki became an occasion for promoting the drink. Since there was no bottler in Finland, company officials organized a quasi-military operation: they sent a rebuilt D-Day landing craft from Amsterdam to Helsinki loaded with publicity material such as 150,000 sun visors bearing the trademark "Coca-Cola" and 720,000 bottles of Coke. Salesmen even managed to get photographs of Russian athletes consuming the capitalist beverage. The cover of *Time* magazine showed the globe drinking a bottle of Coke with the caption: "World and Friend: love that piaster, that lira, that tickey, and that American way of life."[51] Coca-Cola was fast becoming a universal drink.

The chairman of the board of the Coca-Cola Export Corporation at this time was James Farley, a former aide to President Roosevelt and a major figure in American politics. Farley used his political contacts to further overseas affairs and added some Cold War rhetoric to the product's commercial expansion. In 1946 after a global tour Farley declared that the peoples of Europe, Asia, and Africa "look to the American nation to lead them out of difficulties. They look to us for loans, for raw materials, and assistance."[52] Farley was a militant anti-Communist who warned in 1950: "We find ourselves in danger from an enemy more subtle, more ruthless, more fanatic than any we have ever faced. The time has come for Americans to challenge the aggressive, godless, and treasonable practices of totalitarian communism." Coca-Cola was about to mix with Cold War politics.

Almost everywhere in postwar Europe Coca-Cola's arrival provoked opposition. In many cases local beverage interests tried to block the entry of the American soft drink. In Belgium and Switzerland they challenged the drink with law suits alleging that it contained a dangerous amount of caffeine. In Denmark breweries managed to ban the drink temporarily. In most cases the local Communist party led the opposition and described the drink as an addictive drug or even a poison. In Italy *L'Unità* warned parents that Coke could turn children's hair white. Austrian Communists asserted that the new bottling plant at Lambach could easily be transformed into an atomic bomb factory. These disturbances were trivial compared with the controversy that erupted when Coca-Cola arrived in postwar France.

In France the first bottles of Coca-Cola had been sold to American servicemen in 1919. Yet, except for some cafés in major cities that catered to American tourists, French establishments rarely served the beverage during the 1920s and 1930s. With the war sales stopped altogether. After the war the American firm tried to resume operations but encountered difficulties because potential bottlers lacked equipment and the dollars to import the concentrate from the United States. To overcome these obstacles Coca-Cola Export orchestrated an American-style marketing plan for France. The key was constructing a new manufacturing plant in Marseilles to produce the concentrate. A small fraction of this concentrate, the ingredients used for blending the secret formula called "7X," was to be imported from the United States. To promote sales the country was divided into zones with the Paris region and the Midi targeted for initial operations. The company began signing contracts for bottling franchises and allocated a large budget for advertising. Within a few years, it was projected, each French citizen would consume six bottles of Coke annually. The concessionaires were to employ American sales and distribution techniques, including new trucks brightly painted in company colors, free tasting, and endorsements from cinema and sports stars (figs. 5, 6). The American multinational construed this strategy as a resumption of prewar operations, but this claim was rather disingenuous since business before 1939 had consisted of one bottler who imported syrup from the United States. The president of the export corporation was James Curtis and its representative in Paris was Prince Alexander Makinsky, a White Russian émigré, who had become an American citizen and was, like Farley, a staunch anti-Communist.

From the beginning there was trouble. Foreign investments required authorization from the Ministry of Finance, which was empowered to block ventures that might deepen the country's chronic deficit in its balance of payments. Since Coca-Cola Export offered to invest only a modest $500,000 and expected to repatriate its profits while requiring its Marseilles plant to buy certain ingredients from the Atlanta company, the rue de Rivoli denied permission in 1948. Makinsky admitted privately that "the trouble is . . . our investments are negligible."[53] The multinational offered to supply the ingredients temporarily without charge and to delay repatriating profits for five years—to no avail. The rue de Rivoli refused to budge.

The Fourth Republic's motives for obstructing the American firm were, as we shall see, far more complex than aversion to an unappealing foreign investment. Coca-Cola posed serious political problems and raised anxieties about Americanization.

The French Communist party reacted sharply to the news of the Coca-Cola Company's plans. *L'Humanité* asked: "Will we be *coca-colonisés?*"[54] The American company, it was alleged, intended to spend 4 million dollars on publicity and planned to sell 40 bottles of Coke per person annually. *L'Humanité* predicted "the Coca-Cola invasion" would further depress sales of wine, already damaged by tariff reductions demanded by the Americans, and would worsen the large trade deficit while the "American trust" siphoned away dollars. Communists also charged that the Coca-Cola distribution system would double as an American espionage network. And the rumor spread that Coca-Cola intended to advertise on the facade of Notre Dame.

5. Coca-Cola accompanies the Tour de France to Lourdes. (Courtesy the Coca-Cola Company)

Communist propaganda exploited deepening anxiety among the French about the United States. It evoked the alleged submissiveness of the Fourth Republic toward its Atlantic ally and the threat of American economic and cultural domination. The Communists were not alone in expressing such worrries. *Le Monde* and Christian *progressiste* journals also noted the first hints of a new danger as American private investment began to expand.[55] Dollars flowed into sectors like petroleum where American capital had existed for decades. But now there were also "bridgehead" investments like the new plants being built by Coca-Cola and the International Harvester Company. Coca-Cola was only one feature of a multifaceted American "invasion."

Besides the Communists and the *progressistes,* the government encountered heavy lobbying from those economic interests—wine, fruit juice, mineral water, cider, beer, and other beverages—who saw themselves directly threatened by Coca-Cola. Winegrowers were facing the beginning of postwar surpluses in 1949–50, which sharpened their anxiety about foreign competition. The Confédération des fruits et légumes, the Syndicat national du commerce en gros des vins et spiritueux, and similar associations charged the American soft drink with endangering public health and domestic industry. One such association asked: "Is Coca-Cola a poison?"[56] The organ of the Confédération

6. Billboard advertising, 1951. (Courtesy the Coca-Cola Company)

générale de l'agriculture warned that the drink could stimulate "addiction analogous to that observed in the use of drugs and tobacco," which was why, perhaps, the company encouraged free tasting.[57] Wine wholesalers asked that Coca-Cola conform to the health code imposed on all French beverages and complained about American customs' regulations on wine and liquors—a one-sided situation that "may explain, if not justify, the often bitter remarks heard in France when an American beverage enjoys free entry."[58] None of these interests openly demanded a ban on Coca-Cola, but they insisted that the product submit to existing French health regulations.

Pressured from the outside by the Communists and by a coalition of domestic beverage interests, the French government faced opposition from within as well. The Ministry of Finance, after conducting its own investigation of Coca-Cola's plans, advised against allowing a resumption of business by the American firm. As an investment the ministry concluded Coca-Cola would rapidly and permanently become "a disaster" for the nation's balance of payments with the United States.[59] Payments aside, the ministry called the bottling contracts "draconian" because they placed control in the hands of the Atlanta company and assured it the lion's share of profits. And when the ministry tried to force Coca-Cola Export to relinquish control over its Marseilles plant to

French interests, the Americans refused.[60] The treasury also suspected that the beverage, which made individuals loyal consumers after a few drinks, might be addictive either because of its caffeine or because of some secret ingredient. Politically, the ministry warned, the government should expect "extremely brutal reactions" from the winegrowers and from fruit juice and mineral water interests, who all believed they could not match the advertising and financial reserves of the Yankee newcomer. Such reactions would provide "powerful arguments to adversaries of the current majority."[61] Authorizing Coca-Cola, treasury officials implied, would only aid those who charged the government was subservient to America.

Other government bureaucracies were also suspicious of Coca-Cola. Starting in 1922 the beverage had faced a series of legal actions brought by customs officials and by the department for the repression of frauds, an agency of the agriculture ministry. At issue were alleged violations of the health code and deceptive labeling. These charges had reached a climax in 1942, when a court dismissed all the indictments by ordering a *non-lieu* (no cause for prosecution), which seemed to close the case. Yet after the war these legal tests resumed and officials pursued them so eagerly that Makinsky complained that the French administration had a "personal grudge against us."[62]

The incumbent governments, those of Henri Queuille (September 1948 to October 1949) and Georges Bidault (October 1949 to July 1950), rested on a centrist coalition of MRP, Radical, and Conservative parties and enjoyed Socialist support. Like other centrist cabinets of the years 1948–51 who tied their fate to the Atlantic alliance, these governments felt trapped. On the one hand it was essential to maintain good relations with Washington, especially if France expected generous treatment under the Marshall Plan. On the other hand Queuille and Bidault faced demands from their own ministries, the Communist party, and the beverage lobby to block a multinational that virtually symbolized the American way. Admitting Coca-Cola seemed to be a trivial issue and one that should not jeopardize American aid. Yet these governments succumbed to domestic pressures. When Coca-Cola Export applied in early 1949, for a second time, for authorization to import some $15,000 worth of ingredients for its Marseilles plant, the finance ministry again refused.

At this point Coca-Cola Export retaliated. In the summer of 1949 James Curtis, the head of the company, discussed the affair with Maurice Petsche, the minister of finance, who asked for clarification of the company's plans in order to help him "overcome the political considerations which caused the official obstructionism."[63] Petsche promised to raise the issue with the cabinet. The government authorized bottling operations, which began in December 1949, but Petsche's ministry continued to obstruct the company's plans. Unable to obtain clearance for importing the "7X" ingredients, Coca-Cola Export suspended construction of its Marseilles plant and resorted to shipping concentrate to its Parisian bottler from its manufacturer in Casablanca. Since the American ingredients amounted to only 3 percent of the value of the concentrate, it was labeled as a Moroccan product and shipped without an import license.

By late 1949 intense legal battles supplemented the finance ministry's obstructionism. "Our major headache," according to Makinsky, were two suits over the soft drink's ingredients and labeling initiated by the agriculture ministry's agency for the repression of fraud.[64] Much of the argument centered on the presence of phosphoric acid, which the 1905 health code seemed to prohibit, the amount of caffeine, and the nature of the mysterious "7X."[65] Even if only a trace ingredient, "7X" was an unknown and raised the possibility that it contained toxic or addictive elements. There was also the charge that the trademark was fraudulent because coca leaves were not truly present and thus "Coca-Cola" misrepresented the product. Of all these charges, it was the presence of phosphoric acid and caffeine that caused Makinsky's staff the most difficulty. Under the existing code, Makinsky privately acknowledged, Coke was "pretty vulnerable."[66] The wine, fruit juice, and other domestic beverage lobbies joined the department of frauds in its suits. Once begun, these court actions assumed a life of their own, marked by hearings, wrangling, and contested scientific tests. To add to the Atlanta company's worries, the Ministry of Agriculture appointed a special advisory committee, which contained experts known to be hostile to the soft drink, for the purpose of clarifying the code on nonalcoholic drinks.

Blame for all these actions, according to Coca-Cola Export, lay with the government. Farley accused it of instigating criminal prosecution against the sale of Coca-Cola for political reasons, that is, to accommodate the Communists and the special interests.[67] Compounding difficulties for the soft drink company in the winter of 1949–50, major newspapers joined the attack on *coca-colonisation,* and parliament took sides in the affair.

The Communist party and the domestic beverage industry forced the National Assembly to take up the issue at the end of 1949. Parliamentary opponents of the American beverage pursued two paral-

lel, yet different, approaches. The Communist party sought an immediate outright ban on the sale of Coca-Cola for reasons of public health
and on economic grounds, that is, to protect domestic beverages from
the unfair competition of the "American trust." This proposal gathered
little support outside the Communist party itself. Winegrowers, who
would also have liked outright prohibition, took a more indirect
approach to the ban. Paul Boulet, the deputy-mayor of Montpellier and
spokesman for the winegrowers of the Hérault, proposed a general
regulation of all nonalcoholic beverages made from vegetable extracts
under the guise of protecting public health. Coca-Cola was not explicitly named as the culprit, but everyone recognized that the intent of
Boulet's legislation was to extend the definition of harmful substances
in nonalcoholic beverages in order to allow the government to prohibit
the import, manufacture, and sale of the American soft drink. Boulet
apparently omitted naming Coca-Cola because such a proposal would
have violated trade agreements with the United States by discriminating
against a specific product. His proposal assigned responsibility for
determining whether or not the beverage was harmful to the minister
of public health, who would act on the advice of experts from the
Conseil supérieur de l'hygiène publique and the Académie nationale de
médicine. Rather than openly defend the winegrowers, Boulet masked
his purpose by stressing the probability that Coca-Cola was injurious
to public health. That the Coca-Cola Company paraded its product's
alleged wholesomeness and directed its appeal at youthful consumers
seemed to Boulet and his supporters to be especially insidious. Boulet's
project attracted far greater support than that of the Communists. The
latter, preferring a disguised ban to no ban at all, supported Boulet as
did some MRP deputies and those deputies representing rural constituencies.

The government's spokesman in the National Assembly was the
minister of public health, Pierre Schneiter, who like Bidault and Boulet
was a member of the pro-American MRP. The government did not want
a ban on Coca-Cola, and Schneiter insisted that the Boulet proposal was
unnecessary because existing legislation was adequate to protect national
health in the event that the drink was harmful or fraudulent. The minister
of health said the government had no precise stand on the issue but made
light of the affair: "I would rather trust in the common sense of the
country where we have always known how to choose the beverage that
suits our taste and generally drink it under reasonable conditions."[68]
Nevertheless, the government chose not to oppose the National Assem-

bly and elements of the MRP over this issue. Schneiter left the decision to the will of the assembly, knowing that at worst the legislation gave the government the authority to act but did not mandate it.

Opponents of Coca-Cola urged immediate action by the National Assembly, but the government managed to postpone debate until February 1950.[69] The assembly then rejected the Communist proposal for an outright ban but adopted Boulet's bill by voice vote. According to the legislation, if the experts found a nonalcoholic beverage injurious to public health, the minister of public health was empowered to ban it. The assembly submitted to the pressure of the winegrowers, the Communist party, and a small contingent of MRP and Gaullist deputies. The bulk of the deputies who acquiesced probably realized that, given its stand, the government was unlikely to invoke the ban: thus they could give a sop to the interested parties without any harm. Resisting Coca-Cola was a way of expressing latent French uneasiness about American domination.

The assembly's proceedings were an unedifying spectacle of disingenuous debate and weakness. The government and the parliamentary majority surrendered to the clamor of a determined minority of opponents composed of protectionist economic lobbyists and anti-American ideologues. The debate by and large avoided the real issue of growing American economic and political domination. Ostensibly the question was the protection of public health. Only the Communists raised the broader issue. One Communist deputy at the end of the debate complained: "We've seen successively the French cinema and French literature attacked. We've watched the struggle over our tractor industry. We've seen a whole series of our productive sectors, industrial, agricultural, and artistic, successively attacked without the public authorities defending them."[70] In the end the National Assembly, under the pretext of regulating nonalcoholic beverages and without daring to admit its motives, made a gesture of national assertion vis-à-vis the United States.

The Bidault government tried to maneuver between the domestic opposition to the entry of Coca-Cola and the need to avoid a confrontation with the United States. During the winter of 1949–50 internal politics continued to weigh more heavily. In February 1950 customs officials in Morocco denied a routine application from Coca-Cola Export to ship a batch of concentrate to its French bottlers. Still trying to discourage the Americans, the government imposed a de facto embargo that thwarted the company's gambit of importing concentrate from Casablanca.

Surveying the opposition in early 1950, Makinsky concluded there was a formidable array of enemies that were "trying to 'get' us." They included not only the domestic beverage lobbies, the administration, the Communists, and parliament, but French public opinion as well. The Paris chief of Coca-Cola Export thought the French were "as a whole anti-American" chiefly because they resented being dependent on the United States.[71] But the Atlanta company had the will, the resources, and the influence to retaliate. It feared the precedent should its product be banned in France.

Coca-Cola Export relied on its legal staff, hired expert scientific advisers, and used its contacts within the French administration, including the prime minister's office and the Conseil supérieur de l'hygiène publique, to make its case. Those involved in the legal proceedings as well as legislators received memoranda outlining the company's arguments. This documentation stressed that the soft drink was being sold freely in seventy-six countries; that previous investigations proved it conformed to the health code; that its advertising campaign would be neither excessive nor provocative; that the manufacture and sale of the beverage were in French hands; that virtually all the supplies, from the sugar to the delivery trucks, were to be purchased in France; that experience showed its sales did not harm the markets of traditional drinks; and, especially, that there was no connection between Coca-Cola and the Marshall Plan.[72] In addition, the multinational took its case directly to the French government. As chairman of the board of Coca-Cola Export, Farley visited the French ambassador, Henri Bonnet, and, after accusing the government with harassing the company for political reasons, asked the foreign office to persuade the finance ministry and the cabinet to end the embargo.[73]

The Atlanta company also sought the intervention of Washington. Makinsky asked the State Department to take its part, charging Paris with "discrimination, hostility, and unjustifiable delaying tactics," and threatened to withdraw Coca-Cola's business from France.[74] After trying to stay aloof from fear of linking Coca-Cola with American aid, the State Department acted. David Bruce, the American ambassador in Paris, told Premier Bidault that the United States would resist arbitrary discrimination against any American product. Bruce also lodged a protest with the foreign ministry against the Bidault administration's interference with the import of Coca-Cola concentrate from Morocco.[75] The American ambassador warned of "possible serious repercussions" if the harassment of Coca-Cola were to continue and asked the French cabinet to take up the matter.[76]

Farley tried to rally the American public. He exploded before the American press.[77] "Coca-Cola was not injurious to the health of American soldiers who liberated France from the Nazis so that the Communist deputies could be in session today," he proclaimed. Farley noted that the drink was served everywhere in the world except in Communist countries. He complained that the French showed small gratitude for the Marshall Plan. Uncle Sam, he snarled, would probably not condone this insult and the American Congress might be moved to stop economic aid.

News of the affair was carried widely by the American press. Some newspapers were outraged and suggested retaliation such as barring French wines. One editorial said gravely:

France is under a solemn obligation to the United States, as a matter of honor and gratitude for our having saved her independence in two terrible wars, and our having expended so much American wealth for her sake in peacetime, to refrain from enacting any measure . . . that would disclose to us . . . that she is unmindful of America's immeasurable sacrifices and generosity.[78]

Another paper cast the affair as part of the global ideological struggle:

You can't spread the doctrines of Marx among people who drink Coca-Cola. . . . The dark principles of revolution and a rising proletariat may be expounded over a bottle of vodka on a scarred table, or even a bottle of brandy; but it is utterly fantastic to imagine two men stepping up to a soda fountain and ordering a couple of Cokes in which to toast the downfall of their capitalist oppressors.[79]

Others made fun of the affair and called it "a tempest in a glass of Coke." One member of Congress announced rather crudely that if the French would drink Coke it would give them just what they needed since the war—"a good belch."[80] More perceptive observers recognized that Coca-Cola threatened French sensibilities. One such editorialist who did not approve of the National Assembly's regulation also noted that the Coca-Cola Company had been tactless in presenting its product to a people who had become hypersensitive about their way of life since the war. The day when "opposite Notre Dame there is a poster of 'The Pause that Refreshes' and on restaurant tables one sees as many Coke bottles as carafes of red wine, it will be not only the French, but also Americans, who will feel poorer."[81]

From Washington the French ambassador alerted Paris about how the Coca-Cola affair, especially Farley's remarks, had enflamed American public opinion and might endanger economic aid. Outright prohibition, he warned, would be interpreted as "a sign of hostility toward the United States."[82] Indeed, the Quai d'Orsay took the American reaction to the

Coca-Cola affair seriously because of its possible impact on Marshall Plan credits.[83] The foreign ministry was aware that the Coca-Cola Company exercised powerful influence on American opinion.[84] In April 1950 the Bidault government quietly lifted the embargo but asked Coca-Cola Export to exercise discretion and limit such exports to reasonable needs.[85]

In the French press a few critics grasped the full significance of the affair. The neutralist Catholic newspaper *Témoignage chrétien* gave credit to the Marshall Plan for French recovery yet noted "the fear, the worrisome rumors that the Americans are taking advantage of their role as lenders to stick their noses in our domestic affairs."[86] "Not content with supervising the distribution and use of Marshall credits—which is normal—the countless army of ERP [Marshall Plan] bureaucrats has assumed the right to monitor—and to correct—all aspects of our economy and even our policies." The journal enumerated incidents of American threats that would "lead France straight, if we don't guard against it, to pure and simple subjection." "If we are a tired people, we are not an inferior people, a colonial people." How do the Americans treat us?

[as] children who know nothing because we are ignorant of the "American way of life." That the Americans teach us—like nursery-school children—about the civilization of chewing gum, Coca-Cola, and literature in the form of aspirin tablets would be childish if it weren't so exasperating.

Let's not exaggerate, *Témoignage chrétien* concluded. Coca-Cola is not a poison and it's less dangerous than Pernod. Yet "we must call a spade a spade and label Coca-Cola for what it is—the avant garde of an offensive aimed at economic colonization against which we feel it's our duty to struggle."

Le Monde, like the Catholic journal, explored the symbolic quality of the affair. Beuve-Méry revealed his own aversion for American society in the attention his paper gave to Coca-Cola. Robert Escarpit, who often wrote for the paper, contributed a wry article entitled "Coca-colonisation" in which he observed:

Conquerors who have tried to assimilate other peoples have generally attacked their languages, their schools, and their religions. They were mistaken. The most vulnerable point is the national beverage. Wine is the most ancient feature of France. It precedes religion and language; it has survived all kinds of regimes. It has unified the nation.[87]

Here we have Frenchness defined as the fruit of the vine.

In its major essay on the affair, *Le Monde* argued that Coca-Cola represented the coming American commercial and cultural invasion. Already "Chryslers and Buicks speed down our roads; American tractors furrow our fields; Frigidaires keep our food cold; stockings 'made by Du Pont' sheathe the legs of our stylish women."[88] But why, *Le Monde* asked, given this profusion of American products, has Coca-Cola been singled out for such attention? The answer lay not with charges about spies or dangers to public health. "What the French criticize is less Coca-Cola than its orchestration, less the drink itself, than the civilization—or as they like to say, the style of life—of which it is the symbol." The marketing campaign for Coca-Cola submerged the consumer with American-style "propaganda," covering walls with signs and storefronts with neon lights (figs. 7, 8). America has already sent us several fads, mused the reading public, some of which are more threatening than others because they affect the life of the mind—the book digest and the sensational press. These bad habits have spread almost unopposed. What is now at stake is "the moral landscape of France." In mock solemnity the newspaper ran an article entitled "To Die for Coca-Cola" that noted: "We have accepted chewing gum and Cecil B. De Mille, *Reader's Digest*, and be-bop. It's over soft drinks that the conflict has erupted. Coca-Cola seems to be the Danzig of European culture. After Coca-Cola, *holà*."[89] *Le Monde* admitted that the Coca-Cola Company could legitimately feel that it was being unjustly persecuted. Yet as *Témoignage chrétien* did, this paper expressed a sense of foreboding—Americanization was on its way and France might well be the worse for it.

The international quarrel over Coca-Cola subsided as quickly as it had begun. Before 1950 was over the affair, at least for politicians, officials, and the press, seemed forgotten. In June the upper house of parliament, the Conseil de la République, reviewed and unanimously rejected the assembly's proposed regulation of nonalcoholic beverages. The upper house found Boulet's proposal unnecessary and prejudicial to relations with the United States; in general the senators took a more dispassionate view of the affair than the lower house. Léo Hamon remarked, "When it's a question of beverages, it's wise to trust the palates of the French and it's desirable to conserve our energy for more serious issues."[90] Another senator noted that the assembly's bill made France seem singularly "disagreeable" after accepting so much American aid; he denounced the cowardly approach to banning the drink: "It's not worthy of France and will be no honor in the annals of parliament." The Conseil's rejection

7. A prominent ballerina sips Coca-Cola at the base of the Eiffel Tower.
(Courtesy the Coca-Cola Company)

forced a second reading of the bill in the assembly, which promptly
passed the regulation once more and thus made it law in August 1950.
The so-called anti-Coca-Cola bill authorized the government, acting on
scientific advice, to draw up new regulations for beverages made from
vegetable extracts. But the experts procrastinated in setting standards
and subsequent centrist governments delayed issuing new regulations
based on the Boulet bill.

In 1951 the Ministry of Agriculture issued its interpretation of the
health code, concluding that the soft drink conformed to French law.
But the Ministry of Public Health balked. Farley blamed Communist
officials in the health bureaucracy for its continued obstructionism
while the ministry refused to relent until the legal actions were settled.[91]

8. The "Pause that Refreshes" on the Seine. (Courtesy the Coca-Cola Company)

After a series of scientific tests of the drink's ingredients found it to be neither fraudulent nor in violation of the existing code, a magistrate ordered a *non-lieu* in September 1952. The department for the repression of frauds, which had initiated the suit, accepted the decision; then the wine and fruit juice interests appealed and forced further tests, which again cleared the drink. Finally in December 1953 an appeals court confirmed the *non-lieu* and thus terminated legal action. Coca-Cola was found to be free from violating all existing codes and the company was convinced the Boulet legislation was not a serious threat.[92] Coca-Cola Export rejoiced in its "handsome victory" but refrained from publicity, preferring to let the matter rest as long as its opponents "hold their peace."[93]

Why did Coca-Cola's enemies fail? The Atlanta company generated enormous pressure to counter its opponents' efforts, mounting a press campaign, winning the intervention of the State Department, and convincing the French foreign office. It also lobbied forcefully within the government, the bureaucracy, and the legislature. The governments of the Fourth Republic tried to balance between the Americans and the domestic opposition generated by the Communists and the beverage interests and some of its own ministries, but eventually conceded to the Americans. Other than the Communists and the beverage interests there was not, despite all the noise, any serious support for banning Coca-Cola. Once the Communist party had exhausted the propaganda value of the issue and once the winegrowers and others had lost their fear of the American drink, no one remained to champion the fight. In addition, the Coca-Cola Company won all the battles waged against it in the courts. It also moved quickly to establish its operations in France and present its opponents with a fait accompli. By 1952 the drink had moved outside cafés and was available in offices and factories.

Nevertheless, at the cultural level the affair survived. A poll of 1953 reported that only 17 percent of the French liked Coca-Cola either "well enough" or "a lot" while 61 percent said "not at all."[94] Although Coca-Cola expanded in France after the affair, it was never accepted as readily as elsewhere in Western Europe. On a per capita basis the French, even today, continue to drink less Coca-Cola than any other Western European people.[95] Coca-Cola remained a symbol of Americanization and many French families continued to believe the drink was distasteful and possibly harmful. But the "Pause that Refreshes" ceased to be an economic, ideological, or patriotic issue that captured national attention. It became a matter of personal taste or private sentiments about America or consumer society. Even the Communist party eventually had a change of heart, or a loss of memory, and in time its publications carried ads that read: "Drink Coca-Cola: Coca-Cola is the One."

In retrospect the war over Coca-Cola was a symbolic controversy between France and America. Its emotional energy derived from French fear of growing American domination, in a political, economic, and cultural sense, during a bleak phase of French trade and a tense moment of the Cold War. The Communist party and beverage interests were able to exploit concern, at least among politicians, officials, journalists, and, to a degree, among the public about American intrusion into French affairs and American challenges to French traditions of consumption and culture. Coca-Cola aggressively announced the arrival of consumer society at a time when the French were not ready to deal with it. Indeed the Coca-Cola Company was a forerunner of those American multinationals that were to descend on France and provoke another, similar, phobia about American economic imperialism in the 1960s. For all those who opposed the entry of Coca-Cola the affair was, in one form or another, a tiny effort at national self-assertion, a gesture that France might find a "third way" in the Cold War, at a time when the nation had little room to maneuver. As one journalist summed up, "For us fortunate tipplers, the wine of France will do. Neither Coca-Cola, nor vodka."[96]

··········

The first wave of postwar anti-Americanism was a product of the early Cold War years. It did not represent the entire intellectual community since there were those who defended the Atlantic alliance and even the American way of life. But Communist militants and prestigious left-wing intellectuals, who were inspired by socialist or Christian principles and who edited key newspapers and reviews, tapped widespread uneasiness about American presence and policy; they perceived a popular desire for national assertiveness to mount a noisy show of independence from and criticism of the United States. Later in the 1950s, as Washington's influence over French policy weakened and as the Soviet Union's reputation as a progressive force diminished, these two sources of anti-Americanism declined.

But anti-Americanism survived because it had other roots and dimensions. The debate about the American model continued because this was a discussion among the French about their future. It was a debate about modernity, independence, and national identity—issues that would continue to trouble the French even as the days of McCarthyism and Stalin receded along with the danger of the Cold War becoming a hot war.

CHAPTER 4

The Missionaries of the Marshall Plan

In the summer of 1949 a team of sixteen French business-men, engineers, and workers arrived in the United States to begin a six-week tour of plants manufacturing heavy electrical equipment. These were the first "missionaries" sent, under the auspices of the Marshall Plan, to study the secrets of American prosperity. The United States government, acting first through the Economic Cooperation Administration (ECA), the agency that administered the Marshall Plan, and later through its successor, the Mutual Security Agency (MSA), conceived and helped fund such visits. By the end of the program the French had sent some 500 missions and 4,700 missionaries on tour through American factories and farms, stores, and offices. France alone supplied over one-quarter of all trainees sent to the United States from Marshall Plan countries.[1]

The subject of this encounter is these missionaries' assessment of the American economy, especially its prodigious prosperity in the early 1950s. The voices are those of French businessmen, technicians, and workers who visited the United States as well as those of some French and American officials.

What struck these visitors most was the affluence of the average citizen in the United States. It was apparent that there was a distressingly wide gap between the standard of living of an American and a French worker. The parking lots reserved for employees of the Ford plant, for example, seemed like "immense lakes" to the French. One such visitor, who had a flair for precision, counted 75 automobiles in the parking lot of a factory that employed only 130 people. This prosperity, the missionaries were instructed, resulted from the efficiency or "productivity" of American labor. A Studebaker cost a Detroit autoworker nine months of wages, while a Parisian autoworker could not afford a simple Citroën because it would cost two and one-half years of work. The difference between American and French standards of living had its origin in a "productivity gap." The lag in productivity was merely the postwar way of formulating an old problem—why the French economy lagged behind best practice as defined by the United States. In the 1920s the problem had assumed the character of a need to adopt measures of rationalization, or scientific management. But in the 1950s the problem was defined, measured, and publicized as a gap in productivity. As an economic indicator, productivity has several technical meanings, but after the war it most often referred to the efficiency of economic inputs, in particular to the economy's total output measured in man-hours of labor, that is, labor productivity.[2]

This gap, this index of relative economic inferiority, appeared at a moment when the American economy was emerging from a stupendous wartime performance and French recovery was barely under way. The prosperity of the later 1950s and 1960s was not yet visible as the missions crossed the Atlantic. America was bursting with self-confidence and promise; the French economy was struggling with postwar reconstruction. These were the heady days of the Marshall Plan, when American officials sought to persuade Europeans that free enterprise and high wages should replace the Old World's bad economic habits.[3]

··········

After a brief account of the Franco-American effort at closing the productivity gap through the policies, institutions, and operations of the Marshall Plan's technical assistance program, of which the missions were one element, this chapter focuses on how French experts assessed the sources as well as the costs and benefits of American affluence and, in turn, critically assessed their own economy and society.[4]

Productivity was not among the early priorities of the Marshall Plan (officially the European Recovery Program, or ERP, which ran from 1948 to 1952). Initially the Economic Cooperation Administration allocated only a modest sum for technical assistance for Europe.[5] It was not until 1950, when the ERP had run nearly half its course, that American officials became convinced that Europeans had to be shown how to run their factories and farms. At this point the ECA faced a series of problems. It had to find new ways to make Western Europe self-sufficient and ready for trade liberalization before dollar aid terminated. And the fight against communism seemed to hang in the balance. Up to then European workers—the social stratum most sympathetic to Soviet propaganda, especially in France and Italy—had not benefited from reconstruction; economic hardship seemed to offer a breeding ground for communism. In addition, Washington had decided, even before the beginning of the Korean War, to encourage European rearmament. Once the war began on the Asian peninsula, the ECA faced the dilemma of mounting a massive rearmament program on the continent without sacrificing an already precarious standard of living. In the eyes of ECA officials, raising productivity was the answer to all these problems.

In January 1950 the ECA formally invited the French government to participate in an expanded technical assistance, or productivity, program. Although technical assistance had been part of Marshall Plan aid from the beginning, now it was to be extended to include the creation of national productivity centers, exhibitions of American machinery and products, visits by American consultants, and more missions.[6] American officials had been distressed by the slow progress made by the French in mounting a productivity drive. Paris in the early days of the Marshall Plan did not seem to take the program seriously. The head of the ECA office in France complained: "It is disturbing to find so little evidence of any determination on the part of the French to develop the concerted and vigorous productivity program so essential both to permit improvement in the standard of living and to support the requisite military defense effort."[7]

The situation deteriorated further in 1950–51: the hot war in Korea continued, rearmament strained the fragile European economies, labor's condition worsened, and the Communist party heated up its anti-American campaign. Trade unionists told ECA officials that the Marshall Plan might have helped industry but had not brought higher purchasing power to workers.[8] ECA labor advisers calculated that real wages had fallen below prewar levels and that the Communists were successfully exploiting the workers' misery.[9] Richard Bissell, assistant deputy administrator of the ECA, recommended program reforms that would bring labor tangible benefits in order to strengthen non-Communist trade unions as a way of assuring long-term French political and military stability. Such reforms would also move France toward trade liberalization and economic integration.[10]

In the summer of 1951, with the end of the Marshall Plan in sight, Washington notified the Europeans of further modifications in the technical assistance program when ECA's successor, the Mutual Security Agency, took charge. French officials learned that more funds would be made available, but that the focus of assistance would shift "not exclusively but principally" to defense production.[11] "Defense" was broadly defined by the MSA to include maintaining the standard of living. A further condition of technical assistance was that its benefits must be shared with workers and consumers. The MSA was looking for projects that would rapidly demonstrate the benefits of productivity to society at large. Bissell described the new policy this way:

Coca-Cola and Hollywood movies may be regarded as two products of a shallow and crude civilization. But American machinery, American labor relations, and American management and engineering are everywhere respected. The hope is that a few European unions and entrepreneurs can be induced to try out the philosophy of higher productivity, higher wages, and higher profits. . . . If they do so, restrictionism can be overcome at merely a few places, the pattern may spread. The forces making for such changes are so powerful that, with outside help and encouragement, they may become decisive. It will not require enormous sums of money . . . to achieve vaster increases in production. But it will require a profound shift in social attitudes, attuning them to the mid-twentieth century.[12]

Boldness, not sensitivity, would be common among ECA officials dealing with Europeans on the matter of productivity. The Americans were especially impatient with French and Italian industrialists whose conservative and restrictive ways seemed to obstruct progress toward competitive markets. In the summer of 1951 a top ECA official publicly attacked French and Italian business for their "feudal mentality."[13] The head of the French national employers' federation (Conseil national du patronat français, or CNPF) protested the charge and characterized the speech as the "greatest single boost to Communist propaganda in France during the past year."[14]

The Fourth Republic reluctantly followed the wishes of the Americans. It is fair to say that without the ECA there would have been no French productivity drive. In 1950, after much procrastination, the government of Georges Bidault created a Comité national de la productivité (CNP) composed of representatives of employers' associations, trade unions (syndicates), and the state; it included some outside experts as well. The under secretary of state for economic affairs, Robert Buron, a strong advocate of productivity, presided over the new center.[15] While the CNP set policy, the actual executor of the program was a semiofficial agency, the Association française pour l'accroissement de la productivité (AFAP). It used subsidies from the French and the American governments to send missions and publish their reports.

Even though the productivity gap had been recognized five years before by planning experts like Jean Monnet and Jean Fourastié, the French program took form only in 1950–51. This delay occurred for several reasons. The ECA itself had been slow to give priority to technical assistance, and both the magnitude of the gap and the appropriateness of the American model were difficult to demonstrate. A prevailing perception that America was an economically privileged nation seemed to make the American experience irrelevant. Only gradually did the French recognize that American know-how was relevant and that true recovery, including an end to inflation, depended on raising productivity as well as production. In addition, they had the political problem of mounting a French program that would be viewed as independent of American aid. Officials were worried lest the program appear to be American-controlled and thus arouse domestic opposition, especially from the Communists. The republic wanted to avoid appearing subservient and validating thereby the Communists' accusations. Thus the government rejected an ECA proposal to establish a joint Franco-American productivity center modeled after the Anglo-American Council on Productivity, which brought American experts to help administer the program in Great Britain. One top French official recorded his aversion for any "foreign interference," no matter how friendly, in the program and scolded the Americans for harboring the illusion "that the French problem could be solved by simply applying methods used in the United States."[16] Similarly the commercial counselor in Washington informed ECA directors that "a purely French program" constructed to avoid political disorder and assure a national consensus was "the *sine qua non* of a real collective effort."[17]

In fact the Fourth Republic had reservations about the entire Marshall Plan because it infringed on French independence and fed Communist polemics. Thus, the French government refused to honor its obligations to publicize Marshall Plan aid. This refusal prompted protests from the ECA and even from the American Congress. American officials believed that the Communists were winning the propaganda battle over the Marshall Plan and that the French people, including direct beneficiaries of aid, were ignorant of what the United States was giving.[18] When pressed by the Americans to mount a massive publicity campaign, the

French resisted. A top official advised the prime minister in 1948 that "a campaign that escaped his authority would risk, if it failed to take account of our population's legitimate sensitivities, damaging the nation's *amour propre* . . . and, in the end, run counter to its own purposes."[19]

Without doubt the most important cause of government procrastination was the Communists. Early on, the Communist party had taken aim against the Marshall Plan. And after some hesitation the largest trade union federation, the Confédération générale du travail (CGT), which was under Communist control, decided against participating in the productivity program. This refusal robbed the CNP program of vital support and opened it to political blackmail. At the national level the CGT enrolled about half of all unionized labor and at the sectoral or firm level frequently dominated the work force.

From the outset the CGT had been the principal obstacle to a productivity program. Before the Marshall Plan began, Jean Monnet and his staff at the national planning agency had undertaken preliminary productivity studies, but their efforts remained sterile until 1948. As soon as the Americans decided to sponsor technical assistance through the ERP, the problem of the Communist-run trade federation surfaced. Monnet's planners insisted that excluding the CGT would cripple the program. But the minister of industry, supported by business and the non-Communist trade unions, argued that the CGT would wreck the program if it were included.[20] The government, itself divided on the issue, muddled through by creating a complicated set of provisional committees that screened the American-funded productivity missions from possible sabotage by the CGT. As a result the French program limped along from 1948 to 1950, sending only three missions in 1949.

The objections of the CGT and the Communist party to the program were virtually identical. The CGT insisted the drive was aimed at releasing resources to aid rearmament and at weakening the CGT.[21] From the party's perspective the productivity drive was being run for and by the Americans. Its accomplices were the CNPF and the "syndicalist gangsters," that is, the non-Communist unions.[22] The drive, according to the Communists, intended to fortify NATO's offensive capacity and divide the working class by coopting the "secessionist" syndicates with crumbs of capitalists' excess profits. According to this analysis, low productivity levels resulted from the inferiority of French capital equipment, a weak industrial structure, and Malthusian capitalists. Without profoundly altering these conditions, raising productivity could come

9. Productivity drive defeats Stalin. (Economic
Cooperation Administration, P/TA, OD, CSF, box 5)

only at the expense of the health, dignity, and standard of living of
workers.

Like so many other postwar Franco-American encounters, the productivity program fell victim to Cold War political controversy. The
ECA/MSA promoted the drive during the Korean War to facilitate
Western European rearmament and to combat communism in France
and Italy (see fig. 9). The Communist party and the CGT responded by
obstructionism. In the National Assembly the Communists sought to
halt subsidies to the program and the CGT retaliated at the plant level.
On occasion their resistance was passive—CGT workers would walk out
of films being shown at factories when they spotted the credit, "This film
is presented to you by the Marshall Plan."[23] Sometimes the CGT could
be more aggressive. Returning labor-missionaries were ostracized as
capitalist hirelings. In 1952 the ECA sent a traveling exhibition entitled
"The True Face of the United States" featuring a portable cinema and
displaying posters, photographs, and other information about American
efficiency and affluence (figs. 10, 11). When the exhibit reached a small
town in the Cher, the local CGT union called out its members to protest.
Some five hundred demonstrators hurled debris and overturned the
exhibit's canvas top before gendarmes intervened. The following day the
mayor, afraid of further incidents, canceled authorization for the exhibit.[24] Together the Americans and the Communists turned the drive
into a political ideological struggle.

10. Traveling exhibition for the American way visits a provincial French town, 1950. (Archives nationales, F60ter 394)

11. Display from traveling exhibition demonstrates that high productivity means Americans work fewer hours to acquire consumer goods than Europeans. (Archives nationales, F60ter 394)

One can hardly overestimate the importance of the Communists' opposition for the stance of French labor. The CGT's attacks aroused the historic suspicions of labor toward any form of industrial rationalization. Non-Communist syndicates were extremely cautious about participating in the American-sponsored program.[25] These so-called free unions, the Confédération française des travailleurs chrétiens (CFTC), Force ouvrière (FO), and Confédération générale des cadres (CGC), joined the CNP only reluctantly and after setting conditions for their participation.[26]

These free unions faced a double dilemma. First, they were intimidated by the power and fervor of the CGT and the Communists. Cooperating with the Americans made them appear like tools of foreign capitalist interests rather than advocates of French workers. Second, they harbored grave doubts about the entire scheme. In the short run it threatened unemployment and in the long run seemed to offer fewer benefits to labor than to employers. Employers had a bad record as far as the unions were concerned. And, CFTC and FO representatives reminded the ECA, workers were suspicious because after 1945 the employers and the government had asked them to roll up their sleeves and raise output, but as of 1950 they had received few benefits.[27] As one old-timer plainly (and ungrammatically) summed up the situation for an ECA official: "Tell them in the United States that we're not against the Marshall Plan. Tell them that us workers would just like to see a little more of it."[28] Still, rather than spurn an offer made by the ECA and their government that might bring benefits to workers and fortify their unions, these syndicalists gingerly elected to try out the program.

But French employers did not make participation easy for the unions. The CNPF may have proclaimed its unqualified support for the program, but in fact organized business fought a rear-guard action against it. Trade associations did their best to limit the purview of the CNP and make certain the program did not become a gambit for either state *dirigisme* or trade union interference in their prerogatives.[29] The head of the small employers' federation, Léon Gingembre, who had been stung by American criticism of French business, stated his objections directly to the ECA. He complained of "the complete lack of understanding you have of the mentality of our country in general and of small- and medium-sized business in particular."[30] Other than establishing some personal contacts, he concluded, on the basis of the first mission, that "there was little else to retain." Gingembre's federation abstained from subsequent missions. Far more important than Gingembre's defiance, the major trade associations were to earn a reputation for manipulating and obstructing the program.

After the Marshall Plan ended in 1952, the MSA channeled technical assistance toward improving the standard of living as part of a broadly defined defense program for Western Europe. American aid became openly tied to promoting free enterprise and strengthening non-Communist trade unions, especially in France and Italy. Controversy over this program led to the withdrawal of the non-Communist syndicalists and the collapse of the CNP. In 1953 a Commissariat général à la productivité, with Gabriel Ardant at its head, replaced the CNP. At this point interest in the missions faded and Ardant turned his attention toward other means of promoting productivity. The subject of this encounter, however, is the missions.

··········

It is hardly surprising that the AFAP, the operational arm of the French drive, had difficulty in assembling its first missions to the United States. CGT members stayed away, and American immigration policy that refused entry to anyone with a Communist affiliation, present or past, discouraged many labor officials.[31] It was also difficult to get funds from the budget to cover the French government's share of the costs.[32] At the same time employers controlled the selection of delegations, largely because they contributed heavily to mission expenses and were allowed to choose the participating firms. French procedures for selecting delegations did not satisfy the ECA, which complained that the initial missions underrepresented labor and marginalized the role of the trade union federations.[33] ECA officials believed that unless the syndicalists were more involved in selecting labor delegates, American unions would object and the delegates would appear as "stooges"—just as the Communists pictured them.[34] Organized business exacerbated the problem on occasion by choosing delegates from among relatives or other workers who had no standing in the union and were reputed to be management's cronies.

French officials were perplexed about what they viewed as a complicated and delicate matter.[35] On the one hand they wanted a broad range of views. But on the other, the abstention by the CGT and the testiness of the free unions as well as the CNPF made selection procedures difficult. Moreover, it was not easy to obtain a broad range of private firms since only those employers who volunteered and contributed to expenses were represented. Adjustments in procedures during 1950–51 improved team selection in the eyes of the ECA without ever fully satisfying the Americans.

In 1950, after a slow start the year before, some forty missions comprising over five hundred visitors toured the United States and the pace accelerated in the next two years. By the end of 1953, when activity began a long decline, some three hundred missions and twenty-seven hundred visitors had journeyed across the Atlantic to study everything from hybrid corn to antitrust legislation.[36] Some teams were highly specialized, such as delegations of consulting engineers; others, composed of employers, officials, technicians, and workers, studied either specific sectors like coal mining or broad intersectoral topics like industrial relations, accounting, marketing, or personnel training. About two-thirds of the missions studied industrial problems; most of the rest focused on agriculture. Relatively few were devoted to retail trade, crafts, and service. The French tertiary sector drew the fewest participants into the program. In theory a team of a dozen members had two employers, six engineers or foremen, and four workers or employees, though some teams were to include only technicians or workers. In practice management, broadly defined, may have occupied almost half the posts.[37] The missions spent about six weeks on average visiting factories, farms, stores, universities, and research centers; they talked to government officials, labor leaders, trade association representatives, research scientists, farmers, plant managers, engineers, and workers. Most teams covered a limited geographic region like the Midwest, but collectively they roamed over the entire continent. Some of the hundreds of reports they filed were published by the AFAP in as many as ten thousand copies. This effort was designed to administer a shock, to make the French eager to adopt American techniques, and to "produce and foster this 'virus' of productivity."[38]

The record left by these missions tells us both how the French perceived the American economy circa 1951 and how they assessed their own way of life. Yet the published mission reports should not be taken at face value. The AFAP prepared them as it did its radio programs and films—as elements of a propaganda campaign. They were to be useful in a technical sense, but they also preached the productivity gospel. These documents were rarely candid about the missionaries' ambivalence. They often "homogenized" the views of the teams, making those of business and labor indistinguishable, for example. More complete and accurate accounts of the missions' impressions, however, can be found in other records.[39]

The wonder about American prosperity and the self-assessment expressed in these reports were not uniquely French but had, to some degree, a European character. British and Italian productivity reports made similar evaluations of American management, human relations, and markets because all the official reports reflected heavily what the ECA intended.[40] The contrast in economic practice was between Europe and the United States—though there were some peculiar Gallic twists to what these Europeans found.

Despite the laudatory tone of the French reports it would be a mistake to regard the missionaries as naive or uncritical. The cross-Atlantic travelers did not always accept what the Americans claimed about their economy or find the American way of life entirely admirable. Even some of the prime propagandists expressed doubts about America's self-image, as a land of entrepreneurial pioneering, competitive markets, and cooperative trade unions. Skeptics voiced misgivings about the "reality" of the American economy and detected disturbing features in the American way of life. They were unimpressed with American manufacturing techniques, disliked consumer society, or believed nothing could be transferred because American success came entirely from its natural endowment.

Nevertheless, most of those who left a record of their perceptions were profoundly and positively impressed with the American way of life and sought to emulate it. Converts were apt to idealize American ways (fig. 12). These enthusiasts consciously or unconsciously found in the United States everything that was missing in France. They believed Americans possessed the basic human virtues, as one prominent employer put it, of honesty, self-discipline, mutual respect, as well as commitment to work and service. No wonder, he thought, there was so little friction in industrial relations and such high output.[41] Another industrialist described French factories as mirror images of what he found in the States. American plants, even older ones, were clean, orderly, quiet, and well illuminated, while at home there were many "dark, dingy factories, with filthy floors and horrible noise . . . which seem more like prisons than places where men have to spend a third of their lives."[42] Some employers found a natural paradise for business across the Atlantic and thus, of course, avoided criticizing themselves for the shortcomings of European business.[43]

The clean and efficient plants as well as the "lakes" of private cars and the "forests" of TV antennas proved the productivity gap was not the figment of some statistician's calculation. It was the missionaries' task to find the causes of this lag and identify what could be borrowed or adapted to end it. They also wanted to know whether such transfers would put the French way of life at risk. For in this collective examination of conscience the stakes were far higher than manufacturing techniques. The entire social and economic environment in which business and labor functioned was at issue. This self-appraisal tells us what thousands of French businessmen, technicians, and workers held dear about their way of life and what they thought to cast off in order to come closer to the American way of life.

The major analytical issue for the productivity teams was to discern what were the "givens," or natural advantages—the non-transferable features—of the American economy. America was called an "economic aristocracy" among nations because of its privileged endowment. The essentials of this privilege were the continent's wealth of natural resources, especially power, and the enormous size of the market that stimulated the mass production of a narrow range of standardized products and afforded economies of scale. Every mission report attributed some portion of America's productivity to such "natural" advantages. A few credited such advantages with sole responsibility for America's success and concluded little could be reproduced in France. The report of the electronics industry, for example, discerned numerous advantages enjoyed by American manufacturers and concluded that there were some, but not many, feasible reforms.[44] The head of the CNP itself, Robert Buron, in assessing the factors responsible for American productivity estimated only 50 percent were capable of "fruitful adaptation."[45]

In spite of the general recognition that much of America's economic eminence derived from special conditions, most missionaries allowed for a considerable measure of transferable practice. As we shall see, many of the visitors construed what was "importable" in narrow technical terms and confined themselves to borrowing manufacturing techniques. But the most striking finding of the missions was that human factors were the key to America's performance. This impression was, of course, precisely what the ECA wanted the Europeans to conclude. According to the author of an early synthesis, "The great discovery and the great surprise to French investigators was, without question, the role that human factors played in American productivity. Most of the reports give them top priority."[46] To the degree that productivity was a matter of attitudes and will—such as a "scientific" approach to management or more open and trusting relations between employer and employee—

12. French images of American mores, drawn from literature of the productivity drive: Even small American entrepreneurs engage in mass production (*top left*); Inventive Americans find solutions to every problem: "Well, Miss Forrest, if you plan to stay half-dressed like that, you'll have to build a higher wall" (*center*); Economics govern how Americans think: "Well, well! Supply is greater than demand!"(*bottom*). (Claude Foussé, *Traits caractéristiques de la prospérité américaine* [1953], 47, 21, 19)

then Gallic imitation was feasible. This was the 50 percent to which Buron referred. Accordingly the missions, encouraged by the AFAP and the Americans, focused on human factors. Yet the peculiarly hospitable social "climate" in which American productivity flourished was to prove exceedingly difficult to import. That causes were human or psychological or even institutional, the French were to discover, did not make them more readily adaptable.

· If for analytical purposes we set aside the part of productivity attributable to America's natural endowment, including market size (which the missions believed they could not recreate), and the part attributable to specific manufacturing techniques (which the missions freely borrowed), then what remained and what the productivity enthusiasts judged essential to closing the gap was a small number of items all more or less attributable to management and industrial relations. The emphasis on these factors tells us what the French believed was most backward about their economic ways and forms the crux of their self-assessment.

· · · · · · · · · ·

It is no exaggeration to claim that the French discovered "management" during the Marshall Plan.[47] Management, the teams learned, was not the same as *direction*.[48] First, an American manager, like a true *chef,* was recruited not only for his knowledge and capacity to command but also for his ability to persuade, rather than impose his will, on his subordinates. In addition, management was not a matter of experience or aptitude alone; it was a function of continuous training and proper organization. Management was more a learned technique than it was a "business sense" or a "gift of command." American managers, the French observed, were trained at universities or professional schools. It is no surprise that the Harvard Business School was a major attraction for the productivity teams. And training was practical, specialized, and continuous. "American employers know that running a company is a learned skill and they do all they can to improve their education. Management, the technique of *direction* in all its forms, is a scientific discipline."[49] What was also distinctive about management was that American firms were highly structured, often using a staff-and-line system, with precisely defined functions and responsibilities symbolized by an organization table. Authority was decentralized or delegated. And order was provided by the use of collective (committee) decision-making and organization. Finally, American management was "open." There was easy communication among supervisors and subordinates; information was freely transmitted up and down the managerial hierarchy and throughout the entire enterprise so that even the production worker was kept informed.

Unlike the French *patron*, American managers never seemed overworked. They readily executed their tasks because of sound organization, adequate staff, and the heavy use of office equipment. The French were astonished at seeing a telephone on every desk. At the top American managers were able to focus on policy. They emphasized forecasting and supervision (*contrôle*). In the first instance they had detailed statistical data available to them on almost every facet of the economic environment; they stressed functions like market research and product design and development. In the second instance the comptroller, or chief financial officer, used budgetary or accounting techniques to monitor company operations instead of merely documenting the past as in France. Thus American managers left nothing to improvisation. They relied on neither genius nor routine. They were flexible without improvising because they carefully studied and prepared for the new; change too was part of the system. Management was method. And insofar as management was a result of training, organization, and attitude, it could be transmitted.

Implicit in this affirmation of American management was a critique of French *direction* (see fig. 13). The mission reports directly or indirectly criticized French business for its heavy centralization—for its Napoleonic type of *président-directeur-général* (PDG) who refused to delegate responsibility. The typical PDG acted without the advice of his subordinates; was unaware of the grievances of his personnel; and failed to inform his staff of the company's market situation. French managers tried to be expert in all functions and assumed too many tasks. They were overloaded with questions of detail and had no time to reflect.

American consultants confirmed the existence of a "management gap." To the Americans their Gallic hosts seemed to possess a pool of "bosses as good as those in the United States, but their knowledge of techniques of industrial management is less advanced."[50] American specialists criticized the *chef d'entreprise* not only for hoarding authority but also for neglecting long-term planning, marketing, and advertising. The *chef d'entreprise*, the Americans observed, often blamed the state for difficulties caused by his own mismanagement. Moreover, as a basis for recruitment, French business relied too heavily on academic degrees, personal character, and experience whereas Americans insisted that management was a learned skill that must be continuously honed through training and tested by competition.

13. How Americans imagine the office of a European business, according to Marshall Plan literature. (*Rapports France-Etats-Unis* no. 38 [1950]: 14)

What the Americans also singled out for criticism was "the old tradition of secrecy." In comparison the American firm was transparent. French visitors were astonished at the openness of American business. Americans freely allowed foreigners access to every aspect of their enterprise including manufacturing techniques, organizational structure, sales figures, wage rates, and profits. Nor did they hide this information from their employees. Given the behavior of the French missionaries themselves after their return home, the critique of secrecy leveled by the American consultants seems apt.

Above all American management, in the eyes of French converts and American consultants, seemed inherently dynamic compared to the conservative *patronat*. The latter lacked either an "enterprising" or a "methodical" spirit and preferred cartels to competition, paternalism to industrial democracy. One American adviser liked to tell a story about French "Malthusianism":

A prominent French industrialist, who had obtained considerable credit in order to purchase new machinery, asked me for advice. He could select either a type of machine that was antiquated or one that was entirely modern. Despite my advice he chose the first, being afraid, he told me, of acquiring excess productive capacity.[51]

In contrast, American managers sought the new. They were stimulated from outside the firm by competition and from inside it by a promotional system that rewarded merit. "The great American principle is that, whatever an individual's background or academic degrees, the best deserves the best position."[52]

The emphasis on managerial deficiencies did not mean, however, that the missions paid less attention to the technical aspects of manufacture. Quite the contrary. Missions particularly appreciated the generous deployment and use of machinery at near full capacity. "Overall, American factories are better outfitted than ours; it must be added that in general they also make better use of their equipment."[53] Especially striking were the profusion of power hand tools; the use of machinery for the transport, handling, and storage of materials and products; and the extravagant consumption of power throughout the production process. To a lesser extent the productivity teams praised the skillful design of American plants. Most every industrial mission also applauded the dependability and high quality of American suppliers. One experiment demonstrated that the mere use of American raw materials in a French textile mill significantly raised productivity. And the French penchant for tardiness, which at times interrupted the flow of production, inspired a jibe in Washington. "They say that when you give a cocktail party you invite the French at 6:30 and the Americans at 7:30 so that everyone arrives together. This precision in keeping appointments is also the rule in making deliveries."[54]

What the mission reports published about technical matters, however, and what in fact interested the missions were at odds. Published reports minimized the importance of manufacturing processes. And the productivity propagandists insisted that the missions were least impressed by this aspect of the productivity gap.[55] In fact we know many missions focused exclusively on technology—to the dismay of the AFAP. Visitors tended to select only those "elements that immediately satisfied a particular interest and disregarded everything else," according to one summary.[56] What was most readily available to the missions for copying was manufacturing technique. Such tinkering was also most likely to bring immediate gains to employers. But the productivity agency wanted to impress the French with the more "profound" aspects of the problem and tried to focus attention on such matters as management rather than machinery.

Marketing was one of the most noted weaknesses of French enterprise. Almost unanimously the missions perceived that they were behind the Americans in all aspects of distribution. CNPF leaders reported privately that they had little to learn from American firms at the technical level, but much to learn about selling.[57] French business lacked market studies, adequate advertising budgets, attractive product packaging, self-service retail outlets, and consumer credit. If techniques of conducting market research were familiar to the visitors, Americans employed them more extensively and more systematically. In the world of advertising, the French believed they were superior in "graphic imagination"; but American advertising firms were more effective because they were less constrained by their clients. Indeed to the French business ear the term "marketing" was revolutionary not because it was Anglo-Saxon but because it shifted priority and prestige from production to sales.[58]

The goal of American marketing was new: it aimed at creating consumer society. "Americans have had the merit of finding the way to make their entire population live comfortably."[59] Americans had discovered that the motor of economic life was not fulfilling elementary needs but stimulating the desire to live better. Demand was virtually unlimited. French teams reported: "This message of 'Live better,' repeated by all advertisers trying to sell their products, constitutes the background noise for all of American life—a sound punctuated by the ring of cash registers throughout the country."[60] The strategy was to make everyone a consumer and the means were standardized products, market analyses, advertising, high wages, and consumer credit. The distribution of easy credit gave every American the capacity to purchase consumer durables, that is, cars, washing machines, television sets, vacuums, refrigerators. These were high-price items that required generous credit in order to tempt buyers. In the 1950s consumer durables were the most visible manifestation of the productivity gap. The trouble with France, as one report suggested, was that half its population was still outside the circuit of the economy. The peasantry and the industrial workers might contribute as producers, but they still did not qualify as true consumers, as eager buyers of consumer durables.[61]

French business, so it seemed, neglected buyers whereas in America "the consumer is king." The voyagers happened to tour the United States at a moment when retailers pampered customers and supermarkets were in their early ascendancy. Despite this solicitude for the consumer, it was noted, America had far fewer retail distributors than France and the Americans' monstrous advertising campaigns did not seem to raise costs excessively. But the "cultural" and even ethical aspects of advertising were more bothersome, as one report observed: "There is no point insisting on the heavy, obtrusive, and aggressive character of American advertising. Don't they say that it is the art of making someone buy something that he doesn't want with money he doesn't yet have?"[62] Thus the massive marketing of products made some visitors skeptical about the claim that in America the consumer was king—perhaps she or he was more a victim.

Another feature of American management that attracted much attention, but which the French (and even some Americans) viewed with skepticism, was the so-called human-relations technique. Even before the war American researchers like Elton Mayo had demonstrated that psychosociological factors were more important than physical conditions or wages in determining labor's performance. Such findings generated the human-relations method of management, whose principles were open communication and respect for employees and whose symbol was the personnel office. The assumption was that high productivity depended on mutual comprehension by management and labor of each other's contribution to output. The human-relations approach to management personalized intrafirm relations; managers were to recognize that there was an individual in every worker and that relations among employees could be improved through a combination of goodwill and skill. In fact, it encompassed a bewildering variety of techniques. It evoked images of worker and employer shaking hands or eating lunch together. Human relations was one reason why the French likened American enterprise to a "glass house."

French missions were amazed at the lengths to which Americans went as they tried to promote "team spirit." From the careful "orientation" of the new worker to the sponsorship of company sports teams, American business created a sense of community that in turn fostered easy rapport between management and workers. The French were flabbergasted at the sight of employees addressing employers by their surnames or volunteering suggestions on how to improve operations. One company inspired such suggestions by sending holiday greeting cards that read, "Merry Christmas to all . . . and to all . . . Good Ideas!"[63]

On occasion the Americans seemed to have gone too far in cultivating such easy rapport. One mission reported a visit to Barber-Greene, a small enterprise in the Midwest that made material for road construction.[64] This company was unusual in that it applied the principles of a Christian idealist named Melvin Evans. Evans himself related to the French visitors the story of a foreman whose family problems had harmed his work and his health. The company psychologist counseled this worker and soon his output improved. Evans said this example illustrated his contention that the secret of happiness lay in four conditions: job satisfaction; a comfortable home life; leisure; and faith in God. The visitors manifested "some anxiety, for the French temperament appears to be badly suited to such incursions into one's private life." Nevertheless, after seeing the success of the company, the mission supposedly became "really enthusiastic." Its members were amazed at witnessing the company president, in the presence of the union delegate, provide information about profits, dividends, and wages. Workers said they liked their jobs in the company—and four out of five owned an automobile. The missionaries concluded that given the small scale of operations and the company's "climate of cooperation," it should be a model for French enterprise.

Some of the teams were skeptical about the soundness of the human-relations approach and its relevance to France. Visitors detected a certain cynicism in this form of human engineering. They reported the comment of one American expert, "this fraud that they call human relations," and expressed doubts that in itself human relations could alter behavior.[65] One American manager supposedly joked:

Sociology has shown that men seem to produce better if they are happy, and we try hard to make them happy. But if experiments proved that men produce still better if they are furious, we would work it out so that they could be furious all the time.[66]

The missions recognized that the purpose of human relations was to create an open and cooperative climate for work; they saw that this technique served to persuade workers to accept the system of free enterprise and to fortify social peace. But American trade unions, the French noted, had reservations about the technique and argued that some employers used it to substitute "psychotherapy" for high wages. To the skeptics such techniques invaded privacy and concealed the manipulation of labor. Rumors of the "confessionals" at Western Electric, where employees exposed their innermost feelings in group interviews but were subject to unseen observation by supervisors, portended the worst. Even enthusiasts disapproved of some aspects of this human engineering. The signs that reminded everyone to "Keep Smiling" suggested workers should mask their true feelings in the interest of solidarity.

Most missions refused to see human relations as either readily adaptable or as a panacea. France was different. The French generally lacked team spirit. French firms had less internal cohesion, and workers feared exploitation so keenly that there was a veritable sense of class struggle. The teams believed that France had a different, and less supportive, social and economic environment. In contrast Americans had the sense of working in a dynamic economy with the highest standard of living in the world, and American workers possessed the security afforded by strong trade unions and profited from the easy informality and apparent sincerity of social intercourse that inspired confidence. Only by taking into account these differences could these new managerial methods be introduced to France. The missionaries warned that the consequences of adopting American human relations techniques might be "unintended, most often mediocre, and sometimes harmful."[67]

Looking outside the firm, French visitors found an extremely competitive, yet supportive, economic environment in the United States. Missionaries gaped at the price war waged between Macy's and Gimbel's in 1951 that drove down the price of home furnishings by 50 percent. Americans took enormous pride in their free enterprise system, which, they claimed, was largely free of either government controls or internal restraints. The American industrialist was caught between the anvil of competition and the hammer of wage pressure that constantly forced him to find ways of raising productivity. The missionaries were told that Americans enshrined their worship of competition in antitrust legislation. It was no coincidence that the ECA/MSA was doing its best to open the Western European economies by condemning the continent's fondness for cartels. But the obvious existence of oligopoly in many industries clashed with America's self-image and aroused the skepticism of some French teams about claims of perfect competition.[68] Nevertheless, witnessing the relatively high competitive levels of the American economy reminded the visitors of their own sluggish markets at home.[69]

In America the entire national economy was, much like the individual firm, transparent. Statistical economic data, gathered by governmental and private sources, was at everyone's disposal. The display at the Department of Commerce that recorded each new birth captivated the missions. To one observer, Gallic reserve explained the lack of a French counterpart: "French enterprises like statistics as much as Americans do, but they don't like to provide them."[70]

Even more important for explaining American prosperity than this competitive and transparent economic environment was the social context in which American enterprise functioned. Americans, including American workers, agreed on the virtue of free enterprise and they made productivity a national goal. Productivity was "more than a technique; it is a social reality."[71]

The key, according to this analysis, was a cooperative labor force. From the perspective of the CNP, which was directing the drive, labor would determine the success or failure of its campaign. Business, it was assumed, would more readily follow the Americans' lead. Thus much of the drive aimed at selling French workers on the benefits of the American way.

The primary attraction was the affluence of the American worker. The symbol of prosperity was the automobile parked in the working man's driveway. Experts concluded that the living standard of the skilled American worker was far superior to that of the comparable French worker and probably even to that of the majority of French middle managers and professionals like lawyers. The source of such affluence was high productivity. This causal relationship was the crux of all the reporting about the United States. A rising level of productivity not only lowered costs and increased profits, but it also cut prices and generated higher wages. Productivity paid the bill for the workers' automobiles and television sets. High wages, in turn, "deepened" markets for sellers by raising the purchasing power of workers. American wage earners, it was said, realized this vital relationship and thus willingly supported efforts to raise their productivity.

What remained to be overcome in France was labor's fear that productivity was simply a new scheme of exploitation hatched by capitalists. The promise of American-style affluence was one avenue of persuasion. Another was the argument that Americans work "better" but not "harder." The old charge that the assembly line subjected the worker to speedups seemed baseless when one knew American factories. French trade union delegates found that American factory work was no more advanced than their own.[72] The abundance of power hand tools and other forms of machinery reduced human effort. According to one estimate, only 3 percent of all energy used in American manufacturing was derived from manual sources.[73] American workers simply worked more efficiently. And the pleasant ambiance of plants, like the Johnson and Johnson factory—clean, brightly illuminated, ventilated, and automated—was a vision of what could be in Europe.

Even more appealing than the character of physical labor was the mutual trust that existed among all employees. One CFTC official reported, "What distinguishes American economic life from ours is a different state of mind rather than technique."[74] American workers, unlike their French peers, were committed to raising output because they knew the employer would share the benefits with them. Sympathetic syndicalists observed an absence of social class and class conflict.

The United States is really a country without the psychology of class. Americans believe that payment in respect and consideration is as important as payment in wages. The absence of this notion of class explains the behavior of the American worker. The worker, whose labor movement is completely pragmatic, stripped of all ideology (too much so to my taste), has only one worry—that of always getting more.[75]

More skeptical French trade unionists reported that American unions might not cry class struggle from the rooftops but also recognized that their American peers won nothing without a fight.[76] And one missionary complained privately that high American productivity was the result of "ruthless action on the part of management [and] the gigantic war effort."[77]

In the eyes of the syndicalists, American trade unions seemed unbelievably powerful and respectable. The well-furnished offices, technical staffs, and large dues-paying memberships astonished the European visitors.[78] So did the appearance of American labor leaders sporting bow ties and smoking cigars. These former street fighters now controlled funds valued in the millions of dollars, played golf with politicians, and attended classes with managers at the Harvard Business School. American trade unions also enjoyed collective bargaining and closed shops and operated independently of employers, the government, or political parties.

The American labor movement supposedly shared fully in the "religion of productivity." David Dubinsky, head of the International Ladies Garment Workers' Union, told the French, "We have a vital interest in employers' profits and thus in the efficiency of production" because high wages come from high productivity just as high profits do.[79] American workers, Dubinsky said, didn't fear technological unemployment because it was vain to oppose progress and they knew sooner or later that new jobs would be generated. Trade unions in the United States appeared pragmatic to French non-Communist syndicalists, but "life there is not a bed of roses; they quarrel and strikes are tough battles. But when a truce is signed, both sides respect it." Industrial peace came by settling precise issues, like wages, and if conditions changed, the two sides restarted discussions instead of resorting to extreme measures. Above all, both sides never doubted the other's good faith. "They believe in their sincerity. In extreme circumstances they tell each other that they are maladroit, never that they are corrupt or worse."[80]

This idealized perception of American labor relations prompted syndicalists to issue an indictment of their situation. American workers, inside and outside the factory, did not feel "this haughtiness, this self-importance, this contempt or lack of understanding that too often characterizes . . . employers here."[81] As one labor mission concluded:

It's not a question of wanting to introduce brutally and mechanically the methods of American trade unions into France. . . . Nor is it a matter for us of accepting or admiring everything that we found there. We do think, nevertheless, that it would be desirable to see our French labor movement secure for all our fellow workers a situation comparable to that which exists in America.[82]

The New World was far from perfect. And in many respects, at both the technical and the human levels, French industry could instruct American industry. Yet every mission concluded that imitation of some American methods was both possible and desirable. A synthesis of mission reports concluded, "The essential condition for the success of the productivity crusade is the dissemination of an atmosphere of confidence and loyalty."[83]

This conclusion points up an issue that seemed to underlie the entire campaign. Raising productivity, in the eyes of the true believers, required a new French revolution. For those missionaries who earnestly sought to introduce American ways, the question seemed to be, were the French of the 1950s willing to accept radical social and economic renovation in order to raise productivity? To import American methods implied an overhaul of French *direction* and labor relations because the American model was built on mutual trust and respect, open and honest communication, and the delegation of responsibility. In particular, employers would have to make an equitable distribution of benefits gained from raising productivity, and labor would have to overcome its historic mistrust of the *patronat*. There would be no place for communism and class struggle. At the technical level, industrialists and engineers needed to recognize that productivity was not merely a matter of copying some technical recipes. For the real issue was learning how to generate a continuous flow of new techniques. At the macroeconomic level, producers and consumers would have to welcome a more market-oriented economy.

In fact the productivity drive, at least in the short run, failed to bring about a drastic overhaul of either the socioeconomic or the political status quo: markets were not opened and communism was not weakened. Much could be accomplished within existing French structures and without overturning habits. Productivity rates in France improved but without, at least immediately, this seemingly necessary socioeconomic revolution.

··········

It is difficult to assess the impact of the productivity drive, and this issue has not been the principal objective of our analysis.[84] We know that productivity rose dramatically after 1953, with France leading most other Western European nations, and we know also that rising productivity was a major cause of the prosperity of the late 1950s and 1960s. Changes were introduced at the plant level that included everything from installing fluorescent lighting and conveyer belts to redesigning production lines. But how many of these changes came from the productivity movement? If such innovations were not inspired by the drive, they were at least similar to American practice, and they contributed to the stunning rise in productivity rates. And it seems likely, given the scope and energy of the drive, that it did communicate the productivity message to large numbers of businessmen, technicians, labor leaders, and officials. French business audiences, for example, were said to be so saturated with talk of American efficiency that they asked speakers to avoid the subject. But what does the implementation of the drive reveal about the French response to the American way?

Follow-up studies by the ECA in 1951 show a mixed response to the first efforts at introducing American-style productivity measures.[85] In a few instances eager missionaries revolutionized their firm's operations, but others either ignored what they had seen, encountered stiff opposition, or at most introduced piecemeal innovations that yielded little in the way of gains. Some plants with strong CGT unions obstructed anything that resembled productivity reform, but in other factories or offices such changes occurred despite, or with the compliance of, a CGT local.

Much later the AFAP tried to assess the impact of the program that it organized. Questionnaires sent to former participants in 1955–56 revealed only modest results.[86] To be sure, the experience of seeing the American way was a "shock" to everyone and stimulated a general effort to improve operations. Yet the poor response to the questionnaire led the AFAP to infer that perhaps as many as half the missions were "sterile." Among the respondents, however, there was virtual unanimity that the new knowledge gained in America had been applied in some manner. Significantly, however, these applications were only rarely labeled "productivity programs." Such programs were introduced de facto or carried a different appellation because productivity per se encountered such "distrust" that it was wiser to avoid such an identification.

About 30 percent of those attempting innovation encountered interference. The source of these objections was equally divided among boards of directors, managers, and workers—and in most instances the opposition was not overcome. In some cases the returning missionary, according to the questionnaires, faced indifference or even hostility among his peers, which isolated him and dampened his enthusiasm. In other instances once a firm had introduced change and gained a competitive advantage, it had little incentive and insufficient training to continue innovation. Sometimes efforts to raise productivity were blocked by hidebound suppliers and clients. Without cooperation at each stage of the manufacturing-marketing process, prices could not be lowered or competition enhanced. Thus productivity advocates were unable to demonstrate sufficient gains to cause their firms to abandon old routines.[87] In these circumstances, the AFAP concluded, results were inevitably limited.

Too many visitors, in the eyes of the AFAP, preferred copying technical aspects of American manufacturing rather than familiarizing themselves with broader American methods of management or human relations. While the teams perceived the social and psychological aspects of the problem, few, in practice, awarded them priority. The visits, the agency acknowledged, were usually too brief to master the more complex features of American enterprise such as management, organization, and marketing. From the AFAP's perspective there had been too much literal copying of American machinery and manufacturing processes and not enough learned about American methods to enable the French to find their own solutions to their problems.

Even witnessing the "glass house" of American business firsthand did not alter the closed character of the missionaries' own enterprises. Only one-third of the *chefs d'entreprise* (who responded to the questionnaire) had called on outside consultants for advice. The AFAP attributed this reluctance to the secretive ways and to a "certain misplaced amour propre" among heads of family firms.[88] Of these *chefs d'entreprise* only 3.5 percent would allow visits to their plants from competitors. Only 10 percent would accept visits from former mission colleagues!

When asked to quantify the gains made by their innovations, most participants replied that productivity had been raised but that they could not be more specific. Most often the respondents answered plaintively that productivity was "a matter of climate and nothing durable or definitive could be done in this area until the positions of trade unions, workers, and employers were fundamentally altered."[89] But such social changes were beyond the reach of the crusaders of the early 1950s and in this regard the failure of the foundry experiment is instructive.

During 1952–53 a controversy erupted over a pilot program in the foundry industry that revealed labor-management tensions. At issue was the extension of an experimental training program operated by the CNP and funded by the ECA in a handful of companies to another hundred foundries as well as to a small number of manufacturers of men's clothing and shoes. In fact, the foundry experiment was a small operation that had yielded mixed results after a year of operation. By late 1952 it could claim the introduction of productivity bonuses; the setting of wage levels that were slightly higher than those of regional competitors; and the virtual absence of layoffs (or none connected with the program).[90] Yet these pilot companies had not yet shown higher profits or lower prices.

In the fall of 1952 the syndicalists on the CNP asserted themselves. Labor support had always been tentative, but now the free unions—the CFTC, the FO, and the CGC, which had accepted the ad hoc arrangements between employers and workers in the original foundry experiment—demanded guarantees before expanding the program.[91] Workers who had been in the pilot program acknowledged an improvement in work conditions but complained that they rarely benefited from bonuses and, despite rare layoffs, the workers almost unanimously continued to fear unemployment.[92] The syndicalists had become frustrated by the refusal of the employers to bargain collectively; they were unhappy with their nominal role in formulating CNP policy, and worried that the pilot program might be detrimental to workers' interests. The non-Communist unions now insisted on formal agreements between employers' associations and trade unions in order to define the principles of the program and to elaborate guarantees that would cover a wide range of issues such as a share in productivity benefits, participation by trade unions, and job security. No longer satisfied with mere representation on the CNP, the free labor federations wanted to introduce collective bargaining to gain a real say in developing a national productivity program.

Employers were afraid of the drift toward *autogestion* (worker self-management) represented by the syndicates' demands. They knew the non-Communist unions were weak—in most of the pilot foundries the CGT was the largest syndicate and the other syndicates were often altogether absent. Thus business leaders in the CNPF and the trade associations saw no value in reaching an accord at the national level with syndicates who could not control the work force at the plant level. The free syndicates were playing a weak hand, perhaps trying to use the productivity program to strengthen themselves vis-à-vis the rival CGT, and the employers knew it. Trade associations thus opposed any contractual agreements that would assure labor bonuses in advance, and the CNPF insisted that it could not impose collective bargaining and productivity contracts on either trade associations or on individual firms.[93] Individual employers might be willing to cooperate, but organized business was not.

The CNP eventually had to abandon the pilot program because of the rigidity of the trade associations and the united opposition of the labor movement, non-Communist and Communist. The agency could not bring employers and employees together to negotiate; the government refused to intervene. American officials tried, using their control of credits, to force contractual agreements, but failed.[94] The training program thus limped along in 1952 despite the syndicates' opposition, but the following year the FO resigned from the CNP/AFAP over this affair. The resignation of this non-Communist union led to a complete overhaul of the productivity program. Because organized labor and business could not resolve their differences, the state stepped in and appointed Gabriel Ardant as commissioner of productivity to take charge of a new loan-subsidy program.

The foundry controversy demonstrated that when real stakes were at risk—in this case defining the goals, procedures, and benefits of a productivity program—the drive collapsed because organized business and labor disagreed. Weak non-Communist trade unions were unable to force collective bargaining on employers. A weak, and unwilling, CNPF could not impose its will on either the trade associations or individual firms. In this instance those missionaries who had warned that France lacked the "social climate" that Americans enjoyed were vindicated.

Nevertheless, the contentiousness of trade associations and labor federations did not prevent progress at the grass-roots level. Incremental gains occurred in individual firms despite the indifference, even the hostility, of the national trade unions and employers' associations. And in many cases individual firms and local unions worked together to implement the productivity program. The social climate was not uniformly hostile to productivity.

Private enterprise acted on its own, more or less with labor's cooperation, in an incremental way to raise efficiency. Organized business or labor federations often had little to do with this grass-roots change. What really raised rates were the thousands of firms who adapted by doing such things as standardizing their products, retraining their workers and managers, introducing market studies, and remodeling their plants.[95]

Whatever the actual effects of the productivity drive may have been (and the missions were only one part), officials began to take pride in the rising curve of national productivity rates by the mid-1950s. The gap was closing. By 1955–56 overall gains in productivity were unmistakable—advancing at an extraordinary rate of 5 to 6 percent per year. Outsiders began to notice French performance. If during 1955 some sixty missions still visited the United States, France was now the host to twenty-nine missions who arrived from other European and non-European countries. Emulating America ceased being an imperative. The inferiority complex that was so prominent in 1950 disappeared. Productivity seemed to be advancing spontaneously. Commissioner Ardant cautiously expressed the new confidence in 1956 when, after noting the multiplication of private experiments and a "new spirit," he stated:

Within this immense frozen ice field, which has characterized the French economy for thirty years, with its network of false protections, costly routines, and antiquated institutions, these are the first rumblings, the harbingers of renewal, which, if the French want, could shatter it. But it's not always easy to opt for life, to choose imagination and reflection, to prefer new, and thus risky, investments, over outmoded, traditional outlays. Every Frenchman carries within him a formidable old man who is difficult to exorcise.[96]

Clearly, the need for missions was over when officials in Washington quizzed Ardant during his 1956 visit about France's remarkable productivity rates.[97]

As a program, technical assistance under the Marshall Plan was only a modest success because of Gallic reluctance that American efforts encountered from almost every quarter and because of the Cold War.[98] In general French government, labor, and industry doubted that the American model could be readily transferred across the Atlantic. The Fourth Republic feared that the program might make Paris appear subservient to Washington; subservience was a sure formula for failure, given Communist surveillance of the republic's independence. The CGT refused to participate, and the non-Communist labor federations cooperated timidly before withdrawing their support. Trade associations harbored serious reservations and refused to enter into binding contracts with organized labor. Only individual enterprises and local unions proved willing to experiment. Yet, of all the handicaps that encumbered technical assistance in France, the most crippling was its subordination to Cold War politics. Together the Americans and the Communists converted what might have been a nonpartisan technical aid program into an issue of political ideology that took away much of its appeal.[99] The promise of higher wages, shorter hours, lower prices, increased profits, and more goods—in short the promise of the American way that would have benefited French workers, business, and consumers—was damaged, but not paralyzed, by an ideological contest.

....

In retrospect, the revelation of the postwar productivity gap prompted a self-examination of the nation's social and economic status quo. It was this reflection, rather than the drive per se, which has been the subject of this discussion. To ask why French productivity levels were low was to raise questions about why economy and society were resistant to changes à l'américaine. The gap was not merely a matter of manufacturing or selling techniques. It was also, as we have seen, a question of overturning old ways: an authoritarian style of organization; an embittered and distrustful system of industrial relations; and a protected economic landscape. But neither organized business nor labor were enthusiastic about adopting such measures because they judged these measures largely non-transferable, in many ways undesirable, or just unnecessary; nor did the French government fully back the cause.

At another level, the productivity gap posed cultural and philosophical issues. What sacrifices in Frenchness would catch-up entail? How should the French define prosperity and happiness in the postwar world? Was the American way the model?

The missionaries had their doubts: "What other civilizations consider as a concession to the less noble aspect of human beings—enjoyment of material wealth—becomes for American civilization, if not happiness itself, at least a step toward happiness."[100] Virtually every mission wanted to provide the French with a standard of living comparable to that enjoyed by Americans. Yet ambivalence lingered.

Americans, to the missionaries, had "a vigorous collective sense" and a willingness to accept discipline—on the job, in public, and as consumers. "This demonstrates that Americans are not only marvelously gifted to live in society, but also to produce and consume in large quantities practical objects of standardized quality."[101] Americans were conformists, who as a price for their comforts accepted mass-produced, aggressively advertised articles. They sought only superficial variety in order to sustain mass output and were content to buy the latest model of a product rather than, like Europeans, seek an exclusive or unique one. A synthesis of the teams' reports stated:

There exist in the United States a wide variety of climates, landscapes, and people. However, these people live in a city that recurs ten thousand times, inhabit a home that oddly resembles their neighbor's, own the same practical and comfortable furniture, eat the same simple, rapidly prepared, meals at the same time. The American populace gives the impression of a vast middle class.[102]

There was worry about giving up the "nice old habits" and a traditional sense of Frenchness. The head of one mission, reflecting on the sacrifice to collective norms that affluence required, observed that a factor in the American system was the "very simple tastes and habits" of the average American in certain areas such as food. Hot dogs and hamburger cost less than a cut of beef manicured by a French butcher. "When the American tries to leave this standardization, it costs him a fortune—which a Frenchman doesn't hesitate paying because it's his way of conceiving life." To this observer,

Everything depends on defining what one means by a "high standard of living." This expression does not have the same meaning on both sides of the Atlantic. If certain Frenchmen understand it as the Americans do, if they advocate the

"American way of life," they must point out that it can only be attained by profoundly modifying the tastes and habits of our people.[103]

The missionaries of the 1950s worried about the sociocultural costs of importing the American way of life. They harbored an uneasy feeling that material comfort ought not to be the highest social priority—"it is difficult to achieve this material comfort without compromising one's moral stature."[104] Their anxiety was pointed up by their eagerness to emphasize that the United States was not a cultural wasteland. Missions stressed the well-endowed museums and universities. But there were doubts. Even Robert Buron found American intellectual conformity unacceptable. Yet he opted for the American way: "Who could, with good conscience, defend low wages in the name of culture and defend misery as an indispensable complement to the charms of individualism?"[105]

Among even the most ardent proponents of the American way, there was skepticism that the New World was a socioeconomic paradise and apprehension about the accompanying social and cultural costs entailed by Americanization. What is most striking is that even among those who most wanted to bring the American way to France in the 1950s, enthusiasm was restrained by ambivalence.

CHAPTER 5

The American Temptation

The Coming of Consumer Society

At the end of the 1950s French cinemas were showing a film entitled *La belle Américaine*. The heroine of this comedy was not, however, as might be expected, a lovely Hollywood actress. It was rather a General Motors car. The film not only suggests the new prosperity of the French people but also makes the commonplace identification of Americanization with automobiles.

There was a second dimension to the anti-Americanism of the postwar years besides the political-strategic dispute. To be sure, even after the troubles of the Korean War era anxiety lingered about American hegemony. Thus in 1956 a visiting delegation of French political and intellectual leaders that included Gaullists, Atlanticists, and socialists shocked their American colleagues by accusing the United States of being an imperialist power.[1] Nevertheless, after about 1954 a sociocultural critique gradually suffused anti-American discourse, supplanting the earlier commentary about America as a political menace. Worry over America's passion to fight communism and turn the West into an armed camp subsided once McCarthyism vanished, the Korean War ended, Stalin died, West Germany rearmed, and containment yielded, at least rhetorically, to coexistence as Western strategy toward the Soviet Union. If Cold War tension remained, at least the political boundaries of Europe had been stabilized and the central issue of France's place in the new order had been settled. France was firmly Atlanticist and the earlier, more fluid, international situation had crystallized. Even the neutralists of *Le Monde* modified their stance and accepted German rearmament once the Soviets rearmed East

Germany.[2] Moreover, the peak of French dependence on the United States had passed and Washington's interference began to diminish. These changes shifted concern away from geopolitical and strategic issues. Gallic observers might continue to search for signs of latent McCarthyism and militarism, but interest turned to America as a domestic model.

Displayed as in *La belle Américaine*, America offered a sociocultural temptation to the French. This was an attraction many tried to resist. Americanization in the form of mass consumption and mass culture initially nourished anti-Americanism but in the long run also weakened it. This chapter examines the debate during the 1950s about America as a model of the modern society.

· · · · · · · · · ·

What was said or written about America toward the end of this decade reflected the coming of consumer society to France. The remarkable period of economic growth later labeled the *trente glorieuses* had begun. The appearance of *La belle Américaine* on the screen, for example, paralleled growing automobile ownership. The total stock of privately owned automobiles more than doubled between 1951 and 1958 and half these cars were new. By 1958 there was one car for every seven French citizens.[3] In the case of television, at the beginning of the decade there were only twenty-four thousand sets in France. By 1958 there were nearly a million.

Consumption and incomes grew a third between 1949 and 1958 and even more rapidly afterwards. Over this time span all wage earners experienced a sharp rise in purchasing power as incomes rose faster than the cost of living. Family strategies turned away from saving and investment, away from traditional values of building the family patrimony toward more present-minded enjoyment. Total household consumption grew 40 percent between 1950 and 1957, ahead of the annual growth of production, investment, and income. More so than other Europeans, the French pursued consumption at the expense of investment or saving. This powerful pull of demand derived not only from purchasing power but from a rapid proliferation of credit. The "traditional values of caution and frugality crumbled; debt was no longer considered something to be ashamed of," one historian writes.[4] Only the farmers continued to resist the trend toward buying on credit.

The way the French spent their income began to shift in the 1950s (see fig. 14). The major changes were not so much in food or clothes, though dietary ambitions altered and demand for clothes gave more stress to fashion. But far more income went for health and personal hygiene. And the star of the domestic budget was household equipment. Expenditures on domestic appliances rose at an annual rate of 15 percent with the most dramatic progress coming after 1954. In that year only 7.5 percent of French households owned a refrigerator, 10 percent a washing machine, and 18 percent a vacuum cleaner. A survey taken in 1954 confirmed that the French conceived of their new well-being as starting at home.[5] From 1949 to 1957 the stock of home appliances grew 400 percent. The first spending priority was household goods. The next consumer aspiration was automobile ownership. And the third goal, after the achievement of domestic comfort and a private car, was leisure and culture. Spending on radios, television sets, records, games, photographic and sporting equipment grew rapidly.

Rising consumption was not equally distributed. Among the many excluded it aroused frustration and envy.[6] Farmers, for example, were largely outsiders. In rural Vaucluse Laurence Wylie reports that in 1950 villagers had little interest in acquiring modern conveniences. The farmers might have seen new bathroom facilities in American films but were either too poor to install modern kitchens and bathrooms or believed that buying on credit indicated poor household management. Thus farmers continued to invest in the family patrimony rather than in objects that would draw attention to their prosperity—especially the attention of the tax collector.[7]

The picture drawn by these data is of a society largely unequipped with consumer durables in the early 1950s. Only one of every seventeen inhabitants in 1951 had a car, for example. But the buying spree began in the middle of the decade and quickly gathered a momentum that was to carry over into the 1960s. Yet the French did not acknowledge this move toward consumer society late in the Fourth Republic. A poll in 1956 showed that despite a substantial increase in the average per capita income during the year, nine of every ten persons surveyed thought their standard of living had declined or remained stationary.[8] The dawn of consumerism was still shrouded in the darkness of recent shortages and penury.

··········

It would be presumptuous to attempt to map what the French intelligentsia thought about America in the 1950s. Too little scholarly work on the subject exists. And the closed preserve of St-Germain-des-Prés was so subtly, yet sharply, fragmented into circles, hierarchies, rivalries, and influences that a comprehensive and accurate map may

14. Ads for American products, 1950s: Blue jeans (*above*); American television sets (*opposite*). (Courtesy Bibliothèque Forney-Paris)

elude even the most experienced native cartographer. Assessing "influences" of America, for example, on one scholarly field such as the social sciences is a daunting task.

But there was a subgroup of the intelligentsia, one that had lower status than *les grands intellectuels* yet included some of its most celebrated members, whose views of the American social model can be examined. These individuals might be termed the "popularizers"—prominent journalists, literati, and academics who directly and extensively addressed the issue of the American temptation and who shaped opinion. They were the experts who published popular books on America or wrote for strategic newspapers or reviews; they were the authorities on America who captured, if not a wide audience, at least one that counted as an educated elite. They may not have been the voice of France, but they were heard by the political, administrative, commercial, academic, and intellectual elites. These were the intellectuals who worried about America—less as a source of ideas or trends in the rarefied world of philosophy, literary criticism, history, social science, or art—and more as a socioeconomic and cultural model. Their books and articles directly addressed the question of the meaning of American consumerism and mass culture for the French.

This subgroup of the Parisian intelligentsia comprises the principal sources of informed opinion about contemporary America. *Le Monde* was the journal of the intelligentsia. Its editor, Hubert Beuve-Méry, and its reporters, men like André Fontaine and Claude Julien, set the main lines of interpretation not only for St-Germain-des-Prés but also for much of the French elite. Even after neutralism had been eclipsed, *Le Monde* continued to convey its uneasiness about the new society across the Atlantic.[9] *Esprit* under the editorship of Albert Béguin and then Jean-Marie Domenach was one of the most important reviews for the intelligentsia and continued its prewar Christian personalist assessment of America. The distinctive interpretation of *américanisme* by Simone de Beauvoir and Jean-Paul Sartre appeared in *Les Temps modernes,* while book-length studies of America were published by Claude Alphandéry, Cyrille Arnavon, André Maurois, Jacques Maritain, André Siegfried, and Claude Julien. And social scientists like Raymond Aron, Georges Friedmann, and Michel Crozier contributed to this assessment.

During the 1950s the image of America as a sociocultural system was heavily marked by ideology. Unlike the critical assault in the 1930s, in this postwar decade it issued from the left, rather than the right. The grid through which most observers viewed the New World was constructed from Christian and socialist assumptions about America as the archetypical capitalist society. America was conservative, materialistic, exploitative, conformist, racist, and militarist. Visits to the United States rarely overturned the critics' assumptions. America's image was further damaged when visitors and even invited guests were denied entry because of their leftist views. Unmasking the reality of the consumer paradise became the self-appointed mission of most of these popularizers. They were convinced America was not the happy land of material plenty and social progress. A book of photographs entitled *Les Américains* portrayed the American people as joyless materialists immersed in mass culture, evangelical religion, and patriotism. The image was one of lonely individuals in bars, sidewalk preachers, poor blacks, and flag-waving crowds.[10] Nor did Americans unselfishly bring the world the gifts of prosperity and freedom. Americanization was something other than what its apologists claimed.

If St-Germain-des-Prés was stubbornly engagé, other America-watchers left and right either refused to judge American society ideologically or were partisans of Americanization. Among these observers were such literary celebrities as André Maurois, Jacques Maritain, Albert Camus, Claude Roy, André Siegfried, Vercors, and Henri Troyat. Familiar negative themes appeared in their literature but were generally balanced by more positive appraisals of achievements and promise. Whatever the prestige may have been of these authorities, the weight of opinion among the popularizers was still essentially socialist and inspired by *marxisant* or Christian principles.

The debate about America in the 1950s had two other characteristics besides this ideological lens. First, unlike earlier criticism, it accepted that Americanization was at hand. Second, social science began to inform its perceptions.

Most observers now assumed that France was becoming Americanized in a material sense. Affluence, appliances, and automobiles lay round the corner for the French—remote in 1930, possible in 1950, and both inevitable and imminent in 1960. A few prescient commentators like Georges Friedmann had recognized France's future in America in the late 1940s. But virtually everyone accepted it by 1960. In that year Jean-Marie Domenach wrote:

Ten years ago we could still look down on the snack bars, the supermarkets, the striptease houses, and the entire acquisitive society. Now all that has more or less taken hold in Europe. This society is not yet ours, but it—or one that resembles it—could be our children's. The United States is a laboratory exhibiting life forms into which we have entered whether we like it or not.[11]

In the 1950s the technocratic nightmare of the interwar years became either real or irrelevant. But it was no longer a futuristic hallucination. Between the wars Duhamel may have predicted France's future in the guise of America, but he spoke of a distant future and one that might not, with proper resistance, come to pass. But now, "America is coming" was the consensus. And expressions of cultural archaism that had been common in 1930 were scarce two decades later when Jean Cocteau ascribed to industrial society qualities that he did not find in France:

So many disasters, hospitals, desperate withdrawals into the cloisters, flights, suicides, catastrophes. If that changed there would be discipline, order, fear, comfort . . . all those qualities that France doesn't possess and that would cause its ruin. France bristles with contours and peaks. One can't imagine a flat France. France would have everything to lose in aspiring to possess resources that are unsuited to it—for example, to want a large industrial plant. Its prerogatives are crafts, invention, the stroke of inspiration, the accidental.[12]

But Cocteau was out of step at a moment when Americanization was under way. Outright rejection of this future, which was plausible before the war, was now an impossible stance. Only the hidebound like

Duhamel, at age seventy-two, continued to insist that when it came to washing clothes a machine could not match hand laundering.[13] But few were paying attention to him any longer.

A final characteristic of this debate was the introduction of American social science. These empirical studies simultaneously sharpened and deadened the socialist critique. On the one hand, by the end of the decade the *marxisant* observers renewed their critique by drawing heavily on the literature of American social science. They enriched their critique with the exposés of such Americans as C. Wright Mills, William H. Whyte, David Riesman, and John Kenneth Galbraith. Here were the themes of "the power elite," "the organization man," "the outer-directed man," and "the affluent society." On the other hand, at the end of the 1950s sociology began to replace socialist ideology in American social studies. Scholars like Michel Crozier, Alain Touraine, and François Bourricaud came to regard America as a laboratory of the future and looked to American social science for methods and theories in order to study common problems.[14] Searching for the suppressed class struggle in America—a theme of earlier studies like that of Daniel Guerin— became passé.[15] Crozier left behind his former *marxisant* interests in America and became the gadfly of the leftist intelligentsia, embracing modernization as a beneficent force rather than a cover for capitalist exploitation.[16] For Crozier the issue became how best to remove the obstacles to modernization in France. Sociology was no longer the handmaiden of socialism, and studies of America became more "scientific."

....

Debating the American model in the 1950s meant assessing four major issues: consumerism, conformity, mass culture, and optimism. And implicitly or explicitly such discussion raised the question, was America a social model for Europe?

With respect to the first issue French observers weighed the advantages and disadvantages of the coming consumer society embodied in the American dream. On the positive side Americanization promised more leisure and comfort, less drudgery, and greater opportunity for personal improvement. Jean Fourastié's best-sellers, for example, paraded the attractions of the American "revolution" and the technological future.[17] Visitors to the United States during the early postwar years observed with fascination the birth of consumer society.[18] Coming from a society that was still suffering from austerity and one that made saving a virtue, they were astonished at the luxury of hotels and trains and shocked by the spectacle of waste elevated to civic virtue. Even the average American home was full of surprises. The journalist team of Pierre and Renée Gosset exclaimed:

There were three bedrooms; two bathrooms, gleaming, of course; a dining room where silverware was on exhibition; and a kitchen where the family actually ate. Renée mused wistfully in the kitchen with its enormous refrigerator, sensational stove, a sink with built-in cupboards. . . . All was spotless and without a faded curtain.[19]

Whereas interwar travelers seemed frightened by the dehumanizing qualities of mechanization, their postwar successors often welcomed its liberating qualities. Sartre may have found prefabricated housing antiseptic but others believed that emancipation from deprivation, including liberation from squalid housing, enabled the average person to concentrate on more elevated goals.

One of the enthusiasts of America, André Maurois, wrote a dozen popular studies of the United States.[20] He acknowledged that mass production entailed some uniformity but argued that its benefits in liberating human beings from the meanest kind of work far outweighed its disadvantages. Maurois even disputed the stereotype of materialism. Americans, according to him, were obdurate idealists. They idolized men like Lincoln and Einstein rather than tycoons like Rockefeller. At an international conference on Americanization, a diatribe against the coming technical civilization provoked Maurois, as well as several other members of the French delegation, to come to its defense. They argued that technology was a progressive force that had lifted the masses. And if American materialism meant creating universities, museums, and libraries like those in the United States, then they wished Europeans "were a little more materialistic."[21]

But most readings of consumer society were far more negative than those given by Maurois or Fourastié. France might be facing a gadget society, the worship of mammon, and the death of culture. This critical reading predominated in the 1950s as it had in the 1930s. At *Esprit* Jean-Marie Domenach, for example, characterized America as a materialistic society whose dynamism derived from consumer-driven economic growth. He wrote, "This almost unlimited capacity to acquire and to consume is the fundamental characteristic of the American model" and likened it not to the possessive avarice of the European petite bourgeoisie but to an infantile desire to receive gifts.[22] He proclaimed that "money is unable to provide a durable basis for human society. One may well detest societies built on money but hating a society is not hating the people who live in it—one may like the people who suffer there."[23]

One of the most influential examples of this genre was Claude Alphandéry's essay *L'Amérique est-elle trop riche?*, which found abundance to be the defining characteristic of America.[24] In Los Angeles, a city that struck other French critics as a caricature of America, Alphandéry was captivated by the network of highways, the tens of thousands of cars moving from suburb to work, and the ubiquitous Cadillacs. At the same time he cited official data on the pockets of poverty and the precariousness of the average suburbanite's household budget. As for advertising, Alphandéry was less bothered by its vulgarity than by its economic costs and its superfluity—was there much satisfaction from having the airline phone to ask you how you wanted your steak cooked? Citing John Kenneth Galbraith, he noted the contrast between private affluence and the dearth of public services. Higher levels of consumption required more public goods, that is, more cars required more roads; but the United States lagged in this respect. Los Angeles suffered from smog, inadequate public transportation, and a lack of free parking. To make matters worse, Alphandéry noticed the slowing of growth in the late 1950s. He located the problems of the American economy within the engine room of consumerism and attributed the downturn to the expensive marketing apparatus, to the "unproductive" changes in product models, to the unsuitability of American exports for the underdeveloped world, and to the general waste of resources through unbridled competition and rapid obsolescence.

Alphandéry embellished earlier critiques of consumerism like Duhamel's when he proposed a psychological and philosophical "American malaise." Consumerism generated an endless escalation of desires that could not be satisfied. "It is a form of alienation in which wealth, which ought to bring more freedom by liberating those who possess it from elemental constraints, rebounds against them."[25] The mass media contributed to this alienation by exciting appetites and creating a kind of status conformity based on the possession of consumer products. Alphandéry, relying on Vance Packard, called Americans disgruntled "status seekers."

Eager for material goods, anxious about appearances, disoriented by diverse temptations, millions of Americans live without knowing the relaxation and the feeling of liberation that they could hope for from abundance.[26]

Alphandéry found some "antibodies," such as the high rate of social mobility, that might fight this malaise of conformity and greed, but he was not sanguine about alleviating the ills of consumer society.

Alphandéry's doubts about the cornucopia of affluence were matched by others' dismay at American waste. André Fontaine gazed enviously at the sea of used cars for sale on Livernois Avenue in Detroit, but Georges Friedmann, as he flew from a New York airport, saw only neglect in the hundreds of automobiles covered by snow.[27] More distressing was Americans' habit of disposing of usable goods because they wanted the newest model. Claude Julien suggested that America was a privileged society mainly because it wasted not only its own vast resources but those of underdeveloped countries as well.

Affluence had other negative social costs. French visitors noted that high incomes were equated with merit and social status. This was a vulgar equation to the intelligentsia. By 1960 it was also evident that consumerism was creating its own set of problems. Domenach noted that Americans were discovering their air was unbreathable, their water undrinkable, and their cities unlivable.

Of all the issues that consumerism raised for this generation of American observers, right or left, the one that most confounded them was whether French identity would survive the coming affluence. Most intellectuals either hoped or assumed that Americanization did not mean homogenization. Raymond Aron, for example, doubted that the French owner of a television set and an automobile would live like an American. "I hope," he said, "that he will preserve his singularity."[28] André Siegfried also believed that the French, outfitted with consumer durables, would behave differently from Americans. He cited a conversation with an American who showed him splendidly equipped kitchens and invidiously compared them to those of the French bourgeoisie. A friend of Siegfried's interrupted to ask, "But notice, where does the best cuisine come from?" Siegfried added that French kitchens were being modernized rapidly but explained the real difference:

The American confuses means and ends. When he owns a machine he forgets it has a purpose. The machine inspires such boundless admiration in him that he forgets its function. The French woman, in her modern kitchen, doesn't lose sight of its purpose, which is the preparation of pleasant meals.[29]

Civilisation, most insisted, would survive. But what were the salient features of this *civilisation* that they hoped and wanted to defend? That was less easy to specify. Some insisted that at least part of the answer lay in Gallic *bon goût* and the quality of French goods. The equation of quality and crafts seemed a quintessential Gallic trait. Siegfried, one of the oldest and most respected interpreters of the New World, contended that mass-produced goods could never fully match the quality of artisanal production.[30] Americans had a genius for the former but not for the artistic—not for haute couture or luxury textiles, for example.

If consumerism was coming, who was responsible? By the mid-1950s it was difficult to blame America any longer for exporting this phenomenon. Maurois argued that such features of Americanization as advertising, book digests, and gadgets were the adventitious products of an era, of a process of democratization and mechanization that Americans and Europeans were both facing. Raymond Aron also accepted the transformation as universal and inevitable:

This process of "Americanization" is looked upon by many with horror. But in some respects the battle is not so much against Americanism as against the universalizing of phenomena linked to the development of material civilization. If the effort toward increased productivity and the subordination of all usages to the imperatives of greater output is termed Americanization, then the whole of Europe, including France, is indeed in the process of becoming Americanized.[31]

Another observer argued that the process might be a blessing or a curse, but it was "an innovation which we [Europeans] have brought upon ourselves and has not in any sense been forced upon us by the Americans."[32] Europeans freely chose to shave with Gillette razors and eat California oranges. But a Swiss philosopher, Jeanne Hersch, disagreed, saying she was less certain Europeans were free to choose:

The Americans make us uneasy because, without wishing us ill, they put things before us for our taking, things which are so ready to hand and so convenient that we accept them, finding perhaps that they satisfy our fundamental temptations. . . . Masses of American products are imposed upon us by artificial means, especially where films are concerned. . . . Even when we can make a choice between products, we are influenced by a sort of force within ourselves, which we fear because it is indeterminate and indefinable . . . the threat we feel hanging over us, is not something evil; it is a vacuum, such as is produced by rapid movement.[33]

Americanization seduced Europeans. Hersch's psychological interpretation reversed the traditional notion that Europe corrupted American innocence—now the Americans tempted an innocent Old World.

....

The legacy of Alexis de Tocqueville is discernible in the second issue raised by the American model. The postwar left, like the interwar right, castigated America for the malaise of conformity. America was a mass society. Its law was that of rule by majority opinion. This law was so commanding that on occasion it swept away constitutional guarantees of personal liberty. Observers did not have to look deeply to see manifestations of the sameness of this "flat society." Friedmann noted an astonishing similarity in the main streets of all American cities. Everywhere one found a "micro-Broadway" populated by "movie theaters with their illuminated ads, light bulbs that blink day and night, galleries of vending machines, bars and cocktail lounges, drugstores, television sets, [and] signs in gaudy, seductive neon."[34] Simone de Beauvoir after visiting a bowling alley reflected on how differently the game was played in France:

I recall a bowling match in the square of a French village on a July 14 afternoon; the uneven ground laid traps for the players. Gardens, country cabarets, and squares shaded by plane trees are all replaced in America by these great air-conditioned halls where they roll standardized balls on exactly measured alleys without arguments or laughter. . . . It is monotonous to watch.[35]

Most visitors complained about the homogeneity of the food. The drugstore in Cleveland or Albuquerque sold the same ham sandwiches and ice cream. But Claude Roy noted that America had something else to do besides eat. "It has America to build."[36]

In *Les Temps modernes* the young sociologist Michel Crozier observed that American social scientists served their society's mania for conformity by statistically defining what was "normal" in almost every form of human behavior including sexual relations.[37] In *Le Monde* Claude Julien evoked the era of the "gray flannel suit" to describe American management. Drawing on the work of American sociologists, Julien explained how the bureaucratization of decision-making dampened imagination and boldness.[38] American management had lost much of its allure since the days of the Marshall Plan.

The weakness of the American left, a most perplexing phenomenon to the French left, was to be explained by the assimilative power of affluence and the pressure of conformity that immunized the society against radicalism. For its expert opinion, *Esprit* relied on a Chicago labor leader, Sidney Lens.[39] Lens argued that the new "standardized man" took refuge from the real world in his privacy and his consumer goods. Television dominated his leisure. But commercial sponsors and advertisers emptied television programming of any content, paraded a fairy-tale land of plenty, and treated Americans as children. "Standardized man" was capable of only infantile judgments. Nonconformity and creativity were branded "Communistic." Even most trade unionists believed Communists should be deprived of their citizenship. Everything conspired to make Americans accept their high standard of living as paradise. Yet, Lens told his French readers, consumer society did not make Americans content. Unhappiness was recorded in the high number of homicides, alcoholics, and neurotics.

Some of the harshest words about American uniformity came from *Esprit*. In 1951 Albert Béguin, following a visit that he said began without any preconceptions, wrote that daily life impressed him as "an attack against my personal liberty" because of the repetitiveness of advertising, the banality of conversations, the sameness of life-styles, and the uniformity of the environment. Not to acquire the latest model refrigerator, not to own a television set, or not to profess ideas derived from the daily newspaper was to be different, and difference was equated with being "un-American." Béguin acknowledged that there were good reasons, given the continent's need to integrate its immigrants, for this pressure, but the consequence was that America suffered from "a sort of dictatorship without a dictator" exercised by society on society.[40]

Béguin's successor as editor, Jean-Marie Domenach, repeated this indictment a decade later after his own tours of the United States. The only difference was that the "inorganic suburbs, monotonous roads lined with drugstores, and interchangeable motels" were also visible in Europe by 1960. Domenach asserted wildly that "the American state is liberal, but American society is totalitarian; it is possibly the most totalitarian society in the world." Politically an individual is free and that is important. "But in the realm of mores and human relations, difference is proscribed, not by edict or violence, but naturally, functionally. The same air, the same blood circulates through the countless channels of this porous society." Worst of all, from his perspective, America transformed revolt itself into a social function. It absorbed rebellion. "Try a 1960 Chevrolet. Try Zen. Try Jesus. Try whatever you want. You will feel better and better."[41] Domenach held some stubborn hope that this "hypersocialization, this domination by the other" would sooner or later unleash a nonconformist rebellion.[42]

• • • • • • • • • •

Americans' penchant for conformity was obvious in the kind of culture they preferred. The New World, in the eyes of French observers, was a cultural wasteland as well as the land of consumerism and conformity. Leisure entertainment was infantile. They noted the inane content of films, best-sellers, radio programs, and, the new discovery, television. "Come and watch television" was a common invitation extended visitors. But the French were not impressed with this distraction. A Catholic priest, Raymond Bruckberger, wrote, "I always think of Bernanos's words: 'Man has greater need for illusions than he has for bread.' The danger of television is obvious."[43] Commercialization of art was another grievance. Publishers sought neither to educate nor to discover original work—they wanted only to sell books to the masses. The "digest" was the symbol of this cultural deterioration. American culture seemed to be subservient to market criteria and subjected the writer or artist to commercial standards of success. Business profits and popular tastes dictated to the creative few. Even education was compromised by Americans' obsession with efficiency. The American army, *Le Monde* reported, was helping educate its officers by introducing speed-reading machines. But the army, the daily sarcastically noted, was satisfied if its officers could read quickly and comprehend 75 percent of the material.[44]

Yankee provincialism and anti-intellectualism provoked Gallic disdain. While visiting Cincinnati, André Fontaine was interviewed by several local journalists. At the end of the interview he was asked what newspaper he represented. "Excuse me, can you remind me of the name of your newspaper?—*Le Monde*—How do you spell that? Is it two words?"[45] The isolationism of the Midwest bewildered another journalist for *Le Monde*. He reported how an Iowa farmer asked foreign journalists if they wanted food packages sent to Europe. The date was 1952.[46] Albert Béguin reported that American undergraduates knew too little about the past to read French novels.[47] And Domenach was horrified when a businessman asked him if France was bigger than Belgium.[48] Americans distrusted intellectuals in power. Julien noted how the label "egghead" was a political handicap in American politics. He quoted President Eisenhower's definition of intellectuals as "those who use lots of sentences to say what can be expressed in a few words."[49]

Assessing the promise of American mass culture divided and perplexed French intellectuals. Was it to be praised as cultural uplift or condemned as cultural leveling? Unlike prewar literati who despaired over America, this postwar generation, while still sharply critical, saw a cultural transformation under way. If Americans lacked creativity, they were seeking the beautiful. One visitor flatly predicted: "You begin with the Pyramids, and eventually you come to build the Acropolis."[50]

America's colleges seemed like cultural oases and its libraries and concert halls were sumptuous by European standards. An article in *Esprit* marveled at the cheap paperback copies of C. Wright Mills and the thousands of Californians who voluntarily subscribed to an independent radio station.[51] To an apologist like Maurois, it was unfair to denigrate American culture. If Americans had no great tradition in painting, he observed, they produced masterpieces in the other arts and they admired European culture. Maurois quoted a sentimental American professor who, when going off to war, said to him, "Perhaps I shall be able to make my dream come true and re-read *Madame Bovary*, sitting in the shade of Notre Dame and eating a French croissant."[52] Claude Roy said Europeans' cultural snobbery was unwarranted anyway. Roy portrayed the ideal cultivated European who supposedly contrasted with the modern "mechanical man":

Western man . . . with his Christian, humanistic civilization, his ox-drawn cart, his Greco-Latin heritage, his unrefrigerated food, his respect for the human personality, his Hellenistic-classical sense of moderation . . . openhanded and gazing heavenward, dressed in a suit from the Belle Jardinière, tending Candide's garden, surpassing capitalism on the one hand and Marxism on the other . . . huddled in his Henry II dining room lined with flowered plates and works by the church fathers, Proudhon, and Kierkegaard, standing at his window watching the trains go by in steely contempt.[53]

Roy believed that neither Europeans nor Americans corresponded to these stereotypes. Raymond Aron, when faced with the question of whether high culture was sliding down toward mass culture in America or whether the cultural level of the average American was rising, answered judiciously, "I do not think one can entirely reject either thesis."[54]

But the critics continued to express their doubts. Vercors noted that it was too early for these pioneers to prize the beautiful because they were still immersed in the useful. And Alphandéry found certain products of mass culture, like paperbacks, brought cultural uplift, but he thought Americans were still backward:

Undoubtedly one finds in the United States a mixture of good taste and extreme vulgarity, but the dominant characteristic is a will toward cultural self-improvement, an admiration, perhaps a bit innocent and unqualified, for the great works of the mind, and an eagerness to refine taste and knowledge. However, what is missing is the pleasure of thinking in and for itself, the disinterestedness of reflection, an interest in synthesis. . . . There is still a great distrust for systems, for conceptions labeled "ideological," and there is a decided preference for pragmatism and specialization.[55]

The old charge that Americanization brought a "lowering" of culture would not disappear. Everyone was now willing to attribute a certain measure of cultural prowess to the United States and to allow a certain "progress" in American taste. And there was no longer any pretense that the two cultures were altogether dissimilar, though there was as yet little recognition that France itself was about to plunge into mass culture. Mass culture supposedly characterized America, and had an ugly tendency of invading high culture—the infamous American "digests" exemplified this adverse mixing of cultural levels that shocked the French. *Les Temps modernes* contended that "popular culture" was growing in America at the expense of both traditional "folk culture" and "superior culture." Culture became homogenized and denatured when the Book-of-the-Month Club brought Proust to middlebrow readers. Endless repetition of even the most profound experience made it a cliché. Mass media, Sartre's review argued, removed the individual from personal experience and, while appearing to compensate, actually aggravated his isolation from others, from reality, and from himself. It brought "the *déréalisation* of life that is lived for the most part as fiction. Art can deepen the perception of reality, but popular culture distracts us, hides from us its true aspects, and prevents us from living this reality." From this Sartrian perspective, American popular culture was not "authentic" and brought no real satisfaction because one cannot chase solitude or boredom with distractions: "The man who is bored is lonely because he misses his own company and not that of others, as he believes. He is deprived of individuality; he lacks the capacity to live and to feel."[56] The conviction among the intelligentsia that American mass culture was somehow contaminating persisted.

Most common in this effort at distinguishing Gallic culture from American technical or mass culture was to equate Frenchness with *civilisation* and define the latter as Latin humanism. Underlying this argument was a barely conscious form of self-defense for and by the French intelligentsia. André Siegfried expressed the problem this way:

The originality of Europe resides to a large measure in the well-matched association of the Anglo-Saxon spirit, which is synonymous with efficiency, and the Latin spirit, which is expressed in individual intellectualism, a combination of the practical with the critical approach. This balance has not been transmitted to the United States.[57]

"Culture [in the United States] in the true sense of the word," he continued, "with all its personal aspects is tending to be increasingly eclipsed by technical progress." America, according to Siegfried, was oriented toward achievements that required collective action, leaving the self-conscious individual powerless. The American's fanatical respect for method, organization, objectivity, science, and technology makes him "appear to us as Germany's star pupil." Siegfried noted that "the system produces competent people but does not guarantee they should be cultured." Americans, in short, had a technical conception of civilization that produced *homo faber;* to it Siegfried contrasted the humanistic goal of developing *homo sapiens.* Man himself, he concluded, not technical progress, was the essential aim of civilization.

The polarities of culture versus competence, or human beings versus technology, were ways of building a humanistic defense against "technical civilization." But there was another thrust to the Yankee cultural menace besides the technical mentality. It came from mass culture.

One response to the vulgarities and excesses of mass culture was to contrast them with the moderation, good taste, and aesthetic values of *civilisation.* Raymond Aron defined this sensibility by observing that Americans showed a certain indifference to aesthetic values in everyday life. Beauty was ignored or subordinated to other criteria like comfort or utility. The beauty of American architecture was largely functional. In contrast, he wrote, "the cult of form, of aesthetic values remains inseparable from the spirit of French culture—as it is in Japan, where concern with beauty touches every incident in existence, every piece of work, every garden, the fish-platter, the house."[58]

A similar defense was to define *civilisation* as the "art of living." In its most banal form it consisted of *flânerie,* that is, the pleasure of breaking habit, of lounging, of reflecting, even of being idle. *Flânerie* could be construed as a protest against the pace and routine of Americanization. Americans, according to one scornful commentator, construed *flânerie* as "loitering" and thought of it as a crime because it wasted time.[59] At a slightly more elevated level, the art of living became the famous *douceur de vivre.* There was an undefinable gentleness to life in France, a languid, pleasurable, and aesthetic quality about everyday existence that was antithetical to American organization and method. What was exemplary about the French, in Raymond Aron's mind, was this art of living that industry and consumerism would not ruin—"provided the French keep faith with themselves."[60]

In the boldest formulation of this humanistic identity, some argued Europe would civilize the United States. Serge Groussard contradicted the view that America anticipated Europe. Rather, to Groussard, "perhaps it is our own civilization, in its human scale and its logic, that prefigures the future civilization of North America."[61] One day, from this perspective, a technological America would become humanized like Europe. But such hubris convinced only a few diehards. The rest concentrated on the task of saving humanistic culture.

This defense of cultural identity was not entirely selfless and high-minded. There were personal or professional stakes involved in the cultural anxiety of the French intelligentsia. Setting humanistic *civilisation* against Americanization was an implicitly elitist defense. One might even argue, as Michel Winock did, that the guardians of humanistic *civilisation* evoked or exploited nostalgia for traditional society to buttress their own privileged position.[62] Intellectuals' position as gatekeepers of culture was at risk but to acknowledge this would be transparently self-serving. Thus writers evoked the France of artisans, bistros, and *flânerie* to broaden their appeal and conceal their elitist self-interest.

Indeed both technology and mass culture threatened a traditional definition of high culture and those whose careers and self-esteem were predicated on its preservation and transmission. America, with its technical civilization and its mass culture, constituted a double menace to the status and future of the French intelligentsia. Technical civilization imposed *homo faber* on *homo sapiens*. Mass culture raised the prospect of the standardization and the commercialization of culture. Edgar Morin complained that the paperback book and other forms of "mass culture" depreciated the creative act.[63] *Esprit* recalled the story by James T. Farrell in which a fictitious American publisher designed a writing machine that dispensed with authors and royalties and produced four books in eight hours—books that sold because they offended no one.[64] Here was the nightmare of Left Bank intellectuals. An unexpressed anxiety lay at the heart of their uneasiness about Americanization, for they could see no ready accommodation. Americanization and *civilisation* were at war.

....

A fourth issue in the debate, symbolized by the ubiquitous American smile, was Yankee optimism. "Americanism," according to Maurois, was a philosophy defined as belief in human perfectibility and faith in work, equality, and freedom.[65] But Maurois was virtually alone during the 1950s in his unqualified praise for Americans' friendliness, confidence, and optimism.

American optimism, which seemed to border on hubris, was an easy target for Gallic sharpshooters. *Le Monde* mocked a publication of the

United States Information Agency suggesting that America led the world in human endeavor. Beuve-Méry's paper proposed that the agency use a drawing of a Yankee seated on top of the globe with the caption, "The American's position in his own estimation."[66] Following the Soviet launch of Sputnik in 1957 Claude Julien ironically used the phrase "agonizing reappraisal" (after John Foster Dulles's warning of an "agonizing reappraisal" of Washington's policy following defeat of the European Defense Community) to describe America's mood. Julien seized on the Russians' triumph to remind the Americans of their unwarranted self-confidence in Yankee science and technology.[67] The young Philippe Labro, whose fascination with America led him to enroll at an elite Virginia college in 1954, scoffed at the shallowness of his fellow students and likened their behavior at the spring prom to "geese waiting patiently to dance at the gigantic ball of happiness and success."[68]

When Jacques Maritain, a prominent Catholic philosopher who had taught in the United States, blessed American optimism with a spiritual interpretation, he earned the scorn of the left. According to Maritain the "American smile" denoted a happy land; Americans, he believed, were the "least materialistic" of modern peoples.[69] Despite their professed esteem for money and objects and their desire for success, fun, and power, Americans prized generosity, kindness, tolerance, and spiritual values. Maritain defined the "American spirit" as profoundly Christian because it was based on the fraternal recognition of the dignity of human beings. The gospel's message of fraternal love was in the blood of Americans. For him America had the best chance of overcoming "technocratic materialism" because of a deep-rooted religious inspiration that informed secular activity. "If a new Christian civilization, a new Christendom is ever to come about in human history, it is on American soil that it will find its starting point."[70]

Such a benediction of America seemed unwarranted to the left. In *Le Monde* Julien gave Maritain's book a gentle review but undercut its argument by suggesting the author was paying a debt of gratitude to his American friends for giving him asylum during the war and for providing a wider audience for his views than he enjoyed in France. Maritain's talk about the spirit of America was an act of faith in the American people, but he missed "all the weight of a social life centered on visible success, verifiable efficiency, on money."[71] Maritain, according to Julien, may have uncovered the spiritual "leaven" in America but underestimated the "heaviness of the dough." Domenach was more severe. He thought the ubiquitous American smile that Maritain evoked hid anxiety, ennui, and even fear. It masked the banality of human relations and hid a psychological and spiritual malaise.[72]

American optimism to Jean-Paul Sartre and Simone de Beauvoir was both a philosophical escape and a means of social control. Travel in the United States in the 1940s revealed the reality behind such positivistic illusions. While both Sartre and de Beauvoir equivocated in their general assessment—to the question "Do you like America?" de Beauvoir answered, "50–50"—they perceived the hollowness behind the optimism. They admired the dynamism of America. De Beauvoir called New York and Chicago "the most human and most exhilarating cities" she knew because they affirmed the creative power of human beings.[73] Yet she found an emptiness in American life. Americans were bored and lonely. In a philosophical sense they tried to flee the human condition, their solitude for example, rather than draw strength and meaning from it. They lost themselves in the world and the pursuit of the object. Their feverish activity—their incessant demand for distractions—was empty because it represented a flight from self-possession. Their liberty was empty because their social and political condition, "this machinery," victimized them. For de Beauvoir Americans could not escape their solitude and boredom because "they run from themselves; they don't truly possess themselves."

Sartre expressed the same mixture of fascination and repulsion for America as did de Beauvoir. *Américanisme* to him was "a monstrous complex of myths, values, formulas, slogans, figures, and rites."[74] The myths of happiness, freedom, and optimism were a new means of social control. Unlike authoritarian regimes, *américanisme* relied on gentle forms of social persuasion: it was a system of collective indoctrination. America was "a country of 'managed dreams.'" Americans were controlled by neither the government nor the capitalists but by other Americans. This nonconformist existentialist saw American society based on *mauvaise foi* and alienation. Americans became tragic by trying to efface tragedy from their lives.

There are the great myths of happiness, of freedom, of triumphant motherhood. . . . There is the myth of equality and there is segregation, . . . the myth of freedom and the dictatorship of public opinion. . . . There is the smiling belief in progress and profound discouragement. . . . There are those pretty, neat homes, those all-white apartments with radio, lounge chair, pipe racks—in short, paradise. And then there are the tenants of these apartments who, after dinner, leave armchair, radio, pipe, and children and go and get drunk by themselves at the nearest bar. Perhaps nowhere else is there such a discrepancy between the men and the myths, between life and the collective representation of life.[75]

The American dream was the opium of the people.

Behind such unmasking of American optimism was a deep Gallic skepticism, even pessimism. Just as Sartre and de Beauvoir reproached Americans for their rosy view of the human condition, Albert Béguin chided Americans for refusing to discuss problems like suffering and death. He was dismayed when students at an American college suggested he consult a psychiatrist because he lectured on the "fecundity of regret." American optimism came at the price of masks and forgetfulness, stated the editor of *Esprit;* he asked, "Today what American would be ready to hear this remark of Bernanos: 'The adversity of men is the wonder of the universe'?"[76]

A decade later Béguin's successor, Jean-Marie Domenach, complained that a French intellectual felt *dépaysé* in America. America was "foreign" to him and to the rest of the world. In part, according to Domenach, what caused the disorientation was America's boundless optimism. But French intellectuals, he wrote, "we carry in our hearts a cemetery of utopias; tragedy is our kingdom."[77] Even for Raymond Aron, hardly a man of the left, French culture was fundamentally different. He framed the differences broadly, setting American pragmatism and moralism against French universalism, pessimism, and skepticism. Aron described French culture:

. . . conspicuous for its catholicity, its profound pessimism, its undefined tension between faith and skepticism. National consciousness in the United States is pragmatic and moral; it will stay that way in the foreseeable future, at whatever stage of economic progress.[78]

Psychologically and philosophically these intellectuals were at odds with the essential assumptions of Americanism. Such reflections about American society and culture inevitably led these observers to an urgent question. Was America a model for France?

....

It is hardly surprising that the collective answer to this self-inquiry was a resounding "no." In the abstract any society is unlikely to function as a model for another. And given the intensity of French anti-Americanism, a negative answer was predictable. What may be unforeseen, however, was the consensus among the intelligentsia on this question. Enthusiasts like André Maurois and Jacques Maritain did not portray America as a transferable model. And Raymond Aron, who was a partisan of modernization, if not Americanization, expressed strong reservations on the subject. Before the question of whether France would resemble America, Aron balked. Technology might be forcing uniformity, but "when it comes to attitudes toward life, death, the social hierarchy, or society, to questions of philosophy or of religion—here I have not seen the picture of the future in the United States."[79]

The most vehement nay-sayers advocated outright resistance to the American model. Cyrille Arnavon, a professor of American literature who had taught at Harvard and Columbia, called *américanisme* a form of colonialism. The export of American culture was a capitalist oligarchy's conservative global strategy to advance free enterprise, anticommunism, and the existing social order. The basic attitudes of a generation raised on publications like the *Reader's Digest,* according to Arnavon, would be characterized by "flabbiness, intellectual passivity, and an irrationalism that profits vested interests and established privilege." He worried that within twenty years French middle managers would be trained in American methods and know only English as their second language, becoming men and women for whom "truly rational thought and, especially, acute social criticism" would be inconceivable. To this left-wing academic, *américanisme* was incompatible with "traditions, ways of feeling, aspirations, even the very methods for directing one's mind that are at the core of the European, in particular the French, heritage."[80] If France accepted America's cultural manna the French would soon suffer from the same collective maladies of the Americans. For Arnavon the antidote to Hollywood, science fiction, and the *Saturday Evening Post* was a careful analysis of facts. Lucid rationality would unmask the ideological message of *américanisme.*

Le Monde just as surely saw no model across the Atlantic. By the end of the 1950s the newspaper may have modulated its earlier abrasive tone but it continued to emphasize the problems of the American social, educational, economic, and political system.[81] Claude Julien published his reports for the paper in a book he named *Le nouveau nouveau Monde.* Despite an appreciative tone, Julien cataloged the problems of poverty, suburban blight, racism, and the power elite, as well as the shortcomings in public health, public goods, and education. He acknowledged that most of these problems also existed in France, but America offered no answers.

Jean-Marie Domenach was more direct in answering the question. For him America was "incommunicable." America was unique and thus could not serve as a model for others. Americans were foreigners to Europeans and were becoming foreign to the entire world. America was no model for a "civilization of persons." For in America consumerism, assimilation, and mobility dissolved everything holy that formed the basis of human society—authority and tradition.[82] In Europe people ranked themselves according to values or status that came from the past rather than according to incomes or efficiency. The twin tyrannies of money and opinion destroyed the frame that protected the individual. Americans could build lovely houses and organize informal associations but they could not create human communities. Thus for Domenach writing in 1960, Americanization might be spreading—but the rest of the world was repelled by the American style of life that reversed traditional values and structures. America was not a model. It was irrelevant.

· · · · · · · · · ·

While these Gallic critics tried to unmask the reality of Americanism, the historian might try to unmask the assumptions of the critics. What were the stakes of this debate at the end of the 1950s? Why did these French censors pursue their American cousins so earnestly?

The stakes of the game were enormous, and the postwar intelligentsia guarded them both: the revolutionary tradition and *civilisation*. America was the siren of comfort and conservatism to those who wrote from a *marxisant* or social Christian position during the Cold War. The correct posture for these intellectuals was astride the revolutionary tradition. American consumer goods and mass culture coopted the working class and suffocated dissent. Succumbing to the American way was to relinquish a revolutionary posture or, at least, a critical social stance. This stance aimed not only at subverting the French status quo but also at demystifying Western society in general. Should the American way become the European way, then the intelligentsia would have lost its political-social mission.

For almost every Gallic commentator, radical or conservative, there was a second stake in the debate. That was French *civilisation*. If this cause was not well defined, it was a grand and emotional issue. For it expressed a defense of national identity against a modern barbarism. Intellectuals must have been pained to hear Anouk Aimée, the actress, ask plaintively in a popular movie of the time: "Are there any new American films to see?" Either America lacked a culture or had one that debased culture. To the alarmists, American mass culture was a noxious contagion. To others, whether television, Hollywood, and the *Reader's*

Digest leveled or enhanced culture were still open questions. But to most, whatever their political preference, *civilisation* was at risk.

What did *civilisation* mean? To those thinking about manufacturing, it was crafts or the production of quality goods that were synonymous with France. To others, it was a way of life variously defined as *la douceur de vivre,* the joys of *flânerie,* good taste, or a highly developed aestheticism. Or it might mean Gallic individualism and nonconformity. Still others conceived of *civilisation* as an expression of humanism that denoted a classical education, moderation, civic-mindedness, and rationality. Or it might mean a philosophical disposition that was skeptical and critical if not pessimistic. And it assigned intrinsic worth and prestige to high culture and the intelligentsia, not to those who would commercialize cultural products. After all, technology and television scarcely honored the carriers of literary culture. *Civilisation* elevated *homo sapiens* over *homo faber.*

To consider the matter in its most general aspect, it has been said that France and the United States clash because they are the only two Western nations that harbor universal pretensions. They are certain that other nations want to imitate them. Americans believe they possess the secret to freedom and prosperity and the French believe they are the champions of *civilisation.* Inevitably the pretensions, or egocentrisms, of these two cultural imperialists, will conflict. For most of those writing about America during the Cold War this rivalry had two dimensions. The mission of the Parisian intelligentsia was both to project a revolutionary critique and as gatekeepers to export and guard *civilisation* as well. America in the 1950s represented counterrevolution and mass culture. France represented revolution and *civilisation.* The stakes of the debate were immense. Thus the intensity of what was written about the American model.

· · · · · · · · · ·

The year 1956, in retrospect, was a landmark in postwar anti-Americanism—at least for the leftist intelligentsia. In October the Red Army entered Budapest and crushed a movement that threatened to take Hungary out of the Soviet bloc and move it toward Western democracy. Russian military intervention against the Hungarian freedom fighters shook the *progressistes'* confidence in the Soviet Union and communism as forces for human liberation. News of Khrushchev's denunciation of Stalin's crimes in the same year seemed to confirm the worst anti-Communist charges about the Soviet Union. After 1956 the diaspora of French intellectuals accelerated when Claude Roy,

Vercors, Sartre and others broke with the Communist party.[83] In time, rejecting the Soviet model would also make some of these men and women available to America. But the reversal would not come quickly or easily. Ironically it was the misbehavior of the Soviets rather than American efforts at persuasion that sapped the vigor of ideological anti-Americanism.

It would be, nevertheless, too neat to divide postwar views about America at 1956. The socialist and *marxisant* filter that colored how the progressive intelligentsia viewed the New World survived Hungary. In an editorial for *Esprit* entitled "The Flames of Budapest," Albert Béguin vilified the massacre as "the naked revelation of reactionary terrorism."[84] In Eastern Europe revolution had degraded into despotism, and the Soviets had exposed themselves as the enemies of freedom, justice, and national independence. But this setback did not shake Béguin's commitment to socialism. Marxism had simply exceeded its boundaries. It had become a dogma and an "ideological system that can defend itself only by a kind of frightening fury against a revolt representing true humanity." Marxism was not false, but socialism needed to be humanized and freed from the "mortgage of theory and totalitarian idolatry." None of this, however, softened Béguin's views of America. If America more or less maintained political democracy, it tenaciously resisted any steps toward economic and social democracy. Money ruled and created injustice, inhumanity, hypocrisy, and spiritual suffocation. Béguin asked:

If we reproached socialist ideology for idealizing man and remaining blind to his fallible nature, we encountered, just as quickly, the even blinder idealism of the average American. What is there to expect from this civilization that ridicules and caricatures the spiritual traditions of the West and pushes humanity toward a horizontal existence that lacks the internal dimension of transcendence?

St-Germain-des-Prés was to drift slowly away, rather than make a sharp turn, from its anti-Americanism.

As Béguin did, others on the left held firm about America. Domenach's "conversion" would take time. If *Les Temps modernes* began to carry articles by Americans in 1957–58, they served only to ratify the Sartrian critique of *américanisme*. Excerpts from books like William Whyte's *Organization Man* sustained the image of America as a society of alienation and neo-Babbittry. One authority, evaluating the works of American sociologists like Whyte and David Riesman for Sartre's review, concluded that the drama of history had been replaced by a pantomime in which humans were trained to adapt, to respond as if drugged, to the signs that each received through outer-directed "radar."[85]

Nevertheless after 1956 the first indications of a softening of the socialist critique among these popularizers appeared. If this shift was barely perceptible, it was nonetheless important. The left's attack began to lose its coherence and its bite. The *marxisant* filter that once colored America in dark reactionary hues began to lighten. America's changing image reflected several developments besides Khrushchev's speech against Stalin and pictures of Soviet tanks in Budapest.[86] Changes in France and the United States also contributed to the softening. It was about 1957 that French observers first noticed the fact of their own economy's remarkable growth.[87] The French standard of living had improved markedly by the mid-1950s and France itself seemed headed toward its own consumer society. This economic change necessarily made American society more relevant. Furthermore, Americanization was being assimilated without the anticipated destruction of old ways. Pierre Emmanuel, who a decade earlier had damned "Imperial America," now scoffed at the danger of Americanization and wrote of the importance of the American experience in humanizing the machine age.[88] The United States also became more appealing once a stalemate was reached in the Cold War and the Eisenhower administration quietly retreated from its pledge to "roll back" communism.[89] The Soviet launch of its Sputnik satellite contributed to the new appeal. Now the United States was no longer omnipotent, and its vulnerability made it less menacing. Yet another reason for the shift came in 1958 when Charles de Gaulle returned to power because of a crisis generated by the war in Algeria. In time de Gaulle was to launch his own diplomatic effort against Washington that would serve to make the left reconsider its anti-Americanism.

Equally important for the intelligentsia was the realization that America needed to be rediscovered and reevaluated. The new issues of bureaucracy, mindless conformity, mass culture, and consumer society confounded old categories of analysis. To this end the intelligentsia, left and right, began to make extended trips to the United States. Michel Crozier, François Bourricaud, Jean-Marie Domenach, Edgar Morin, Raymond Aron, and others became regular visitors on American college campuses.

At *Esprit*, Domenach confessed that his ideological and sociological categories did not fit America. Class, race, and nationalism, all imported from Europe, did not apply. Domenach acutely diagnosed the way the left's conventional attack on America now seemed to backfire.

"Try a left-wing critique of American society and in the end you realize that it becomes a right-wing critique; that you attack democracy, popular culture, [and] mass consumption . . . and that you call into question your own ideology." Domenach now wrote with more emphasis on American diversity, with more satisfaction about American open-mindedness and dynamism, and with more hope for the future, recalling the serious yet eager faces of the undergraduates he taught—"the wonder of America is its receptiveness."[90]

For all these reasons the leftist consensus about the American model began to loosen at the end of the 1950s. The socialist critique became increasingly diluted by impartial description or systematic collection of data and analysis. Social scientists like Michel Crozier and Alain Touraine entered the discussion and interpreted America in a less ideological and less literary way.[91] In 1955–56 Raymond Aron presented his lectures at the Sorbonne on industrial development, which coolly analyzed the common principles of all industrial societies, including America and the Soviet Union.[92] When the popular *Que sais-je?* series published its guide to *La Vie américaine* the French reader discovered descriptions, in neutral language, of American suburbs, household budgets, holidays, food, and education, as well as accounts of social problems like juvenile delinquency. But the tone was optimistic.[93] *Le Monde* moderated its censorious tone; Claude Julien wrote of the common destiny of France and America and called the inventiveness and lack of complacency of Americans their true wealth and hope.[94] At the end of the decade *Esprit* devoted an issue to American social science, with articles by authorities like Edward Shils and Daniel Lerner.[95] And while this review was condemning "standardized man," it reported in an essay on America that McCarthyism had disappeared without a trace, that democracy in America, unlike in France, was real, and that mass society was creating its own antibodies.[96]

The "air-conditioned nightmare" (as Henry Miller once labeled America) was beginning to dissolve before "facts" and new forms of analysis as well as before economic and political developments at home and abroad. It would take another decade before this critique of America inspired by socialist and Christian principles changed, but a start had been made.

CHAPTER 6

The Gaullist Exorcism

Anti-Americanism Encore

The French encounter with America during the 1960s had several dimensions. There were the troubles in international affairs generated by President de Gaulle. The political and strategic sources of these tensions will be presented here, and the economic and financial aspects of Franco-American relations will be examined in the next chapter. In this discussion of Gaullist policy toward the United States we shall hear de Gaulle himself, the political class, and, to a lesser extent, elite and popular opinion. In addition to Gaullist diplomacy the Franco-American encounter had a second dimension. The process of Americanization within France reached the point that it gave rise to a spirited debate about the merits of the American social prototype. This debate, reminiscent of yet different from that of the 1950s, will be treated in a later chapter.

Anti-Americanism revived during the 1960s in part because of the foreign policy of Charles de Gaulle. After Washington rebuffed his proposal to overhaul the Western alliance and once he ended the war in Algeria, de Gaulle launched a forceful attack on what he called the "American protectorate." The West's nuclear strategy, the structure of NATO, and West German dependence on Washington were only some of the issues that fell subject to Gaullist revisionism. And, to the dismay of officials in Washington, in 1966 at Phnom Penh the French president denounced American military intervention in Vietnam. French public opinion endorsed this new aggressive stance against America;

at the height of troubles between the two allies, half the French agreed that the Fifth Republic's posture was "as it should be."

Meanwhile expressions of anti-Americanism were commonplace in the 1960s. One combative Gaullist tract, after listing the ills of American society—its violence, racism, vulgarity, moral laxness, and seductive materialism—quoted Montherlant, "I accuse the United States of being in a continuous state of crime against humanity."[1] On the left, opposition to what was termed American imperialism in Vietnam erupted in bombings of offices of companies like American Express and burnings of the stars and stripes. Representative of this defiant French mood were three best-selling books whose titles convey the message: *L'Empire américain, Parlez-vous franglais?*, and *Le Défi américain*. And audiences in the Latin Quarter were alternately amused and horrified with images of racist lynch mobs, police brutality, and seemingly idiotic public officials in a purportedly documentary film, *Pourquoi l'Amérique?* But such attacks concealed an equally important, but less dramatic, drift away from anti-Americanism—a shift that was obvious by the end of the decade.

In comparison to the activity of the preceding decade, anti-Americanism of the 1960s lacked intensity and scope. Criticism of the United States most frequently occurred as an analogue to praise for de Gaulle's show of independence against the American colossus. Of course cultural purists continued to denounce creeping Americanism, and groups on the left, especially students, pursued the struggle against "American imperialism." Yet this struggle looked to the Third World rather than to the West for its battleground. Student radicals, other than protesting against the war in Vietnam, were not much concerned with the United States or Americanization. As for the posturing of leftist intellectuals against the United States, much of this was only a way of dramatizing their dissatisfaction with trends in France—and before the decade was over they were less certain than they had been in the 1950s that they should aim their critique across the Atlantic. Similarly, while there were serious interests at stake between Washington and Paris, much of de Gaulle's policy was pure spectacle.

Antipathy for America was balanced by contradictory expressions of affection, such as the enthusiastic reception awarded President and Mrs. John F. Kennedy on their visit to Paris in 1961 (fig. 15). Less noticed, but more significant, the issues and forces that accounted for anxieties and resentments during the early Cold War years began to fade. The 1960s unobtrusively prepared the way for the turnabout in the 1970s and 1980s that saw France shift to a far more positive appreciation of

15. Presidents de Gaulle and Kennedy, 1961. (*Charles de Gaulle, 1890–1970* [1970], 309)

America. Once the pyrotechnics of the Gaullist display subsided, observers noted that France was moving toward an accommodation with Washington and Americanization. Thus the principal paradox of this decade is that de Gaulle's policies served to dampen anti-Americanism. In this sense the 1960s performed an exorcism of the American devil.

··········

As president of the Fifth Republic, Charles de Gaulle dominated his decade as perhaps no other French statesman had since the nineteenth century. After his return to power in 1958 he presided over the republic he created in a manner reminiscent of the Bourbons and the Bonapartes. Until his resignation in 1969 he captured the attention of his fellow citizens, Europe, and sometimes even the world. But he especially made the United States take notice.

The Fifth Republic, unlike the Fourth, adopted an overtly anti-American foreign policy. De Gaulle's energetic effort to make France master of itself and to overturn the bipolar system of East-West hegemony that divided Europe and, increasingly, the world—a system that, in his view, subordinated French interests to those of an American-dominated Atlantic community—brought him into conflict with Washington and the American people. He struggled to give France greater independence than it had possessed under the Fourth Republic and to restore its global role. In the Gaullist lexicon he aspired to *grandeur*. His grand design challenged the status quo in Western Europe and made his opposition to the hegemonic power that guarded the status quo inevitable.

There was, to be sure, considerable continuity between the policies of the Fourth and Fifth Republics toward the United States.[2] While the general may have fulminated against the supposed subservience of the Fourth Republic and contrasted its self-effacement with his show of independence, France before 1958 had demonstrated its unhappiness with American policy. Paris and Washington had been at odds over many issues, including economic and military aid, German recovery, European defense, Indochina, and North Africa. On occasion the Fourth Republic had successfully manipulated Washington and, in other instances such as the European Defense Community and Suez, had openly opposed the United States. It had also taken the first steps toward constructing a French nuclear deterrent and, in the final days of the republic, expressed its determination to control American nuclear weapons stockpiled on French territory. The French people meanwhile had demonstrated their dislike of American military bases, voiced misgivings about American leadership of the Western bloc, and, in general, expressed resentment about Washington's treatment of France.

Yet the Fourth Republic, much to de Gaulle's dismay, had also subscribed to an integrated and Atlantic-wide defense community and to the inception of a supranational Europe. To de Gaulle both these communities, NATO and the European Economic Community (or Common Market), deprived France of its independence and encouraged American hegemony. NATO prevented France from exercising the primary attribute of sovereignty, national defense; it jeopardized French security by submitting strategic planning and, especially, the use of the nuclear deterrent to American decision-making. NATO's integrated command structure precluded French control over its own defense. Furthermore, as the Soviet Union moved toward constructing a credible nuclear retaliatory force and as President Kennedy adopted a more flexible military posture toward an attack on Western Europe, American nuclear protection seemed less assured. Similarly European supranationalism, launched with the inception of the Common Market just before the general came to power, led France in the wrong direction. A supranational or "technocratic" structure, De Gaulle believed, lacked the cohesion or the will to act and would inevitably become a feeble organization subject to manipulation by the American superpower. In his view, only the nation-state could be a viable actor in world affairs. European unity should thus be constructed around a loose confederation of nation-states. The president tolerated the new Common Market and worked to mold it to his goals, which included separating Europe from the Atlantic community.

Gaullist policy aimed principally at securing independence and status for France as a player in world affairs. Beyond this goal was a grand design for remodeling Europe. It was predicated on the assumptions that the bipolar world in which the two superpowers competed against each other was inherently unstable and dangerous and that a multipolar system of independent decision-making centers was more secure. An alternative international system was not only desirable but possible because Western Europe had recovered its strength and because the burgeoning Sino-Soviet conflict and the diplomatic defeat over the Cuban missiles signaled the retreat of the Soviet Union. And there were stirrings of independence in the Third World and possibly even in Eastern Europe. In his grand design the American and Soviet hegemonies over Europe were to be relaxed, though Western Europe would still need a reliable American guarantee. A European Europe, one led by France in tandem with West Germany, would play an independent role and negotiate a détente with the Soviet Union, leading to a loosening of the Kremlin's control over Eastern Europe.

As a prerequisite to implementing this grand design, de Gaulle would first have to rebuild French political institutions and end the war in Algeria. He would then try to reorganize NATO so as to give France full partnership with its Anglo-American allies while also building an independent nuclear defense system. Then would come the construction of a European Europe complete with economic, political, and defensive capabilities. Of course there was no plan for these changes; de Gaulle moved only as circumstances and opportunities permitted. Blocking the path to this Gaullist future lay Washington.

De Gaulle charted a different course for France than his predecessors did. Whereas the Fourth Republic, for example, saw a unified supranational Europe as the way to independence, the Fifth Republic saw it as a pawn in America's game. Where the pre-1958 regime found security in an integrated American-led defense system, the post-1958 regime saw NATO as undependable, perhaps dangerous, and possibly expendable protection. Where the Fourth Republic welcomed the United States because it provided security for Western Europeans, de Gaulle thought the United States was exploiting its excess of power.

In his mind the United States had been an imperialist force since the war and cloaked its expansionism in the guise of an altruistic crusade for freedom. Washington, in his view, wanted to retain the bipolar status quo because it guaranteed American hegemony and turned Europeans into dependents. For this reason Washington did not want to share decision making, especially over nuclear strategy, with France. The *force de frappe*, or French nuclear strike force, threatened American control over deterrence. The Gaullist grand design would, if implemented, fundamentally alter the status quo—especially with respect to Western defense, European unification, and East-West relations.

If the substance of policy differed, so did the style. De Gaulle more openly challenged the United States. His assertive and seemingly arrogant diplomacy contrasted with the more manipulative and conciliatory demeanor of the Fourth Republic. He demanded rather than negotiated and, when blocked, resorted to obstructionism. He patronized American leaders and publicly criticized American policy.

While the issues dividing Washington and Paris were formidable, there was also a broad area of agreement. In the last resort France and the

United States were allies. When the Soviets became aggressive, as they did over Berlin and Cuba in the early 1960s, de Gaulle gave President Kennedy his unqualified support. Ideologically, France and the United States were on the same side. In his speech to the United States Congress in 1960 the French president proclaimed:

If, in a material sense, the balance between the two camps that divide the world might seem equal, it is not the case morally. France, for its part, has chosen. It has chosen to be on the side of free peoples. It has chosen to be with you.[3]

The Franco-American dispute was a family feud.

The initial Gaullist confrontation with the United States occurred in 1958–59 during the waning days of the Eisenhower administration when the French president tried, in vain, to reconstruct the alliance system embodied in NATO. De Gaulle had grave reservations about NATO's integrated command structure that subordinated the French military to de facto American command. In memoranda written to President Eisenhower, de Gaulle urged substituting a tripartite—that is, joint French, British, and American—control over the West's nuclear arsenal as well as over global strategic and political planning. If accepted, the French proposal would have ended America's centralized control over both NATO and the West's nuclear strategy. By elevating France to a new inner oligarchy, it would also have ended the United Kingdom's privileged position within the alliance and subordinated other Western Europeans. In practice de Gaulle sought a veto (except in the case of national defense) over the use of American strategic arms in order to prevent the United States from beginning a nuclear war outside Europe that might engulf NATO and Europe and to advance France's status in world affairs. He also wanted assurance that American nuclear weapons would be used to defend French interests. Memories of America's tardy entry into two world wars haunted most French statesmen. While using memoranda diplomacy to effect this restructuring, the French president also continued to build the *force de frappe*. In 1960 France exploded its first atomic device. In this way it opened both avenues. If Washington did not accede to joint control over Western strategy, France would soon have the means for its own national nuclear deterrence and could safely modify its commitment to NATO.

Neither Washington nor London had any interest in granting full partnership to France either in formulating nuclear defense strategy or in creating an intergovernmental network outside NATO to resolve international crises. The Eisenhower administration refused to allow

France a veto over decisions concerning the use of American strategic nuclear weapons.[4] While Washington rejected de Gaulle's demands, it tried to show some flexibility in order to avoid provoking the French president into taking independent action against NATO. But de Gaulle knew a rebuff when he encountered one.[5] At the same time, the general contested Washington's tepid support for French policy in Algeria (since France believed U.S. arms deliveries to Tunisia and Morocco ended up in the hands of the Algerian rebels) and its denial of France's preeminent political role over North Africa.

Rebuked by Washington over restructuring Western defense, de Gaulle began, step by step, to limit French participation in NATO. One reading of de Gaulle's rationale is that since he could not acquire a say in when and how the American nuclear arsenal would be employed in the defense of Europe, he concluded that Washington was not dependable. The Cuban missile crisis of 1962, in this version, further persuaded the general that Washington might give priority to American, rather than European, security or, worse still, might involve Europe in a conflict of America's making. And the Kennedy administration's formulation of a new conception of nuclear defense (the so-called flexible or graduated defense) deepened French concern about the uncoupling of the American nuclear arsenal from Europe. An alternative reading is that de Gaulle, after the Soviet retreat over the Cuban missile affair, felt safe to act independently, knowing that if a crisis occurred, the United States could and would protect Western Europe. Whatever de Gaulle's reasoning, Washington's policy toward Western Europe irritated the general. Under President Kennedy the United States tried to halt France's development of an independent *force de frappe*, continued to give the United Kingdom a privileged position within the making of Allied nuclear strategy, and maintained its centralized control over European defense.

Lyndon Johnson's succession to the presidency in 1963 did not make the United States more accommodating, and Johnson's deepening commitment to a "hot" war in Southeast Asia worried Paris. Viewed from the Elysée (presidential) palace, American intervention in Vietnam underestimated the force of Vietnamese nationalism and concealed American expansionism under the guise of anticommunism. It was one more reason for France to distance itself from the United States. This policy had become possible since the Algerian war ended in 1962, the *force de frappe* was in the making, and the Soviet danger had diminished after the Cuban missile crisis.

Unable to transform the alliance into a tripartite partnership and increasingly dissatisfied with the direction of American policy, de Gaulle acted unilaterally. After a series of actions that disengaged French military forces from NATO, the climax came in 1966 with the announcement that France was withdrawing from the integrated command structure and demanding the removal of United States military installations and personnel from French territory. Few, if any, of de Gaulle's other diplomatic moves seemed more anti-American than this decision. France did not leave the Western alliance, but de Gaulle may have considered that one day he would take this final step toward neutralism.[6] In the end he went no further than withdrawal from the integrated command.

Parallel with his effort at restructuring NATO, the general labored to remodel the emerging European Economic Community. Here too he tried to strip away the Atlanticist and Anglo-American facade of European integration. In 1961–62 de Gaulle proposed to the nations composing the Common Market that they replace the supranational structure with a confederal arrangement in which intergovernmental consultation would make economic policy. De Gaulle also suggested adding European defense to the confederal body's responsibilities. His drive toward creating an independent European Europe free of Anglo-American control, though still sheltered by the American nuclear umbrella, was confirmed by his veto of British entry into the Common Market in early 1963. A parallel initiative in 1962–63 aimed at tying West Germany to France and weakening Bonn's dependence on Washington reinforced the anti-American direction of Gaullist policy. A Gaullist Europe would have encompassed economic, political, and defense strategy and permitted Europe to mute the tension and right the imbalance in the allegedly dangerous bipolar system. Europe with its own defense, that is, one pivoting on the French *force de frappe*, might one day rival the superpowers and be able to effect a détente with the Soviets and Eastern Europe. But de Gaulle's Common Market partners rejected his proposals and the West Germans failed to embrace the Paris-Bonn axis. In retaliation de Gaulle resorted to obstructionism. During 1965 he tried to slow down or halt the move toward building a centralized, supranational European community.

The climax of the Fifth Republic's diplomatic offensive against the United States came during the mid-1960s. Gaullist initiatives, economic and financial policy aside, included granting diplomatic recognition to mainland China (when the United States hoped to isolate China); visiting the American preserve of Mexico, Latin America, and Canada; pursuing détente toward the Soviet Union and Eastern Europe; rejecting the

"AFTER QUEBEC FALLS—"

16. De Gaulle's notion of *grandeur* extends to the
United States, according to Herblock. (*The Herblock
Gallery* [Simon and Schuster, 1968])

American-sponsored nuclear nonproliferation treaty; and publicly criticizing growing American military engagement in Vietnam. At the same
time France took giant steps toward becoming an independent nuclear
power.

By 1967 it was evident that within the Western alliance Gaullist France
was the principal obstacle to American policy. By then the American press
and the public were howling about French "ingratitude" and "arrogance." There were boycotts of French products by American stores and
a motion in Congress for the return of the remains of American soldiers
buried in France. President Johnson's break with his predecessor's style
of entertainment at the White House, which featured French cuisine and
wines, appeared to be part of this anti-French campaign. In Paris Sartre
and other leftist intellectuals tried to stage a war crimes trial against
Americans responsible for the war in Vietnam. Antagonism peaked on
both sides of the Atlantic in 1967–68 (fig. 16).

....

Did the French people approve of their president's diplomatic offensive against the United States? The answer has to be "yes." For to a considerable extent de Gaulle expressed popular desires and grievances. But he was also leading and shaping opinion—though not always successfully, since some of his anti-American projects were greeted with considerable skepticism.

There is no question that de Gaulle's affirmation of French independence vis-à-vis the United States was welcomed by much of the country's elite. Politicians, administrative officials, military officers, business leaders, and intellectuals, including those who opposed the president's foreign policy, expressed pride in de Gaulle's assertiveness. They justified his policy by stressing their nation's uniqueness, for example, its civilizing mission and its European vocation.[7] They also expressed ambivalence about the United States. Within a context of friendship the elite complained about American imperialism and capitalism and argued that France and Europe no longer needed to depend on the United States as they had in the past.

Among left-wing politicians and intellectuals, where anti-Americanism was common, Gaullist policy toward the United States, as might be expected, had a certain appeal. Distancing Paris from Washington earned quiet applause from the Communists. And the so-called groupe des 29, which included several intellectuals who had openly opposed de Gaulle, published a manifesto in support of his withdrawal from the NATO command structure.[8] Certain socialists, such as Jean-Marie Domenach and Serge Mallet, expressed hope that de Gaulle was leading Europe toward independence and integration. Domenach accepted Stanley Hoffmann's reading of Gaullist policy as a step toward European autonomy and disengagement.[9] Domenach categorized himself as a "leftist anti-American"—though he admitted he had come to like much about America—who believed Europe should not abandon itself to "American supervision." He wrote:

The entire question is knowing if through its foreign policy Gaullism expresses only an outdated nationalism, or if beneath the nationalist language other demands, such as the political independence of Europe and a planned European market, are being broached.[10]

The *force de frappe* might, in Domenach's view, be stripped of its nationalist character in order to serve Europe and eventually disarmament. Speaking of the goal of European autonomy, Domenach wondered, "Is de Gaulle the last sign of this will before Europe sinks into comfort and Americanism?"[11] Serge Mallet, a sociologist who wrote for *Esprit,* endorsed the Gaullist premise that France should and could free itself from American tutelage, arguing that capitalism would stifle any future evolution of Europe toward socialism.[12]

Such "left Gaullists" went beyond what others on the left would support. Some Socialists shared Domenach's and de Gaulle's aversion for American dominance but were more skeptical about the European credentials of the Elysée. Thus Gaston Defferre, the Socialist would-be candidate for president in 1965, credited de Gaulle with calling attention to the problem of American hegemony, but he argued that the general wrongly offered outdated nationalism rather than European integration as the solution.[13] Only a strong supranational Europe could force Washington to accept Europe as a player.

At *Le Monde* Beuve-Méry, the editor who had once advocated a neutralist posture and grudgingly came to accept the American alliance as a prelude to détente with the East, found fault with many of de Gaulle's positions as well as his style.[14] Beuve-Méry denounced the general's illusory pursuit of independence. He argued that, given the nation's modest means, atomic weapons would not make France truly independent. The *force de frappe* was ineffective, dangerous, and immoral to boot. The journalist also criticized de Gaulle for trying to build Europe around French hegemony and, failing that, resorting to obstructionism. While *Le Monde* endorsed de Gaulle's attacks on American imperialism and applauded his withdrawal from the NATO command, Beuve-Méry also chastised the president for his vanity, his nationalism, and his authoritarianism. "Tirelessly, the old man pursues his pipe dream: to restore full and complete sovereignty to France and to force his way into the group of global powers equipped with nuclear arms."[15] In short, Gaullist policy toward the United States divided the left while appropriating part of its foreign agenda.

The public, according to opinion polls, welcomed the Fifth Republic's display of independence from the United States. American military presence on French territory had not been popular. Even before de Gaulle's return to power more people wanted the troops to leave than wanted them to stay. Opposition continued to mount in the 1960s.[16] Some reasons given for this opposition were that the GIs were no longer necessary; or the troops represented a "foreign occupation"; or that "everyone should stay where they belong." Only a few said the GIs' presence was provocative toward the Russians or that the soldiers were badly behaved. In this respect "Yankee Go Home" was the people's will.

With regard to reforming NATO, de Gaulle had support—up to a point. Under the Fourth Republic nonalignment had been a popular position, but this was more a vote to stay out of a future war than it was a vote against Washington.[17] Restructuring NATO was popular, but there was no majority before or after 1958 to relinquish either American protection or the alliance. As long as de Gaulle's search for détente retained the cover of the Atlantic alliance, he reflected the wishes of a majority of the French people. A 1967 poll taken after French separation from the integrated command revealed that 54 percent wanted to retain NATO while only 12 percent preferred withdrawal from the alliance. Much of this allegiance to the alliance merely expressed acquiescence to necessity. Nevertheless, about two-thirds of the voters from every political party—including the Gaullists but excluding the Communists—wanted to retain the alliance.[18] De Gaulle would not have enjoyed popular support had he actually withdrawn from NATO.

There is no question that de Gaulle led the French to adopt a more negative stance toward the United States. If a majority of the populace was visibly angry with Washington over Suez and Algeria during 1956–57, those voicing a "good opinion" of America became increasingly numerous after 1960, despite Gaullist policy, and reached a high of 52 percent in 1964.[19] But once de Gaulle became stridently anti-American, opinion followed. In 1965 when asked which country they considered to be "the best friend of France," French citizens ranked the United States a poor third behind West Germany and the United Kingdom. A year later when asked whether French and American interests were close or different, almost half said they were either "rather" or "very" different. Approval of de Gaulle's adversarial stance toward the United States grew from about a third to half of the population after 1962 and remained high throughout 1966.[20] At the peak of Franco-American troubles, when asked whether de Gaulle's policy toward the United States was too harsh or too conciliatory, half those surveyed said it was "comme il faut"—just right.[21]

It seems then that if de Gaulle enjoyed a consensus on his American policy, he helped build it. He capitalized on popular misgivings about American influence, especially the stationing of American troops, and he exploited yearnings for independence and grievances about how Washington had treated France since the war. But America was generally liked, and it was the general who shaped and mobilized opinion to assume a more anti-American stance in the mid-1960s.

Yet there were limits to realignment and independence. A total break with the Western alliance would have encountered serious resistance. Moreover, as President de Gaulle's policy hardened toward America so did the views of his opposition. He polarized opinion. From 1962 to 1966 those who opposed his stance toward the United States increased from 15 to 29 percent.[22] And his criticism of Israel in 1967 and his theatrical behavior in Quebec offended many. Equally important, the proportion of those who believed that independence was possible for France diminished steadily between 1965 and 1968.[23] In the early 1970s, after de Gaulle's resignation, skepticism about national independence, especially among French elites, only deepened.[24]

··········

Was then de Gaulle "anti-American"? Not in the sense that he harbored some visceral dislike of Americans or American institutions, though it seems he did not approve of the American way of life. In fact he expressed admiration for American vitality, power, and love of freedom. He referred, in a press conference, to the United States as Europe's "daughter."[25] Whatever personal antipathy he may have felt about American society or civilization, it is not evident how such feelings shaped his policy. They probably mattered rather little, given his hard-edged realism in international affairs. Nor was he anti-American in the sense that he was an unreliable ally during moments of international crisis. This argument was one that he employed to deny the charge, as in a television interview in 1965:

In reality, who has been the Americans' ally from beginning to end if not the France of de Gaulle? It could not be otherwise. And if the case arises, if misfortune were to happen and if the world's freedom were at risk, who would automatically be the best and most natural allies if not France and the United States, as they have often been in such cases? Besides, as for me, I don't say that the Americans are anti-French and yet. . . . In 1940 they weren't there and we were overwhelmed by Hitler. . . . I am fully aware of the immense service that they have rendered, to themselves, to the world, and to us, by going to war in 1917 and again in 1941. I know it well. I don't say they are anti-French because they haven't always accompanied us. Indeed. I am not anti-American because at the moment I don't always go along with the Americans, and in particular, for example, with the policy that they are conducting in Asia. It's entirely true that I don't approve it. But on that basis to say that I am anti-American! I can't prevent it, but that's the heart of the matter![26]

Ambassadors to Washington and to Paris during the 1960s, respectively Hervé Alphand and Charles Bohlen, concurred in the view that de Gaulle was not anti-American.[27] Yet none of these arguments are conclusive. We retain the impression that the label still fits.

For de Gaulle was anti-American in two significant ways. First he challenged the bases of the Western system of containment that pivoted on American power. He tried, but failed, to overturn this global bipolar order that the United States had constructed after 1947 through a kind of dialectic with the Soviets and that Washington labored to maintain— pending the ultimate demise of the Soviet threat. This system included a centralized and integrated Western defense structure dependent on American nuclear weapons and controlled by the United States; a federated European community open to the Anglo-Americans; a West Germany dependent for its security on the United States; a global commitment to isolation and containment of the Communist bloc; an international monetary order in which the dollar enjoyed a privileged position; and, in general, a France relegated to the position of a secondary ally in a Western bloc not only dominated by America but one that also gave precedence to the United Kingdom and West Germany. Each element of this system faced a Gaullist challenge. Above all, de Gaulle deplored America's excess of power, which he considered dangerous for America and for others. De Gaulle was anti-American in trying to subvert this international order that the United States believed served its best interests. In addition, any judgment on this question cannot dismiss his gratuitous attacks and rebuffs to the United States, such as his refusal to attend commemoration ceremonies of D Day in June 1964 or to assist, in case of need, in the recovery of the Gemini space capsule in the Pacific. These were acts of spite.

Second, he harbored a certain antipathy for what America, as a society, represented. If we lack a substantial and coherent body of data about de Gaulle's views on America—at least until his private papers are opened— the historian can still piece together what the general said about America even if his observations were often casual and spontaneous. Because a remark was impromptu, however, does not in itself invalidate it; quite to the contrary, being less rehearsed it may more accurately reflect his feelings. As a second source we can look at what those, both French and American, who were closest to him have said his views were. Finally, we can compare this record with what we know about his values, principles, and outlook.

The evidence suggests two conclusions about de Gaulle's view of the American way of life. First, he held an unflattering stereotype of American society as soulless and materialistic. We were a commercial empire.

Second, de Gaulle found us to be a society without history and thus without an identity.

In the first instance he occasionally voiced the conservative Gallic caricature of America. Writing in 1934 about how nations mobilized their economies for war, he noted that even in wartime Americans relied on the profit motive to stimulate production; more broadly, he observed that in the American social system, "material gain is the motive for all activity and the basis of all hierarchy."[28] Thirty years later in a discussion with an Arab journalist, de Gaulle observed:

If we wish to create around this Mediterranean—the cradle of great cultures—an industrial civilization that does not follow the American model and in which man is not merely means but purpose and aim, then our cultures have to open up toward each other.[29]

It is likely that in his innermost convictions he, like many other conservative Frenchmen, frowned on the uprootedness of American society and its obsession with gadgets and consumer comforts. In his memoirs he expressed his disappointment that the immediate issue of the 1960s was "not victory or annihilation, but living standards."[30] Geopolitics, not consumerism or *américanisme*, was his arena. Of consumer society, de Gaulle warned that inevitable dissatisfaction accompanied it: "Despite the variety and the quality of the food on every table and the clothes everyone wore, the increasing numbers of appliances in homes, of cars on the roads, of aerials on the roofs, everyone resented what he lacked more than he appreciated what he had."[31] Here before the fact he seemed to sense the troubles of 1968 rooted in this Americanized society.

In contrast with the individualistic way of life that many generations of their ancestors had followed as farmers, craftsmen, merchants, and rentiers, contemporary Frenchmen found themselves, not without some distress, forced into a crowded and mechanized existence. In factories, workshops, construction sites, or stores, their job demanded uniformly mechanical and repetitive movements with always the same companions. . . . As for commerce, it was carried out in identical supermarkets, with rows of shelves and imperious advertising. Everyone's housing now resembled a cell in some nondescript block. Gray anonymous crowds traveled in public transportation. . . . Even leisure now was collective and regimented: meals efficiently served in canteens; cheers in unison from the grandstands of sports stadia; holidays spent in crowded sites among tourists, campers, and bathers laid out in rows; day or evening relaxation at fixed hours for families in identical apartments, where before bedtime everyone simultaneously watched and heard the same broadcasts on the same wavelengths. It was all a matter of circumstance, but I knew that it weighed more heavily on our

17. De Gaulle, the traditionalist, at his desk. (Jean Lacouture, *De Gaulle: le Souverain* [1986], 3:444)

people, by reason of their nature and antecedents, than on any others, and I felt that a sudden addition of annoyances one day might well touch off an irrational crisis.[32]

A leader who celebrated heroic values of sacrifice and public duty, who tried to move the French toward the "high road" of heroism and *grandeur* and away from concern with self-interest, who was wedded to such traditional economic values as the gold standard, who celebrated the virtues of historical continuity and social stability, and who loved the land and the old ways, was sentimentally at odds with the American way of life (see fig. 17). During his visit to California in 1960 the president of France was taken to see a new traffic cloverleaf where hordes of vehicles crisscrossed above and below. He commented to an American aide: "I have the impression that all this will end very badly."[33]

Perhaps the key to explaining the general's sentimental distance from America and his disapproval of America derives from a perception common among conservative members of his generation—that America had no continuity, no identity. He was a traditionalist steeped in history who was forced to confront a hegemonic power that, to him, lacked a sense of history. He made the following offhand remark about the American past: "America was a virgin land where the pioneers found only the bones of some 'redskins' who'd been 'done in.' And a bit later they had to have a civil war and it continues."[34] Ambassador Bohlen, who was close to the French leader, thought de Gaulle did not understand the United States because it lacked the elements necessary for stability— such as a military tradition and a unifying religious heritage.

We were immigrants from dozens of countries—in his eyes, a somewhat messy collection of tribes that had come together to exploit a continent. He felt we were materialistic without a solid, civilizing tradition of, say, France.[35]

Or as one of his oldest and most intimate companions, René Pleven, observed:

The reason that General de Gaulle misunderstood the United States and Roosevelt is that he was a man for whom history counted more than anything else. In order to understand states and policies, his natural and unvarying tendency was to resort to history. That was why he was so successful in describing and dealing with Britain, Germany, or China. But where the United States were concerned he was at a loss; he found no historical keys. Not that the United States possess no history. But de Gaulle was not acquainted with it . . . and did not think it could be compared to that of "real" nations.[36]

In short, de Gaulle could not conceive of America as a nation on the same scale as France—a serious misperception on his part. "Anti-American" is an appropriate label for a statesman who struggled consistently and mightily to upend an international order built by and for America, who disapproved of America's "arrogance of power," who harbored personal misgivings about American civilization, and who incited, even if indirectly, anti-Americanism.

At the end of his presidency de Gaulle retreated from his earlier anti-American stance. He endured several diplomatic setbacks, including the Soviet invasion of Czechoslovakia, which frustrated his aim of creating a European Europe. There were lost skirmishes with West Germany and the Common Market. Then in May 1968 came massive civil disorder at home. Government mishandling of the student-led demonstrations damaged the president's stature. In the midst of these troubles de Gaulle told the new American ambassador that the two countries "were bound together in all the great tragedies" and "must remain so." For "at the bottom we are, you and we, in the same camp of freedom."[37] When President Nixon visited Paris in early 1969 de Gaulle was especially cordial. At this point de Gaulle's interests seemed to be shifting toward internal affairs. The Gaullist storm over the Atlantic was subsiding.

....

At the domestic level the Gaullist years witnessed the efflorescence of consumer society. Paradoxically it was de Gaulle's administration with its deep respect for tradition that pursued economic modernity and in so doing ushered in the new age of Americanization. Just as he led France away from Washington's political and strategic tutelage, de Gaulle moved *la vieille France* toward economic affluence and international competitiveness. Yet the consequence of this departure was to promote the Americanization he personally disliked.

The debate over Americanization figures in a subsequent chapter, but the nature of this socioeconomic and cultural transformation under de Gaulle's presidency merits some discussion here. De Gaulle's republic sought economic growth even more assiduously than had the Fourth Republic. Among its economic objectives, the Fifth Republic promoted financial stabilization; industrial mergers into "national champions," especially in high-tech sectors like aerospace and computers; the massive demographic exodus from the farm; the struggle against hidebound vested interests; European economic integration; and national economic planning. Since the bounty of prosperity brought rising levels of income and consumption, de Gaulle was clearly a champion of what the United States had been promoting in France since the days of the Marshall Plan. He took credit for the high productivity rates that the Fourth Republic and American officials had extolled as the route to the American way of life a decade earlier. In 1967 de Gaulle boasted that France had surpassed other Western European countries in per capita national product and was second only to the United States in this respect.[38]

The economic mechanism that generated abundance in the 1960s was quite simple.[39] Prices for most goods and services (in terms of hourly wages) fell while purchasing power rose rapidly. Transfer payments through the welfare state were substantial, and credit buying finally caught on—as did the slogan "Jouissez d'abord, vous paierez ensuite" (Enjoy now, pay later). Per capita income increased 80 percent from 1958 to 1974 under Presidents de Gaulle and Pompidou.

A manager from Sears and Roebuck visiting France in 1963 as a member of an American commercial mission compared French buying to what he had seen eight years earlier:

I was astonished by the space allotted to kitchen appliances, to washing machines, and especially to leisure. From year to year the French are changing their style of living. They have picked up the habit of eating lunch in three-quarters of an hour and of working five days a week. Offices are being modernized more rapidly than residences. The efficiency of the service sector is improving. . . . The French are beginning to make themselves comfortable. . . . They are starting to like things typically American and we think we can sell more leisure products: camping equipment, luxury and scientific toys, sport clothes.[40]

The data confirm this manager's impressions. France was experiencing the consumer revolution. The part of household spending devoted to subsistence, for example, food and rent, fell from one-half to a quarter between 1954 and 1975 as spending increased for health, comfort, communication, and leisure. Thus if French consumers spent more on food and clothing in value and in volume, the share of spending on these items regressed. What began in the late 1950s was virtually completed in the 1960s. If one in four households had a refrigerator in 1960, fifteen years later nine out of ten owned one. If one in four households owned a washing machine, three out of four did (over the same period).[41] If only three in ten households owned a car in 1960, over six out of ten did so in 1973, and the market had become virtually saturated.[42] By that year 85 percent of households had a television set. Dishwashers and freezers arrived more slowly, as did bathtubs, while telephones were still to come (only one of four families owned one in 1973).

The consumer revolution of the 1960s reached the countryside. If the 1950s had brought kitchen stoves, gas heaters, electric irons, and the like to villages, the 1960s brought indoor toilets, refrigerators, washing machines, and television. The rural home began to imitate the urban home. One sociologist of a Breton town observed: "The urge for consumer goods was still considered scandalous in 1950. It was associated with the extravagance of sailors, who introduced what was once regarded as a life of luxury, later as a life of comfort, and now—more and more by the young—as ordinary life." Spending replaced hoarding. One Breton woman commented, "It's better to have things rather than a lot of money. If you don't spend money, you never have anything, you die without ever having had anything."[43]

The new abundance brought a flood of novel American products to France during the 1950s and 1960s. To the familiar names of Gillette razors, Singer sewing machines, Carnation milk, Frigidaire, Johnson wax, Simmons' mattresses, Columbia records, Addressographs and IBM office machines, Hoover appliances, Mobil petroleum products, Colgate toothpaste, and Kodak cameras that date from before the war came jeans by Levi Strauss, Coca-Cola, Tide soap powder, Camay bath soap, Quaker Oats, Q-Tips, Ronson lighters, 3M Scotch tape, Black and Decker electric drills, Hollywood chewing gum, Marlboro cigarettes, Jantzen swimsuits, Playtex brassieres, Firestone tires, Timex watches, Libby's canned foods, computers from Texas Instruments, Tupperware, Tampax, Polaroid cameras, Culligan water softener, and Formica kitchen counters. Magazines and newspapers routinely carried ads for such products. One American clothes manufacturer advertised the "Kool shirt: la première chemise de sport air-conditionnée." A Frenchman could now stay at a Hilton hotel in a room cooled by a Honeywell air conditioner and rent a car from Hertz. American advertising companies set up business, as did American banks, management consultants, accountants, and similar firms to serve their American manufacturing or commercial clients. In 1963 *L'Express* devoted an issue to France's coming affluence, predicting that by 1975 the French standard of living would equal the American standard of the 1960s and that the gap between the two countries would disappear entirely by the end of the century.[44]

For decades America had influenced French popular music, dance, film, and, to a lesser extent, literature; in the postwar era radio and television programs, science fiction, and language itself joined the list of American exports. (In contrast, certain areas of creativity proved highly resistant to influences from the United States.)[45] *Sélection du Reader's Digest* continued to sell over a million copies in the 1960s. In the film industry several genres became exclusively Americanized—musicals, children's films (Walt Disney), and movie spectaculars. Hollywood steadily increased its share of films projected in France. The first American dramatic series appeared on French television in 1964 and films from across the Atlantic quickly dominated foreign films shown on French television.

As if to cap the Americanization process, at the end of the 1960s McDonald's opened its first outlet for American fast food. And now the dictionary contained words like "le weekend," "self," "jeans," "look," "minijupe," and "le standing" (status). According to ad agencies, it was the muffled sound of a closing car door that conveyed "le standing." The title of a popular record was "Le Temps du plastique," and Georges Perec's "story of the sixties" entitled *Les Choses* portrayed a young modern couple wandering through a world of material objects in which "joy was confused with possessing."[46] A product was more chic if it was described in English: "New, Smart! C'est Dacron"; "Night Cream pour la nuit." One newspaper ad in franglais evoked California-style living for its new luxury homes: "Les tennis-quick . . . avec des amis; piscine . . . pour goûter la détente d'un 'crawl'; centre commercial, lieu plaisant du shopping; barbecue chez soi." To one British observer, France in the 1960s surpassed its neighbors in Americanization: "It is this glossy, restless, hedonistic new surface of French life, much of it American-inspired, that as much as anything differentiates the mood of the late '60s from the struggling, cautious, riven France of the '50s."[47] Some manifestations of the craze for America were not only banal but ludicrous. In one resort there was a mock Wild West town with a sheriff who greeted visitors with "Hi ya, pardners, *comment ça va?*"

Oddly enough the rush of abundance did not mean the French believed their daily life was more comfortable. Polls showed the majority did not perceive that either their standard of living or their purchasing power had increased. Only 20 percent saw an improvement in their purchasing power and 30 percent saw a decline, while 50 percent noticed no change. Compared to their neighbors, the French were extraordinarily pessimistic about economic progress and far more likely to expect the future to be worse than the present.[48] "Consume without thinking about it" was the sentiment of most, according to one historian.[49] The French failed to credit de Gaulle with improving their lives. At the end of his presidency in 1969 only 5 percent of those polled believed their standard of living had improved while 41 percent said it was unchanged and 49 percent thought it had declined.[50]

Abundance did not necessarily translate into support for de Gaulle or inevitably bring satisfaction. But, as we shall see, it certainly brought intense self-examination.

··········

The 1960s mark the weakening of postwar anti-Americanism. Given that the Gaullist decade also represented the highest level of a second wave of criticism that surged around Gaullist foreign policy and the war in Vietnam, this result may appear paradoxical. Nevertheless, the experience of these years went far toward exorcising the American demon.

De Gaulle's affirmation of national pride served in the long run to dampen French combativeness toward the United States and subdue the country's assertiveness in world affairs. Perhaps what the nation needed was a strong dose of self-confidence before it could gracefully accept its diminished rank. After all, de Gaulle did remove some of the irritants to French self-esteem such as American military bases. He also liberated the nation from its colonial past and gave it the means, in nuclear weapons, to acquire a respectable national defense. Since the general also wanted to lead the French in certain directions that made his compatriots uneasy, such as a break with the Atlantic alliance, his successors could jettison much of the Gaullist program without neutralizing the psychological boost he had provided. Then in the 1970s the United States, after Vietnam, seemed a less arrogant and a less dangerous power while the Soviet Union, after Czechoslovakia and Afghanistan, assumed a more threatening posture. American protection was more welcome. For all these reasons, France after de Gaulle seemed more content with its place and less eager to assert itself at the expense of the United States.

Since de Gaulle's resignation in 1969, France has behaved more independently than it had under the Fourth Republic. In this sense he altered the course of French foreign policy. No matter how much his successors might retreat from his position on certain issues, like the Atlantic alliance or the shape of Europe, a Gaullist posture has survived, but without the open confrontations with Washington that marked the 1960s.

At the same time that de Gaulle was correcting the imbalance in Franco-American relations and thus removing an essential source of anti-Americanism, Americanization was advancing within France, and America itself was becoming less odious and less central to the domestic debate about modernity. De Gaulle's deliberate promotion of economic growth, technological leadership, and affluence facilitated this domestic Americanization. And with American-style consumption and the proliferation of Yankee products came a passive acceptance of the American way—even if this was not what the chief of state sought. Taken together, Gaullist foreign policy, Gaullist-sponsored affluence, and a new, blurred, even appealing, image of American society account for the exorcism of the 1960s.

CHAPTER 7

The American Challenge

Dollars and Multinationals

Le Défi américain (The American challenge) appeared in bookstores in the fall of 1967. By Christmas Jean-Jacques Servan-Schreiber's book had sold 400,000 copies and went on to become the best-selling title in France during the 1960s (fig. 18). *Le Défi*'s author became an instant celebrity whose lectures attracted full houses; some observers were shocked that Servan-Schreiber outsold literary giants like André Malraux, whose *Anti-mémoires* appeared at the same time.

The message of this American challenge was simple. Next to the United States and the Soviet Union, the emerging economic power was not Europe—it was American business in Europe. American managers knew better than Europeans how to exploit Europe's resources and markets. If nothing changed, Europeans would soon become subcontractors for American subsidiaries. The author was no Gaullist, but he exposed and expressed a national anxiety—one that the Gaullist regime tried to address.

Among Western European nations France was unique in trying to control American investment during the 1960s. There may have been grumbling elsewhere about the flood of dollars that poured into the continent, but the Fifth Republic alone actively tried to channel and even discourage this influx of capital. And nowhere else did public opinion become so disturbed by the issue. American investment even figured in a minor way in the presidential election of 1965.

The defensive reaction of France to American investment parallels the offensive that de Gaulle launched against Washington's political-

18. Servan-Schreiber, with his wife, at a party honoring his best-seller. (Courtesy New York Times Pictures)

strategic hegemony. And, like his effort at upending American political domination, de Gaulle's resistance to the inflow of dollars resulted, unintentionally to be sure, in bringing France and America closer together. For by the end of his presidency the Fifth Republic and the French reached the conclusion that a certain measure of borrowing from the New World was necessary to meet *le défi*.

The Fifth Republic's response to American money seems puzzling, since the level of American investment in France was below average within the European Common Market. Gaullist resistance was not commensurate with the volume of dollars. Why was France under de Gaulle so different from other Western European nations who eagerly welcomed American dollars and firms? Why did France respond to American investment as a challenge rather than as a boon?

Answers to these questions start, but do not end, with de Gaulle. The attempt at control may have been the president's decision, but he commanded considerable support both within and outside his government. He may have led the way in combating American investment, persuading some to adopt a harsher stance than they would have done otherwise, and he certainly dramatized and politicized the issue. Yet there was also a broad consensus based on ambivalence about American capital that supported a policy of monitoring incoming dollars.

Agreement existed that American capital constituted a challenge that had to be met. If dollars were a source of growth and modernization, they also bore certain undesirable consequences. Thus foreign investment, it seemed, should be screened or channeled. De Gaulle's government, many experts, those economic interests most directly affected, even prominent left-wing politicians, as well as ordinary private citizens, agreed on the need to guide the flow of dollars. Explaining government policy and this consensus of ambivalence are the subjects of this chapter.

....

In the summer of 1962 the Frigidaire plant of General Motors near Paris laid off almost seven hundred workers without prior notice. Ten days later Remington Rand-France discharged eight hundred workers at its typewriter factory near Lyons. Local trade unions complained that the massive dismissals at Remington were teletyped from the United States. Small businesses perceived the American multinationals as "a threat to the economic and social order." One newspaper denounced the "dollar's magic spell" and concluded, "The American, if not the enemy, is the accused." The minister of industry, Michel Maurice-Bokanowski, denounced the multinationals' "casual policy" that ignored the French "social contract," according to which employers, not employees, bore the costs of such layoffs; he announced that future investments, particularly from American firms, would be closely examined.[1] The reproach to Remington Rand was especially sharp since the company had built its plant with capital loaned by a government fund. These events announced the coming storm.

On 18 January 1963 came the news that Chrysler had purchased a controlling interest in Simca, the country's third largest automobile manufacturer. With eighteen thousand employees, Chrysler became the largest American company in France. The Simca takeover irritated and alarmed the government. Chrysler had informed authorities only two days before of its purchase of Simca shares on the Swiss stock exchange. De Gaulle, shortly thereafter, upon meeting the head of Simca at an Elysée reception, supposedly rebuked him by saying, "You could have anticipated it."[2]

It was this series of events that brought the American challenge to the attention of the Fifth Republic and the French people. For some time the government, behind the scenes, had been concerned about the problem. Other incursions, such as the project of Libby McNeill in the Languedoc, were pending. But the Chrysler purchase galvanized officials into action. Recall that only days before the news about Chrysler-Simca, de Gaulle had announced his opposition to the entry of Great Britain into the Common Market. A principal reason for his veto was to protect the European community from losing its identity and coherence in a vast Atlantic free-trade area dominated by the Anglo-Americans.

Two weeks after the Chrysler takeover, the Fifth Republic decided to get tough with American investments. The minister of finance, Valéry Giscard d'Estaing, announced, "It was undesirable that important economic sectors of the Common Market should depend on outside decisions."[3] Any attempt to curb foreign investment, however, had to take into consideration the Treaty of Rome, which obligated the six member states (France, West Germany, Italy, Luxembourg, the Netherlands, and Belgium) to eliminate any discrimination against foreign capital. Accordingly, the first step was for Giscard to raise the issue with his fellow finance ministers from the Common Market.

As we shall see, Gaullist attempts at channeling foreign investment through a national policy were to clash with Gaullist commitments to the Common Market. At one level de Gaulle's twin goals of disengaging France from Washington's hegemony and of building a European Europe seem complementary. The first goal sought to liberate the French and the second to protect all Western Europeans from the American colossus. Both efforts would move Western Europe away from an Atlantic community subservient to Anglo-American, rather than European, interests. Yet in practice these seemingly parallel aims proved to be contradictory—at least with respect to meeting the American economic challenge posed by the flood of investments. De Gaulle's attempt at controlling American investment conflicted with his parallel effort at constructing European unity through the community of the Six. The goals proved incompatible.

De Gaulle's dilemma in the 1960s occurred because in 1958 he had made two important decisions. The first was to join the new European

Economic Community, which was going to reduce the republic's room for maneuver in fending off the surge in American dollars, and the second was to invite American investment. With respect to these issues, as well as the main lines of economic policy, President de Gaulle made the decisions.[4]

The next-to-last ministry of the Fourth Republic, which immediately preceded de Gaulle's, had notified Brussels that France would not be able to meet its treaty obligations on 1 January 1959, the day the first round of tariff reductions was to go into effect. But de Gaulle's government, in the fall of 1958, officially confirmed an earlier promise to apply the Rome treaty on schedule. Why did de Gaulle decide against following his predecessor's use of the treaty's escape clauses?

The historian is seldom on sure ground when assessing de Gaulle's motives, yet on this matter evidence points to endorsing the general's account, which says he elected to abide by the treaty in order to stimulate the French economy by plunging it into the cold waters of European competition. There were other reasons for this choice, such as honoring commitments and strengthening the new continental community at the expense of a rival British-sponsored trade scheme, but they seem less important.[5]

His principal reason for entering the community was that it would serve to renovate the economic and financial structure of France. In 1958 the new government faced large deficits in its budget and in the balance of payments, high inflation, a substantial debt owed to the United States, and an impending rendezvous with the Common Market and the Organization for European Economic Cooperation over reducing controls on trade. Externally, France had lagged far behind the rest of the Six in shedding protectionism. Internally, the market was still encumbered with so many obstacles that there were doubts about its future growth and competitiveness. De Gaulle was determined, in his words, to terminate "the mess, the inflation, the begging," and the policies that over the years had brought a dozen devaluations and an indebtedness that reduced the nation's rank in world affairs.[6]

He opted for a bold program of economic and financial reform to ready France for economic leadership in European and world markets. Central to this program was renovation through competition. He later explained: "Expansion, productivity, competition, concentration—such, clearly, were the rules that the French economy, traditionally cautious, conservative, protected, and scattered, must henceforth adopt." In this program the Common Market was instrumental:

I was concerned with international competition, for this was the lever which could activate our business world, compel it to increase productivity, encourage it to merge, persuade it to do battle abroad; hence my determination to promote the Common Market, which as yet existed only on paper, to support the abolition of tariffs between the Six, to liberalize appreciably our overseas trade.[7]

Accordingly in December 1958 de Gaulle's government introduced a complex program of economic and financial reforms, two of whose "levers" were entry into the Common Market and convertibility of the franc. These measures aimed at relieving the deficits in trade and balance of payments and at attracting foreign, especially American, investment. Thus de Gaulle made the second fateful decision to seek American capital as a remedy to France's economic and financial weaknesses.

Given subsequent events it is ironic that in 1959, as part of the program of economic and financial reforms, France actively began courting American investment. Prime Minister Michel Debré expressed his desire that American firms set up shop in France rather than elsewhere in the Common Market.[8] A new Franco-American Convention of Establishment encouraged mutual investment and accorded nationals and companies of both countries equal treatment. Whereas the Fourth Republic because of its internal political and financial difficulties had discouraged investors with onerous procedures for capital exchange, the Fifth Republic reduced these regulations to a formality. Antoine Pinay, the minister of finance, went to New York in May 1959 to reassure Wall Street that its capital would be safe in France. And his ministry set up a welcome center to encourage investors. Attracting dollars to offset the deficit in the balance of payments was the overriding need.

In 1963, however, following the Chrysler takeover and the layoffs by General Motors and Remington Rand, the republic did an about-face. For the next three years the government adopted a hard line toward American investment. Why was American capital perceived as a danger whereas four years earlier it was being solicited?

First of all France was running a surplus in its payments and no longer needed help. But that alone does not account for the new resistance. In 1963 President de Gaulle with his veto of British entry into the Common Market launched the most active phase of his effort at asserting French independence from the United States. Independence and status in world political affairs depended on economic autonomy—a calculation that had prompted his reforms in 1958. But American capital threatened that autonomy. A host of arguments emerged against the American challenge, including charges that dollars went into buy-outs of profitable firms without bringing any advantages; that American firms were too big and would overwhelm French competitors; that excess capacity was being built; and that American companies violated French rules of the game. Behind this smoke screen, at least from the government's perspective, lay the real danger: American control of key economic sectors. If un-regulated, it was feared, vital branches of industry—some critical to national defense—would fall into the hands of American subsidiaries who were controlled from corporate headquarters across the Atlantic. The fact (still unknown to the French public in 1963) that Washington had blocked the sale of a special computer deemed vital for the French nuclear program demonstrated the consequences of such technological depen-dence. Moreover, the Fifth Republic had awarded priority to national economic planning and outside capital might upset the designs of the planners and the ministries.

American capital came in a rush after 1958. Its biggest surge arrived in 1961 and the peak occurred in 1962–65. To assess the magnitude and type of foreign investment is difficult in this instance.[9] Rarely do studies agree on precise quantities of investment, but at least we can chart its general flow. Quantitative analyses suggest why the French perceived a problem. Of the total stock of foreign investment, which reached about five billion dollars as of 1965, over half came from the United States.[10] Over three-quarters of this took the form of "direct" rather than portfolio investment, meaning that it carried some form of continuing control by the investor such as a substantial share of equity ownership or transfer of patents, technology, machinery, or manage-ment. If by almost every measurement the volume of American invest-ment in France was no more than average for Common Market countries, most of it had arrived recently and the number of transac-tions was relatively large. Most important, it was concentrated almost entirely in manufacturing and much of this was in the most dynamic industrial sectors. Whether the target for American capital was a leading sector like computers or a traditional activity like food pro-cessing, it was among the growth industries of the day. One source estimates that 84 percent of foreign investment between 1960 and 1964 saturated four sectors: chemicals, mechanical-electrical, oil, and farm machinery-food processing.[11] Some industries where Americans acquired a dominant role during this period or several decades earlier were synthetic rubber, petroleum, office machines, tractors, photo-graphic supplies, sewing machines, elevators, telegraph and telephone equipment, and computers.[12] From the perspective of national interest, some of these sectors were strategic; others, such as razor blades, were not.

First to expand their holdings were the big corporations, many of which had been doing business in France for years: IBM, Standard Oil-Esso, and General Motors. A second wave of medium-sized firms, many in the food and service sectors, then entered the French market. Much of this new investment transgressed the so-called traditional boundaries of American presence. For subsidiaries of Standard Oil or IBM to raise their capital stock was acceptable. But for new entries to expand outside traditional areas, as Chrysler did by entering automobile manufacture or as Libby did with food processing, made it appear as if the Americans had cast off all restraint. In addition American subsidiaries, especially in the later 1960s, borrowed capital from European banks that held increasingly large stocks of dollars. In this way corporate America induced Europeans to finance American business expansion. Although the rate of private capital inflow slowed after 1964, dollars continued to arrive.

The reasons for this capital outflow are numerous, but in the last analysis it was attracted by the opportunities offered in the rich new European market. American companies wanted to take advantage of a market of 170 million people who were entering consumer society. Corporate America could, for the first time, export the mass production and marketing techniques it had developed at home. Establishing operations within the European community avoided the common external tariff and allowed free movement of capital and goods across the borders of the Six. A host of related reasons such as earning higher returns on investment, raising market shares over a competitor, or acquiring raw materials contributed to the outflow. In France a stable government, a convertible currency, low inflation, and a balanced budget heightened the appeal.

If the magnitude of American investment in France was significant, though not extraordinary when compared to that in other European nations, it was, nevertheless, widely perceived as a challenge. This reception marked the French as unique among Western Europeans. A consensus of ambivalence, at least initially, supported de Gaulle's restrictive policy. It derived from three deeply held popular aspirations or fears.

As we have seen, postwar France displayed an irrepressible national assertiveness toward the United States. This sentiment had occasionally become strident during the Fourth Republic, and the Fifth Republic both nurtured and excited it. In this instance national assertiveness translated into a refusal of American domination via investment. A second element of this consensus was a fear of Yankee capitalism. American business had a mixed reputation. The interwar years left a caricature of American gigantism, impersonality, regimentation, and ruthlessness that lingered despite the French pilgrimages to the paradise of human relations during the Marshall Plan era. American capitalism was antithetical to an assumedly more humane French way of economic behavior. The French left added an ideological gloss that stressed the exploitive, expansive, and "colonizing" aspects of the American system. A final ingredient of this consensus was a fear of economic decline. In the race for international competitiveness, the postwar generation worried about falling further behind the leaders. The United States was both an agent and a reminder of this relative retardation. In the midst of unprecedented economic growth there occurred doubts that France was abreast of its rivals and fears that Americans would like to keep France in a subordinate position by controlling its dynamic sectors. This consensus dampened enthusiasm for the capital boon from the New World and provided de Gaulle with support for his intervention against the dollar.

··········

The government's opening move to curb the American challenge was to appeal to the European community. In late January 1963 Giscard d'Estaing announced that he would raise the issue of foreign investment at the next meeting of the community's finance ministers. Giscard stated that unless a European solution were found, the autonomy of certain sectors in the community was at risk.[13] But before June, when the ministers gathered in Belgium, Vice-Chancellor Ludwig Erhard of West Germany and André Dequae, finance minister of Belgium, had already declared their opposition to regulating American capital.[14] France's partners were displeased with de Gaulle's veto of the British membership in the Common Market and disinclined to side with Paris on the investment issue. When the finance ministers met at Spa, Giscard tried to soften his tone and proposed drawing up a sectoral inventory of foreign investments with an eye to limiting them should they appear dominating. But his partners' reactions effectively killed any hope for instituting a common policy. They agreed only to study the problem. The Italian minister, Guiseppe Trabucchi, said the Six were committed to a policy of free capital movement.[15] The Commission of the European community was not eager to become involved in a problem that seemed to worry only the French.[16] France would have to act alone and against the policies of its partners, all of whom welcomed American capital. De Gaulle found no help in Brussels.

Following this setback the French government tightened up existing regulations and procrastinated. Rather than rewrite the rules, which risked an open clash with the European community and the United States over existing treaties, the government of Georges Pompidou (which had succeeded that of Michel Debré in 1962) simply stalled. Requests to the Ministry of Finance for authorization gathered dust. Prime Minister Pompidou told the American Chamber of Commerce in Paris in early 1963 that the spread of American investments needed further study in order to prevent surprises in the future.[17] A few months later Pompidou stated:

France is not hostile to foreign investments; however, a limitation appears desirable in practice. France does not wish that the industry of a particular region or a particular branch of industry be dominated by foreign capital, for example, American.[18]

Heads of American banks in Paris were told the government wanted primarily to discourage French firms from seeking American bailouts.[19]

While the government discouraged unwanted investors through bureaucratic delay rather than outright refusal, Giscard and his colleagues groped for a policy. The finance minister first tried to distinguish investments that were "productive" from those that were "exclusively financial," but this made little sense.[20] Over a year passed before the Pompidou government produced criteria for selecting investments. According to the minister of industry, Maurice-Bokanowski, "good" investments improved employment and the balance of payments, raised national income and tax revenues, and aided economic modernization and competitive capacity. "Bad" investments compromised healthy domestic competition, concentrated on the most profitable sectors where they created excess capacity, laid off French staff, ignored national interests, endangered the trade balance, and discouraged French research.[21] Such a list only demonstrated that multiple criteria needed to be employed on a case-by-case approach.

Within the government the partisans of rigor, such as the Elysée and the *ministères de tutelle* (guardian or supervisory ministries), especially the Ministry of Industry, were more strict in their judgment of applications than were the Finance Ministry and DATAR (Délégation à l'aménagement du territoire); disagreements were common. The latter agency championed regional development and eagerly sought foreign investment. But its stance was exceptional. The Commissariat général du plan stood between the extremes, advocating a liberal policy in principle but endorsing restrictions for strategic sectors like electronics.[22] Ultimately selection was in the hands of Pompidou, Giscard, and de Gaulle; this trio often vetoed recommendations from below for authorization.

Many applications after 1963 faced endless administrative obstruction, and some were rejected outright. Weyerhauser offered to buy a box company that was on the verge of bankruptcy. The government tried without success to find a French purchaser yet eventually rejected Weyerhauser's bid because Americans were considered already too powerful in this sector. This rejection was also intended to be a signal to other French firms in distress not to look abroad as an easy way out.[23] The United States Treasury Department only fueled the fires when it pressured the Fruehauf trailer company to make its French subsidiary cancel a contract with Automobiles Berliet. The latter had ordered trailers from Fruehauf-France for sale in the People's Republic of China. This contract raised a jurisdictional issue over which country controlled Fruehauf-France. A court action by Berliet eventually forced the sale. In the first nine months of 1965, out of 164 requests 40 were turned down.[24] The most controversial cases involved two American multinationals, Libby McNeill and General Electric.

Libby became interested in establishing a food-processing plant in the Bas-Rhône-Languedoc in 1961 when it learned of the development of this area. The government was sponsoring a massive irrigation project and also trying, without much success, to build a major canning industry by regrouping the fragmented local food-processors. France had nearly a thousand canning companies, of which most were tiny and none was large enough either to compete in the Common Market or to stimulate change in local agriculture. By January 1963 the Ministry of Agriculture and Libby McNeill had drafted a tentative agreement: Libby would build a large plant in the Bas-Rhône-Languedoc for processing local fruits and vegetables and would export 85 percent of its output. Part of the package included contracts with French farmers, who would grow crops according to Libby's rules and receive guaranteed prices.

In the midst of the outcry over Chrysler-Simca, news of the Libaron (the name of Libby's subsidiary) project leaked to the press. Opposition came from a wide range of political groups, especially on the left, as well as farm associations. Farmers objected to being disciplined by American experts. Local canneries protested against unfair competition from the

American giant. And the fact that an American firm would benefit from an irrigation project built with public funds aroused protests.[25] *Le Monde* suggested that because Libby said it might at the outset need to import some fruits and vegetables from the United States, Libaron might well become a "Trojan horse" the Americans could use to flood the Common Market with their commodities.[26] This was especially galling considering France's own large agricultural surpluses. Defenders of Libaron, how-ever, argued that since Libby entertained Italy as an alternative site, it was better that Libby's cans should contain beans from the Languedoc than from the *mezzogiorno*. And the Fifth Republic needed the cannery to implement its plans for the region. The government suspended action on Libby's proposal and asked the Chicago firm to yield part ownership to a French bank and to modify the growers' contracts. Libby executives complied and authorization was granted.

Of less notoriety than Libaron were projects by American companies to penetrate the French market for animal feed. In 1964 Duquesne-Purina, a subsidiary of Ralston Purina, opened a large slaughterhouse for poultry in Brittany and incurred a storm of opposition. The poultry market suffered from a glut and the contracts let by Duquesne-Purina endangered the local cooperatives. A Breton farm leader complained of the "underhanded American attempt to seize the French poultry market and put our farmers in servitude" and threatened to dynamite the slaughterhouse.[27] Ralston Purina agreed to curtail its output and the affair subsided, as Libaron had. A similar project submitted to the government by the giant feed-wholesaler Cargill was discovered by farm associations before a decision had been rendered. Farmers sent a delega-tion to the minister of agriculture; the government, already under fire from farmers for its approval of the Common Market's new agricultural policy and worried about Breton votes in the 1965 presidential elections, tabled Cargill's request.

The affair that captured most attention, however, occurred in the computer industry.[28] Machines Bull was the only serious competitor for IBM-France, which had long dominated the industry. Bull was owned by the Callies family and had specialized in office calculators. In the early 1960s it embarked on an expensive expansion program absorbing sub-contractors, developing new product lines, and building an international service and distribution network. Only belatedly, however, had it begun to shift to all electronic computers. For some time Bull had been manufacturing electronic machines under license or importing them from the United States; its own research and development could not provide the designs. And the new electronic computers were leased rather than sold, adding further strain on the firm's financial health. By 1963 the company was in need of capital and a technological infusion. General Electric stepped in late that year and offered to buy a 20 percent interest at above market price and to provide technological and managerial assistance as a way of getting into the European market. GE offered Bull not only $28 million in cash but product designs and technicians to help it develop new computers.

The Ministry of Finance, however, in February 1964 refused to authorize the joint venture and called for a "French solution." De Gaulle took a personal role in settling this affair.[29] After much prodding a group of French investors that included two banks and two major electronics firms offered to buy shares in Bull for $7 million, and the government promised public contracts to the company. But there was no technical aid.

In April the government reversed itself and allowed Bull to reopen negotiations with GE. Advice coming from the two electronic firms that formed the French alternative and from the Ministry of Industry was negative. Without the technical and managerial skills and more cash, the "French solution" would break down in the long run. De Gaulle himself judged the scheme designed by the finance ministry unworkable.[30] And, even though the Callies family accepted the ministry's proposal, many of the shareholders and some of the family did not; the situation might have led to a formal vote against the venture and either bankruptcy or nationalization—alternatives the government wanted to avoid. GE knew it had the upper hand and tendered a new, complicated offer that strengthened its position in the merger.[31] In July the government capitulated and allowed the GE-Bull joint venture.

....

Looking outside the offices of the ministries in Paris, we cannot generalize about how major interest groups—much less the French people—viewed American investment. Reactions were immensely varied, sometimes derived from personal experience with an American firm. But there was no important opposition to Gaullist screening policy, at least at first. Criticism grew only as monitoring and stalling turned into a de facto freeze.

Peak employers' associations like the Conseil national du patronat français (CNPF) and the Confédération générale des petites et moyennes entreprises (CGPME) adopted no official stance. Given their diverse constituencies, this is no surprise. The closest approximations to a position were the declarations of Georges Villiers, the head of the CNPF. If at one time this confederation had encouraged American investors, by 1964–65 Villiers tactfully asked Americans to respect certain limits. Speaking at a reception for the United States ambassador, Villiers first praised the benefits of this capital influx, then warned that it was in the interest of neither country that this movement develop in "an excessive manner." French industry, he declared, needed to adapt by itself to international competition; it would be harmful if the centers of technical progress or decision-making were to be concentrated in the United States. "We should be aiming for an exchange of industrial experience—toward stimulation rather than substitution." Sounding a political note, the president of the CNPF remarked that the magnitude of this financial and technical movement "risks producing economic, social, and, as an indirect consequence, political effects . . . that we should try to forestall."[32]

Similarly when top managers of French firms and American subsidiaries, like Ford-France, met in 1964, the Americans pointed out the Europeans' need for capital and warned that if France closed the door, the dollars would go elsewhere within the European community. French executives spoke of an unequal struggle. General Electric, they pointed out, produced two hundred thousand different products; General Foods, should it choose to, could merely cut its prices 10 percent and force out every French candy manufacturer. Outside capital was wanted, but Americans must respect certain limits. They should, for example, invest in existing companies without demanding control and make full use of French middle management, French techniques, and French subcontractors. Otherwise, the French industrialists warned, a nationalist reaction could take place.[33]

Other French business leaders disapproved of the way American firms violated the Gallic code of behavior—especially with respect to competition and personnel practices. Instead of accepting the status quo, Goodyear and Firestone, for example, tried to win a foothold in the original-equipment tire market by offering unparalleled discounts to French automakers.[34] Some American affiliates ruthlessly replaced managers and laid off workers without helping them relocate. Gallic anxiety about the "savage" aspects of American business, which had been repressed in the 1950s, emerged a decade later when American subsidiaries "misbehaved"—allegedly showing their true colors.

Business and financial journals stressed the several advantages of American investment, warned against xenophobia, yet accepted the need for vigilance.[35] This press, like business itself, complained that American capital targeted certain sectors—of which some were vital to national independence. It also reported the "brutal" layoffs at Remington, the contracts at Libby that made farmers work "à l'américaine," and American penetration into the food industry that threatened artisanal manufacture. What raised anxiety in these observers was the colossal size of American enterprise. The press reported that while the sales of the entire French electronics industry were 5.5 billion francs, those of General Electric alone were 27 billion. With respect to business turnover in 1965, General Motors was nineteen times bigger than Renault, U.S. Steel five times bigger than Schneider, Goodyear four times larger than Michelin, and Du Pont three times the size of Rhône-Poulenc. And profit margins for big business were estimated to be on the average double that of their French counterparts. One of the most common comparisons was that General Motors' annual business exceeded the Dutch gross national product by 10 percent.

These business reviews disapproved of the melodramatic way the government presented the problem and the political and anti-American overtones of its policy, yet they urged the Americans to avoid seeking controlling interest. They opposed a strict protectionist policy, recalling how opposition to General Electric's initial offer to Bull had backfired, and looked to Europe, either at the level of European-wide mergers or European Economic Community regulation, for a solution. But as many experts advised and as one business paper declared, "France has a duty to protect itself against inordinate American investment."[36]

The weather vane of the intelligentsia, *Le Monde*, at first displayed Gaullist alarm about American investment and then became more forgiving. Days before de Gaulle's rejection of Great Britain's bid for entry into the Common Market, Maurice Duverger called attention to the other dimensions of the American design on Europe besides the British "Trojan horse."[37] Europe, according to this columnist, faced a "neocolonialism" that threatened to transform an emerging independent Europe into Washington's dream of an open, capitalist Atlantic community. The "true Trojan horses," following this logic, were American companies that had already been welcomed, mistakenly, into the Common Market. These corporations transferred decision-making across the Atlantic to "economic groups" that formed part of the inner circle that ran Washington. Duverger reminded his readers that the American mentality combined extreme generosity in charitable matters with "utmost severity" in business. The way out for Duverger was a planned, autonomous European community.

Two weeks after Duverger's "Trojan horse" column, *Le Monde* divulged the Libaron scheme. But as the investment issue gained attention, the newspaper began to present a more nuanced position, mildly praising the behavior of American subsidiaries, blaming the capital inflows on French weaknesses, criticizing the government for "ambushing" investors, and looking to Europe for a solution.[38] By 1967 *Le Monde* was cheering on American companies for their market-guided behavior and their constructive influence on French firms while continuing to worry about growing outside control. "At a time when capital is increasingly without a homeland, French industry must be sufficiently effective so that foreigners continue 'to invest in France without investing France.'"[39]

In the mid-1960s the American challenge attracted popular attention. Foreign investment was no longer dull reading in economic journals. General-interest periodicals carried the story, and the topic assumed national stature with reports on affairs like the General Electric takeover of Bull. One report said that if the average consumer had learned to accept Mobil Oil, Coca-Cola, Gillette, and O'Cedar, American acquisition of companies making automobiles, snacks, and other foods evoked "a certain mistrust."[40] Public opinion surveys from the mid-1960s do little more than verify a substantial degree of reserve about foreign investment among the French—more so than among other Europeans.[41]

Except for discussion of the nation's long-range economic plan (the fifth since the war), the issue never became the subject of a major debate in the National Assembly. But the left tried, halfheartedly, to use it against de Gaulle by demanding even stiffer measures against the Americans.[42] The Communists attacked the government for selling out French industry to the Americans; the Socialists asserted that the Gaullist regime favored class interests over national ones. François Mitterrand reproached the Pompidou government for authorizing "the colonization of France by foreign capital."[43] Socialist intellectuals like Serge Mallet argued that if European integration was not accomplished, then Europeans would end up working in factories whose managers and technicians were Americans.[44] Gaston Defferre, who made a bid to be the left's candidate for the presidency in 1965, denounced the government's handling of the Simca and Bull affairs and accused it of accepting colonization by the United States. He called the Bull affair "the most striking event of 1964 by virtue of both its symbolic value and its practical consequences . . . it marks in fact the abandonment of a sector that controls the future of all our key activities."[45] Defferre blamed the

Gaullists for mistakenly seeking a French solution to a problem that could be resolved only at the European level. Gaullist errors, the Socialist candidate declared, were leading not to independence but to economic and political "enslavement."[46]

But trying to outbid the Gaullists by playing the nationalist-protectionist card did not work, because the aims of the Gaullists and the left converged. The government was already doing what almost everyone wanted, that is, it was monitoring foreign investment; the left had no real alternative to offer at the European level because Europe had refused to cooperate with de Gaulle. The Gaullists allowed the left little space for its outflanking maneuver. All that could be requested was a more effective screening policy. In the end foreign investment was only a minor issue in a campaign that earned de Gaulle his reelection.[47]

· · · · · · · · · ·

The way the Fifth Republic chose to restrict foreign investment from 1963 to 1966 proved defective. In the cases of Machines Bull-GE and Libby McNeill, the Pompidou government, failing to find an alternative, succumbed to American offers. This was not unusual. In fact, in most cases the *ministères de tutelle* were unable to find French substitutes for American investors.[48] Weaknesses in French industrial structure and capital markets undermined Gaullist policy. Equally important, without a common policy among the Six, American capital found havens elsewhere within the Common Market. In this way France lost jobs, tax revenue, technology, exports, and research facilities—and the products arrived across its borders anyway. Faced with interminable bureaucratic delays, Phillips Petroleum and Rhône-Poulenc, for example, chose Antwerp as the site of their new plastics plant rather than Bordeaux. Ford shifted its proposed new factory from Metz to the Saar. Giscard supposedly made the president of General Motors wait for twenty-four hours, leaving the American executive so angry that he swore he would never invest in France; in fact, General Motors abandoned its plan for a plant in Strasbourg to build one in Antwerp. American executives complained that they could not understand what government policy was other than deference to the pressure of special interests.[49] Discouraged in advance by ministerial arbitrariness and delay, companies ceased even to apply for authorization. This tack deprived the government of its option of screening applications and approving "good" investments.[50]

Official fumbling now prompted press and political criticism because France was losing out in the competition for American capital. Screening, to the critics, was desirable but the way the republic implemented it forfeited advantage to other Europeans. An official report concluded that foreign investment had actually fallen in 1965, that it represented at most 10 percent of domestic capital investment, and that within the European community Germany, Italy, and the Netherlands had received more American capital than France had.[51] Most critics, many of whom were economists, advocated a European rather than a French solution.[52] But that option, at least at the level of a common European community policy, was not available to Paris.

Another report, this one commissioned by the Ministry of Industry in the summer of 1965, noted that foreign investment was not excessive and, in fact, was declining. The report, which expressed views of a select group of officials, bankers, and industrialists, argued that in international markets, in which only a few multinationals could compete, to force an enterprise to depend on French capital alone was unsound.[53] Better to have a French company triumph in such markets, even if it was under American control, rather than have it disappear waving the *tricolore*. The issue was not resisting foreign investment, according to the report, but meeting a lag in technology and management. Foreign investment would help close the technological gap in the race against the real rival from across the Rhine. The report recommended against "uniform ostracism" of foreign investment that would, in addition, be legally and diplomatically impossible and invite reprisals. In June the minister of industry began to bend. He praised American subsidiaries for obeying the French social contract in contrast to their behavior in 1962–63, but he also announced new guidelines, which included French control over a firm's decision-making and industrial research.[54] By mid-1965 the restrictive policy pursued since 1963 had miscarried and was in need of overhaul.

·········

While the administration struggled to define a policy for selecting investments, President de Gaulle pursued a different, but parallel, strategy. The head of state chose to strike at the alleged source of American investment by opening the issue of international monetary reform at his press conference in February 1965. In fact the interconnections between American payments deficits, American overseas investments, and European inflation had been discussed within the highest governmental circles for years and had also been raised at the international level.[55] In July 1963 de Gaulle first spoke in public of "the dollar problem."[56] The following year Giscard addressed the International Monetary Fund (IMF) about the problem of excess international liquidity and recommended the creation of a new reserve unit linked to gold. But it was the dramatic 1965 presidential press conference that triggered a new Gaullist offensive against the dollar.

On this occasion the president sharply attacked the status of the dollar as a reserve currency. The operation of the Gold Exchange Standard, de Gaulle argued, permitted the free financing of foreign investment that led, for some countries, to "a kind of expropriation" of their enterprises.[57] The president recommended overhauling the international monetary system by substituting the gold standard as a means of imposing discipline.

As a reserve currency, the Gaullists contended, the dollar escaped the discipline of international payments. Under the Gold Exchange Standard the dollar was a privileged currency; its use permitted the United States to dispense with the rule of regulating payments deficits by reducing its stock of gold. The Gold Exchange Standard allowed the United States simultaneously to spend lavishly on foreign aid and defense (including Vietnam), imports, and foreign investment without experiencing unbearable repercussions on its balance of payments. For years, according to the Gaullist critique, the United States refused to face its growing payments deficit while corporate America took advantage of the dollar's special status to send capital abroad, further amplifying the deficit. Americans also borrowed from the local stock of Eurodollars to finance their subsidiaries. Moreover, the Gaullists argued, this system allowed the United States to export inflation by printing dollars at will without having to pay in gold for its excesses. In short, the privileged status of its money served to reinforce America's industrial dominance in Europe. Such an arrangement was incompatible with an independent France and a European Europe. If after the war, given the shortage of dollars and America's hoard of gold, there was good reason for foreign banks to hold the currency, such was no longer the case because dollars were plentiful. Without reforms, the system was in such disequilibrium, according to de Gaulle, that if creditors ever began collectively to convert to gold, a global financial upheaval would follow.

Jacques Rueff, one of de Gaulle's principal financial advisers, explained the problem this way:

When a country with a key currency has a deficit in its balance of payments—that is to say the United States for example—it pays dollars to the creditor country, which end up with its central bank. But the dollars are of no use in Bonn, or in Tokyo or in Paris. The very same day, they are relent to the New York money market, so that they return to the place of origin. Thus the debtor country does not lose what the creditor country has gained. So the key currency country never feels the effect of a deficit in its balance of payments. And the main consequence is that there is no reason whatever for the deficit to disappear, because it does not appear. Let me be more positive: if I had an agreement with my tailor that whatever I pay him he returns the money to me the very same day as a loan, I would have no objection at all to order more suits from him.[58]

Whatever the intrinsic merits of this argument—its deficiencies led some Americans to criticize it for being incomplete and self-serving—it formed the basis of policy. Moreover, de Gaulle's arguments evoked sympathy among the French business elite, as the policy of monitoring investment did.[59] The Bank of France in 1965 doubled the volume of surplus dollars it converted into gold and de Gaulle insisted that French gold reserves held by the United States Treasury be transferred to Paris.[60] In 1966 France withdrew from the "gold pool" (an international consortium whose function was to restrain speculation in gold). These words and actions further antagonized a United States that was already displeased with the head of the Fifth Republic. Americans asked if de Gaulle was contesting the hallowed proposition that the dollar was good as gold. Meanwhile the United States Treasury grumbled over the costly operation of repatriating gold across the Atlantic. In response to de Gaulle's press conference, the Treasury defended the existing international monetary order (though acknowledging the need for study), claimed that the gold standard would be too rigid and deflationary, and asserted that no other government would follow the French president.[61]

Before the quarrel over the dollar subsided, exasperated congressmen were demanding that France pay its war debts—from the First World War—before the Treasury changed more gold for dollars. American businesses threatened to boycott French imports. One bar owner in New York invited television cameras to film him "cleansing" his wine cellar by pouring bottles of Bordeaux down the drain. The humorist Art Buchwald advised those who could not afford expensive French products to join the boycott by refusing to eat "French Fries." And the cartoonist Herblock, parodying a James Bond film about a villain named Goldfinger who tried to rob Fort Knox, called the chief of state "Gaullefinger" (fig. 19). Even at the White House, where President Johnson had tried to stay aloof from the quarrel, French wines were no longer served at state dinners (though this practice had more to do with Johnson's "Buy America" campaign than it did with retaliation against de Gaulle). Stinging stories about the "anti-French" boycott filled the French press.[62]

GAULLEFINGER

19. De Gaulle attacks the dollar, according
to Herblock. (*The Herblock Gallery* [Simon and
Schuster, 1968])

For de Gaulle the gold standard was a means to an end. The end was
elevating French rank in international affairs. His defenders argued that
he proposed the gold standard not from some belief in its intrinsic worth
but because he merely wanted to make all countries submit to the same
rule, so that no one currency could create unlimited international
liquidity. He told one of his financial advisers, "I proposed gold but I
could have accepted something else provided it was a standard independent of the Anglo-Saxons' currencies."[63] In retrospect the campaign
against the dollar seems to have been less a genuine debate about money
than a Gaullist tactic to curtail American economic penetration of
Europe and elevate France and Europe over the Anglo-Americans in
running the international monetary system.[64]

For three years following his 1965 address, de Gaulle tried to force more discipline on the United States. International monetary reform involved both economic and political issues.[65] In the first case was the question of liquidity levels and their effects on inflation as well as the question of the proper means for creating liquidity. On these issues the Anglo-Americans sought only to modify the IMF mechanism, and the French wanted to impose strict rules on everyone and thus eliminate the fluctuations caused by the freedom of key currencies. In the second instance monetary reform expressed European, mainly French, determination to end Anglo-American domination of the IMF.

Washington seized the offensive on reform and offered its plan for adding to the world's monetary reserves through new Special Drawing Rights (SDRs) in the IMF. Michel Debré, as finance minister after 1965, struggled to line up his Common Market partners much as his predecessor had tried in 1963 over the issue of American investments. The most Debré could accomplish was a tentative and ambiguous agreement in 1967 over using SDRs as new instruments of credit. But crises in the pound and the dollar demonstrated that the French had been wrong in claiming an excess of reserves. In November 1967 de Gaulle again publicly attacked "an American seizure" of French enterprise that he attributed, in good part, to the export of dollars through the Gold Exchange Standard.[66]

When the central bankers and finance ministers of the principal industrial nations met at Stockholm in March 1968, the French delegation found itself isolated. Debré alone refused to sign the communiqué and told the press that the SDRs were a mere "expedient" and more like money than a form of supplementary credit; he complained that the basic problems had not been addressed since privileged currencies still existed.[67] In private, de Gaulle complained:

We must wait for the collapse of the dollar. The Americans spend too much on Vietnam, research, and space for their own good. We shall be forced to cover the American deficit. They will take up a collection and our partners will give in to American influence.[68]

Once again, France's European partners had deserted it on a question of meeting the American challenge. They refused French leadership because it was too risky. From their perspective the dollar, rather than gold, represented Europe's trade and capital needs.[69]

The controversy over the dollar quieted in 1968 once the franc itself was in danger. By the summer of 1969 the United States had won the struggle over monetary reform. Modifications in the operation of the IMF had been made, but Washington did not comply with the French prerequisite that the United States end its payments deficit.[70] Three months after de Gaulle's resignation, the French government joined the others and accepted the scheme for SDRs.

··········

At the same time that the French government was trying to curtail the source of American dollars, it continued its efforts to control their entry through selective authorization. By 1965, however, Giscard's restrictive policy had proved ineffective. His freeze discouraged desirable investors who simply found welcome elsewhere. Every member of the European Economic Community, except France, actively courted American capital. Thus the French share of direct American investment within the community fell after 1963 while it rose elsewhere—especially in Germany.[71] On 6 January 1966 Albin Chalandon, a former Gaullist party official, wrote in *Le Monde:* "Ford, which has been set up in the Saar on the other side of the French frontier, is going to manufacture German cars with French labor. Wouldn't the reverse be better for us?"[72] Three days later, when de Gaulle reorganized the Pompidou government, the two ministers most closely associated with protecting France from the dollar, Giscard d'Estaing and Maurice-Bokanowski, were left aside.

Michel Debré became the new finance minister in 1966 and received a free hand to deal with foreign investment. He immediately discarded the restrictive policy that had been in effect for three years. De Gaulle consented to the shift in policy rather than ordering it.[73]

Now the issue changed from a political problem of outside control of French industry: it became more a technological matter. France seemingly faced a "technological gap" that the Americans could help remedy. It was no coincidence that 1966 also marked the start-up year of the fifth plan. One of the plan's major goals, which de Gaulle fully shared, was to raise the economy's global competitive stature. Yet the planners faced declining total investment levels. The answer once again was to open France to those who could bring both cash and technology. Debré observed that "within the framework of the plan, which is the charter for government action . . . , it is better to have American investment than none at all. It is rather difficult to imagine how national investment could be a substitute."[74] When quizzed about American investments, Debré acknowledged that the government was not entirely free to respond because of its commitment to competition and because of the warm reception given dollars within the Common Market. Moreover, Debré said, France lagged in technology and its financial market did not match the level of its industrial ambitions.[75] Debré also complained that if the government refused foreign investors, the political opposition would accuse it of "blind nationalism."[76] And, sotto voce within the government, the view was expressed that American companies were preferable to European firms because the Americans gave their subsidiaries more autonomy.[77]

Both the procedures and the atmosphere at the finance ministry changed. A new interministerial committee reviewed applications. Within a year new legislation governing all foreign exchange was in place.[78] Selectivity remained, but instead of delay and uncertainty there was prompt action. New investors needed only to give the ministry prior notification and, if the government did not object within two months, authorization was automatic. This veto power was used sparingly from 1966 on. Foreign investment was once again encouraged. Only a loose form of monitoring remained, except for direct investments made by French corporations under foreign, that is, American, control that now fell under ministerial surveillance (prior law had regulated only original investment from abroad). Debré spoke of replacing a system of restriction with the principle of freedom. He told the American Chamber of Commerce in Paris that even if a review were indecisive, he would still approve the investment. In the first half of 1966 no investor was refused.[79]

The ministries applied multiple criteria to each potential investor and issued their decisions after careful deliberation.[80] High on the list of requirements was that research facilities be located on French territory. Investments that carried technological transfers or aided regional economic development or forced sectoral mergers, especially to raise French firms to the level of international competitiveness, also received priority.[81] When Motorola decided to build a semiconductor facility near Toulouse, a region in need of new industry, it received instant approval. Similarly Alcoa was welcomed at Châteauroux, where the American military base had been closed. General Mills, Nabisco, and Pillsbury received permission to buy into French companies in order to strengthen French shares of a market (cookies) run by European firms. When the perfume industry refused to use synthetic fragrances, Universal Oil Products was allowed to buy Chiris and introduce the innovation to France. Companies like Phillips Petroleum and General Motors that had deserted France for more hospitable sites in the mid-1960s were welcomed back. General Motors decided to put its new $75 million automatic transmission plant near Strasbourg, and Henry Ford II, while attending the road car race at Le Mans, was invited to Pompidou's residence and told how pleased France would be with a new Ford plant.[82] Nevertheless, the new hospitality failed to raise the volume of American private capital in France.

Not all dollars were welcome under the new dispensation. Debré explained he favored closer collaboration between American and European firms but not under conditions that would constitute "economic colonization." Claiming that history would praise the French as "the best Europeans" for their efforts, he insisted that in joint ventures European firms must retain their freedom of action, their technological capacity, their freedom to export, and their control over personnel promotions.[83] And, he declared, there were key sectors that must remain French—especially when some foreign investors represented "an important power" that had "political objectives."[84] Thus in late 1969 Westinghouse was prevented from acquiring Jeumont-Schneider because the latter, as a producer of equipment for nuclear reactors, fell into Debré's reserved zone. Similarly IT&T was denied its bid to take control of France's largest manufacturer of industrial pumps. And when American businesses offered little advantage, as was the case when Revlon and others tried to purchase perfume companies, they were rejected.

As Debré struggled to find an effective way to attract "good" investments and discourage others, Servan-Schreiber caught almost everyone's attention with the publication of *Le Défi américain* in the fall of 1967. What is at issue here is the popularity of this best-seller (its content will be discussed in the following chapter).

To explain why a book becomes a best-seller may be a difficult enterprise, but a major reason for the enthusiastic reception given Servan-Schreiber was the anxiety about the invasion of dollars and multinationals that made Gaullist policy French policy in the 1960s. To be sure, part of the book's success came from the glamour of its author: his courageous stance during the Algerian war, his success at remaking the glossy newsmagazine *L'Express*, his Kennedy-like physical appearance, and his associations with eminent politicians like Pierre Mendès France. Equally important was the book's novel marketing that used means similar to those perfected by American publishers to create publicity and excite and sustain interest.[85] But there was also the warning.

Le Défi américain sounded an alarm. It was the eleventh hour: unless the French, and the Europeans, launched an immediate counterattack, it would be too late—Europe would become a satellite of the United States. Europeans were on the verge of forfeiting their last chance at staying abreast of the technology and skills that accounted for America's dynamism. In a generation, if Europeans remained passive before the challenge, the United States and a few other countries like Canada and Japan would attain the rank of "postindustrial societies" while Europe would fall to the status of an underdeveloped region. European firms would become mere subcontractors and American subsidiaries would employ Europeans as clerks and workers. The decisions about how Europeans worked, lived, and even learned would be made in cities like New York and Chicago.

Following in the government's footsteps, Servan-Schreiber shifted attention from a preoccupation with American capital to technology and management. He noted that "putting an end to American investment . . . will only weaken us further." The problem by 1967 was one of organization, of research and development, of innovation and creativity. The problem was human capital, not investment capital. Stealing yet another page from de Gaulle's list of complaints, Servan-Schreiber stressed that increasingly Americans financed their subsidiaries by borrowing on local markets, exploiting stocks of Eurodollars, winning subsidies, and reinvesting profits. "Thus, nine-tenths of American investment in Europe is financed from European sources. In other words, we pay them to buy us."[86]

The answer lay in imitating the Americans and building Europe. Much as the Gaullists did, he evoked the taste for independence—but within a European context. Thus *Le Défi* criticized Gaullist policy for being too timid and defensive in facing the challenge and for trying to meet it on the national, rather than the European, level. The best-seller attacked de Gaulle for his opposition to further European integration and antagonized the Gaullists by warning:

We can no longer sit back and wait for the renaissance. And it is not going to be evoked by patriotic rhetoric or clarion calls left over from the age of military battles. It can come only from subtle analysis, rigorous thought, and precise reasoning. It calls for a special breed of politicians, businessmen, and labor leaders.[87]

It should be no surprise then that when President de Gaulle was asked at his press conference for his opinion of *Le Défi* he answered, "Here, we don't advertise literature."[88]

Servan-Schreiber's warning touched a common Gallic fear—that the Americans were taking over France and Europe. Evidence had been accumulating that France might be slipping into the American orbit. And the Gaullists had politicized the incursion. But Servan-Schreiber dramatized the issue in a book that combined a catchy title with the drama of an apocalyptic warning, the authority of some carefully selected economic statistics, and the consolation of obvious solutions. He addressed both aspirations for independence and fears of economic backwardness. He struck what was worrying a nation.

The best-seller's fame was brief. The events of May-June 1968 overshadowed it. For several months the book sat on booksellers' shelves as the public's attention shifted to domestic social and political issues raised by the students and strikers. Then in the spring of 1969 came the resignation of President de Gaulle, which ended the attempt at screening foreign investment designed by Michel Debré.

After de Gaulle, the controls on foreign investment largely reverted to what they had been ten years before. The European community intervened by means of a legal action that dragged on from 1968 to 1971, eventually forcing the Fifth Republic to relax the mildly restrictive policies enacted by Debré.[89] Once again Europe blocked France from doing as it pleased to counter the American challenge. President Pompidou, de Gaulle's successor, de-escalated and depoliticized the issue. Only days after de Gaulle's resignation, by coincidence, DATAR established a "Welcome Center" for investors in New York.[90] In February 1970 the government decided to "liberalize" the Debré policy even further, hoping to attract capital and technology. The principle of selection survived but was henceforth rarely invoked.[91] Given the results of a poll of heads of American and European multinationals, which confirmed the reputation of France as the least hospitable country in Europe for foreign investment, it is no surprise that further action was necessary.[92] A month later at the Waldorf Astoria Pompidou spoke on foreign investment before an audience that included President Nixon. The French president reiterated the Gaullist axiom that his country wanted to avoid letting certain sectors fall under foreign control but also observed,

In my eyes nothing would be more prejudicial to French interests than to see American companies set up business only in other Common Market countries. If England becomes a member of the community, this stance will become even more clear.[93]

He proclaimed himself a "partisan of the circulation of capital" and told American business leaders like David Rockefeller that France and Europe sought American investors.[94] And, as if to reverse matters completely, Pompidou notified the Americans that France intended to take up the offensive and develop its investments in the United States.

By 1970, however, the danger of the American challenge was fading and other issues obscured it. As early as 1965–66 there were more applications for authorization from within the Common Market than from the United States.[95] In 1968 intracommunity direct investments (in value) were twice those coming from the United States (though the community total included investments by American subsidiaries in Europe as community investments).[96] American private investment accelerated again after 1968 and the United States remained the principal foreign investor through the early 1970s, but Europe was closing the gap.[97]

··········

Gaullist policy and the response of the French to the influx of American dollars and business in the 1960s was unique among Europeans. The president of Ford-France told a reporter in 1965 that France was the least welcoming country in the European community.[98] Such an admission testifies to the peculiar stance Gaullist France assumed with respect to dollar imports. Nowhere else in Western Europe was there such official, and probably unofficial or popular, resistance.[99] Prime Minister Harold Wilson may have preached against American economic hegemony, yet he allowed Chrysler to take control of a major British auto manufacturer. Some important West German bankers and industrialists and at least one major politician, Franz-Joseph Strauss, spoke out against the American invasion. A few tactless American incursions also aroused concern, but the government in Bonn took no action.[100] Like the other members of the European community, the West Germans welcomed, even sought, American capital. Attempting to channel foreign investment is a common policy among nation states, and in this respect Gaullist France was not unusual. But in the context of Western Europe in the 1960s, France was unique.

Can this Gallic resistance be attributed to the nature and magnitude of American investment in the hexagon? Was there a peculiarly strong American challenge in some objective sense? In fact, France received a smaller share of dollars than other Common Market countries did yet made the greatest effort at controlling them.

Direct American investment in France in the 1960s was comparatively modest in volume and limited in scope. After reaching a peak between 1961 and 1964, the rate of inflow slowed until 1969 when it resumed under Pompidou's presidency. By 1963, of total United States investment in the Common Market, 40 percent went to West Germany, 25 percent to France, and 15 percent to Italy.[101] By the end of 1967 the total value of direct United States investment in France was $1.9 billion, but this was much less than the amount (in billions) in Great Britain ($6.1) or in West Germany ($3.5), and not much above that in Italy.[102] On a per capita basis France was about average for the European community.[103] At the sectoral level dollars may have been focused on French growth sectors, but levels of control were no more concentrated than in West Germany and elsewhere within the Six.[104]

While the rate of American investment in France slowed in the mid-1960s, it continued to grow elsewhere in Western Europe, at least until 1966. In 1958 France and West Germany received dollars at about the same level but a gap steadily opened so that in 1965 France received only $163 million and West Germany $349 million. In the decade 1959–69 the distribution of American capital among the Six shifted to France's disadvantage.[105] By 1969 only one of five dollars invested in the community went to France.

How much of this fall resulted from the Fifth Republic's restrictive policy is difficult to assess. But it seems likely that the selective policy had a considerable effect on restraining capital flow.[106] The shift to a more pragmatic approach in 1966 was too late, given the deceleration of American investment in 1967–68, to have much effect. In the end Gaullist policy deprived the French economy of valuable capital, technology, and research facilities.

If the American challenge involved no greater quantity of dollars in France than elsewhere, then it seems fair to conclude that the Gallic response was a matter of perception and politics. De Gaulle initiated and led, but the French public accepted the need for control.

President de Gaulle's motives in resisting the American investment challenge were primarily political. At risk was French control over its economic future. The timing and development of policy in this area correspond to the contours of the president's grand policy toward ending the American "protectorate." Resistance emerged in 1962–63, peaked in 1964–67, and then receded. In 1966 de Gaulle set aside politics and accepted economic priorities when he allowed Michel Debré to pursue a less restrictive, and more successful, course in screening American capital. But this was a tactical concession toward a strategic political goal. For in welcoming American investors, de Gaulle was trying to close the economic and technological gap with France's competitors in order, one day, to possess the capacity to behave independently. The Americans could remedy the very weakness that made the French dependent.

In resisting the dollar, de Gaulle employed both a French and a European strategy. When his European partners proved uncooperative, he tried a French solution. But in whatever direction he looked, he encountered restraints. At home there was the weakness in industrial structures and capital markets that forestalled French alternatives to American incursions. From the European community came legal, diplomatic, and economic restraints that instead of serving the Gaullist policy of independence obstructed it. Ironically de Gaulle's initial decision made in 1958 to spur French growth through a strategy of international competitiveness via interdependence with Europe denied him the capacity in the 1960s to employ national solutions. In the end Europe gave de Gaulle no help in meeting the challenge of American investment and helped dismantle French schemes at channeling it. Denied either a national or a European solution, de Gaulle and the Gaullists moved toward accepting American transfers.

Resisting the American challenge remained the Gallic consensus even after the end of de Gaulle's presidency, but the conception and answer to the problem evolved. American subsidiaries still stirred French fears of dependence and economic decline. But American investments were now welcomed because the need for modernization took precedence over fear of outside takeovers. Economic priorities precluded a restrictive policy that blocked foreign investment. Outside investment was beneficial; if France was to meet the American challenge, it would do so not through selection and protection but through more competitive French manufactures. Thus the way out was for the French to adopt American ways, for example, to import dollars, management techniques, and technology, as well as to foster mergers and homegrown research that would allow France to stay abreast of and maintain independence from the Atlantic colossus. Even a more open society free of the rigidities that obstructed the free movement of resources might be necessary. Just as de Gaulle himself by 1967 continued to complain about the dollar but accepted economic priorities, so French attitudes moved toward accepting American investment and, more important, certain American techniques, as means of resistance and independence. Both Gaullist policy and consensus advanced toward a more pragmatic and less politicized stance that incorporated a certain measure of Americanization. The outcome of the controversy over the American challenge in the 1960s was, paradoxically, to bring France and the United States closer together.

CHAPTER **8**

Détente

Debating America in the 1960s

In the 1960s the American social model continued to excite a lively, and mostly acerbic, response among the French, especially the intelligentsia. These expressions of anti-Americanism, unlike those set off by troubles in the Western alliance or by foreign investment, were not for the most part generated by the Gaullist government. Yet the domestic debate about America moved the nation toward détente, as did the outcome of de Gaulle's efforts to end Washington's hegemony and curb the import of dollars.

Anti-Americanism attained a virulence in the mid-1960s that had not been seen since the early years of the Cold War. It was fueled not only by persistent French anxieties about the American way but also, to a lesser extent, by de Gaulle's attacks on the foreign policy of the United States and by student radicalism that erupted in massive civil disturbances of May–June 1968. Intentionally or not, Gaullism sanctioned anti-Americanism, and the student revolt targeted America's "imperialist" war in Vietnam as it intensified discussion about consumer society. Despite such assaults, anti-Americanism receded and the controversy over the American way abated.

The debate in the 1960s about the American socioeconomic model was far more diffuse than it had been during the previous decade. While America still represented consumer society, discussion of *la société de consommation* itself began to formulate the issue as "consumer society" and also as "industrial" or "postindustrial" or "technological" society, even as a "technocracy." Each of these terms suggested different aspects of social modernity. Thus the debate extended its scope and introduced issues such as the technological imperative, rule by technocrats, environmental concerns, or the limits of the earth's resources. America became less the perpetrator of some universal crime and more a fellow victim of a global dynamic.[1] The American model was usually close at hand when the intelligentsia addressed these subjects, but America was no longer central to the discussion. Critics were less eager to single out the United States and blame the contemporary malaise on American greed or on Yankee-style buccaneering capitalism. For the historian this diffusion makes the debate harder to follow. But it represents a de-escalation of the controversy.

The debate not only became more cosmopolitan, it also became more French. Those who reflected on this problem were no longer speculating, as they had been as recently as the early 1950s, about an Americanized future. France was in the throes of Americanization (see fig. 20). The benefits as well as the costs of affluence were apparent. The French now enjoyed more comforts, easier communication and mobility, greater leisure and prosperity; but they also experienced a life-style centered on acts of purchase, instant obsolescence, incessant advertising, a profusion of foreign companies and products, congested cities, empty villages, a faster pace of life, pollution, and the corruption of language. The discussion was now less about America and more about what was happening to France.

If the debate evolved because the consumer revolution had arrived in France, it changed also because the reputations of the superpowers crisscrossed. America of the 1960s was different. Compared to the 1950s, the United States seemed simultaneously more imposing and yet more vulnerable. On the one hand, American power and presence were expanding on a global scale. If the American military vacated French territory in 1967, everywhere else American power seemed in the ascendancy. And the Western superpower was willing to use or threaten force in regions like Central America, the Caribbean, and, above all, Vietnam. One American senator could now speak of "the arrogance of power." American investments and popular culture accompanied the new global reach. On the other hand, American society was under attack from within. It appeared to be experiencing its own revolution marked by an upsurge in political radicalism, an emerging youthful counterculture, racial violence, and civil disorder associated with the war in Vietnam. The complacency of the 1950s vanished before a new mood of self-criticism. French observers of the American scene studied this

20. Americanization arrives: McDonald's on the Champs-Elysées. (Courtesy François Lediascorn/New York Times Pictures)

"American revolution" and read the analyses of John Kenneth Galbraith, David Riesman, C. Wright Mills, Vance Packard, and Michael Harrington (all of which were now available in translation) as well as the criticism emanating from leaders of the new counterculture such as Herbert Marcuse and Jack Kerouac. President Johnson's Great Society called attention to the existence of poverty. Soviet scientific successes called into question the eminence of American science, if not the entire educational system. America was a troubled giant.

As the United States became less dangerous, the Soviet Union became more so. For the left, in particular, the Russian invasion of Czechoslovakia damaged confidence in the progressive nature of the Soviet model.

The debate about America in the 1960s, finally, differed from that of the early Cold War years because there were new names and a different balance among the disputants. There were some familiar faces such as Raymond Aron, Jean-Marie Domenach, and Maurice Duverger, but most of the protagonists were new. André Siegfried had died; Jean-Paul

Sartre and Simone de Beauvoir, except for their indictment of American policy in Vietnam, were silent. The Communists were quiescent. There were fewer literary mandarins and more social scientists, and the tone was less hysterical and less personal. There was still plenty of politics and passion, but on the whole assessments were more shaded and restrained. And Gallic commentary on America seemed more balanced when the advocacy of the Americanizers became at least as ardent as the argument of the critics.

This final encounter between America and France focuses on how the intelligentsia viewed American consumer society. As in a parallel chapter on the 1950s, I concentrate on the popularizers, that is, the major intellectuals, and on books, reviews, and strategic newspapers like *Le Monde* that interpreted America for the French in the 1960s. However, in this encounter intellectuals share the rostrum with public officials and business managers.

....

If anything, the intelligentsia's vilification of consumer society escalated while America receded as the target of this scorn. It would be impossible here to explore the views of all those who attacked the new abundance, but such an analysis would include individuals like Jean Baudrillard, Bertrand de Jouvenel, Alain Touraine, Georges Elgozy, and Henri Lefebvre as well as literary and philosophical schools like that of the *nouveau roman* and structuralism.[2] These observers predicted that abundance would heighten alienation. They decried the valuation of objects over social intercourse, of personal gratification over the work ethic, and of prefabricated desires over real needs; they demonstrated how the act of purchase became an acquisition of social signs. Baudrillard spoke of consumerism as a pact with the devil in which individuals sacrificed their identity and transcendence for a world of signs. For these critics America became a reference point. The New World was often evoked as an example of this universal phenomenon but was now only rarely accused of being its progenitor. France had become like America. Thus France, it was said, had been victimized by advertising or become a giant suburb—just like America. Or consumerism had coopted the French working class, as it had American labor. Or it had "proletarianized" the youth of both societies. As one observer noted, given the French fetishization of the automobile, the slogan, "What's good for General Motors is good for the United States," now also applied in France.[3]

The issue of consumer society formed part of the radical student agenda in the 1960s. The so-called student revolution of May–June 1968 brought student occupation of the Sorbonne, generated a massive strike movement among the working class, paralyzed Paris, aroused widespread interest and comment, and momentarily frightened de Gaulle himself. Anti-imperialism, in this case opposing the intensified American military engagement in Vietnam as well as glorifying revolution in Third-World countries, was a major feature of the students' ideological discourse. But Americanization or consumer society were not the principal targets of the protesters of 1968. A general sense of disenchantment with the society of abundance informed the most radical members of the student movement, who had learned about this social evil from such leftist critics as Henri Lefebvre and Guy Debord. But the striking workers apparently wanted to participate more fully in the new abundance before they rejected it. And only a tiny fraction of the rebellious youth saw consumerism as an issue. One survey taken after the end of the spring disorders inquired into motives. With respect to *la société de consommation,* only 7 percent of those polled classified it as an issue of first importance while 80 percent relegated it to the status of a minor issue.[4] Topics like university reform and a general libertarian challenge to established authority—be it academic, administrative, political, or social—were more central to these dissenters.

Consumerism, like America, was a marginal issue in the social upheaval of the spring of 1968. After all it was the young, rather than adults, who had most quickly absorbed much of the new consumer culture imported from America. In 1961 when a bomb planted by the Organisation de l'armée secrète (OAS), the diehard secret military advocates of a French Algeria, wrecked a popular commercial establishment on the Right Bank called le Drugstore, an "enormous crowd of young Parisians gathered to mourn," according to Janet Flanner.

The Drugstore had been the most vital center of Americanization for them, for it was a complete replica of what an American drugstore is and means in the American way of life, and had more influence on Paris youth than any American book translated into French, or any Hollywood film ever shown here.[5]

Some might disagree both on how truly American le Drugstore was—in many ways it was a chic Parisian boutique—and with Flanner's estimate of its influence. But the reaction to its bombing does suggest the new prestige of American consumerism—at least to some Parisian youth. For the adolescents of the 1960s were the first generation to have grown up in prosperity. They simultaneously absorbed and rejected consumer culture. They were, in the catch phrase of the time, "the children of Marx and Coca-Cola."

....

This discussion centers on the American way rather than on philosophical discussions about consumer society. Such reflections would lead away from my inquiry because consumer society during the 1960s, unlike during the 1950s, was increasingly treated as a phenomenon apart from America.

As a people Americans were, as in the past, liked. They were praised for their efficiency, dynamism, youthfulness, and generosity, even if they were also supposedly tyrannized by advertising and materialism, plagued with broken households, drugs, violence, and racism.[6] Nevertheless, the French, at least according to a poll of April 1968, saw themselves as resembling other Western Europeans far more than they did the Americans.[7] As a social stereotype, America as a gadget civilization—materialistic, conformist, optimistic, and soulless—persisted.

Such an interpretation appeared in Alain Bosquet's *Les Américains sont-ils adultes?* whose very title evokes the caricature of Americans as *les grands enfants*.[8] Bosquet, a novelist and poet, created an imaginary couple, the Browns, who lived in suburban Chicago, to portray Americans as slaves of material ambition. The Browns were eager consumers who defined themselves by their possessions and who purchased what everyone else owned. Suzy Brown was loyal to her brands—Kelloggs, Colgate, Avon—and learned about life by reading selections from the Book-of-the-Month Club. The Browns stayed at Holiday Inns and ate at Howard Johnson's so that their vacations held no surprises. This suburban couple had no passions. Even their God was, like them, "affable and boring," according to Bosquet. They strove to please everyone and avoided introspective or philosophical conversation. The Browns had no interest in such discussions because America itself was a dream; it was an ideal. This innocent idealism led the French novelist to conclude that Americans might be ahead of Europeans in a material and technological sense, but that intellectually or emotionally they were not adults.

A common lesson drawn from this stereotype was that America continued to be a cultural menace. For the French on both left and right, this persistent fear formed the exception to the growing détente. If other reservations about America faded, culture and *civilisation* remained at risk. On the left, for example, Maurice Duverger, the eminent political analyst for *Le Monde,* published an interview in 1964 dissociating himself from what he called the currently fashionable idiotic anti-Americans, yet declaring:

It must be said, it must be written. There is only one immediate danger for Europe, and that is American civilization. There will be no Stalinism or communism in France. They are scarecrows that frighten only sparrows now.... Today, all that belongs to the past. On the other hand, the pressure of American society, the domination of the American economy, the invasion of the American mentality—all that is very dangerous.[9]

He compared American drivers on a busy Sunday to insects isolated in the shells of their cars moving together in close rank without touching. Once again we hear echoes of Duhamel's *America the Menace.* Duverger declared that in American society the basis of values was "money and gadgets." Contrast that, he said, to the situation in a country like France:

The employee who reads your gas meter possesses a scale of aristocratic values. He can distinguish perfectly among a nouveau riche, an intelligent man, and a poet. Whether he knows it or not, the cultural ensemble that is at the core of his attitudes is shaped by a completely different historical legacy. I think this element will help us resist pressure from America.

Duverger concluded that Europe's problem was to reach affluence without passing through the "transitory phase of Americanization."

On the right, in the eyes of many French traditionalists, Americanization also signaled the degradation of culture. This reaction only reiterated what had been voiced as far back as the 1920s, if not earlier. In the 1960s Gaullism, and not only because of its anti-American foreign policy, inspired some of this conservative counterattack. De Gaulle, for example, appointed André Malraux as his first minister of culture. Malraux, who had once declared that America was a country without culture, busily promoted a traditional conception of high culture. It is not surprising that this atmosphere nurtured polemics against American cultural colonization.

The most discussed tract of this genre was René Etiemble's *Parlez-vous franglais?* Etiemble, a professor of comparative literature at the Sorbonne and former fellow traveler who had studied in the United States, warned his countrymen that they were being subtly colonized by the creation of a synthetic tongue that he dubbed franglais. Words, syntax, grammar, and even meaning were being corrupted by American exports. As an example of this barbarism Etiemble cited the report of a journalist written during the Algerian war:

21. Ads in franglais. (Courtesy John Ardagh)

J'étais au snack-bar! Je venais de prendre au self-service, un bel ice cream; la musique d'un juke-box m'endormait quand un flash de radio annonça qu'un clash risquait d'éclater à Alger. Je sortis, repris ma voiture au parking et ouvris mon transistor. Le premier ministre venait de réunir son brain-trust.[10]

The perpetrators of this linguistic bastardization were numerous. They included NATO, scientists, doctors, journalists, advertisers and retailers, magazines like *Elle,* sports, television, and restaurateurs. But significantly not the intelligentsia. Servile merchandisers abused the French tongue to be stylish—"It's new, it's different." Noting how prepositions and articles disappeared in slogans like "Buvez Coca-Cola," Etiemble commented, "Soon, the partitive will disappear from French so that Coca-Cola earns lots of money in France" (239). Once the French language was a precise tool of analysis, but now it was becoming a synthetic tongue fit only for suggesting immediate sensations. The phrase becomes a word, the word an object—obviously the better to sell the object (see fig. 21).

For this academic the issue was far more than linguistic purity. *Parlez-vous franglais?* was patently a Gaullist polemic.[11] NATO publications, for example, urged European officers to speak American so that they would come to think like Yankees. For Etiemble linguistic chauvinism was a means of cultural defense against America: "As long as the French still speak French and think like Montaigne or Diderot, they can't easily make them swallow, like so many thrushes, all the affronts of the American way of life" (235). First comes "Buvez Coca-Cola," then comes "Make love like a cowboy" (239). Language was essential to cultural identity. This Sorbonne professor, who was not highly regarded by the intelligentsia, was not above sheer nastiness when describing the United States. He related personal incidents that demonstrated Yankee anti-Semitism and racism, suggesting that in borrowing language one also imports another society's vices. There was even an invidious comparison with the Nazis.[12] In his view Americans offered the French a choice—either speak franglais or disappear as a nation. To which Etiemble preached cultural resistance. Indeed not only de Gaulle's government, but also those of his successors in the 1970s and 1980s, made efforts to guard the language. This theme of a cultural war was to gather momentum in the next decade.

Expressions of Gallic cultural superiority, like those of Etiemble and Bosquet, were commonplace. Even prolonged visits to America did not always allay such astringent perceptions. When a congressional advisory committee in the early 1960s assessed the State Department's overseas cultural activities, including its academic exchange program, it found that of all the nations involved France was the exception.[13] The reaction of French participants to the exchange was distinctly less favorable than the attitudes expressed by any other nationality. A higher proportion of French exchange scholars criticized American education, art, and music and doubted that the experience had been personally or professionally rewarding. Why were the French the exception? The answers given by the congressional report are familiar: French esteem for their own culture bred disdain for other cultures, damaged national prestige, and bred defensiveness; humanistic training made them unappreciative. The State Department, according to one recommendation, should modify its exchange program by inviting scientists and engineers rather than humanists. The latter seemed overly defensive about their superiority and made anti-Americanism their favorite sport.

· · · · · · · · · ·

Political assaults, as well as cultural aversion, persisted in the 1960s. Charging the United States with imperialism was a course available to both right and left. On the right there were Gaullist polemics against the hegemonic pretensions of the United States in Europe and around the world. One Gaullist tract claimed Washington's diplomacy was subservient to corporate giants, making NATO a "colonial pact." American capitalism, from this partisan perspective, was a danger to world peace because its boundless desire for profits and power could escalate into war, genocide, and even a nuclear apocalypse.[14]

The left, as much as the Gaullists, targeted the United States as an imperialist danger. Colonial wars fought by the French in Indochina and Algeria and by the Americans in Southeast Asia heightened sympathy for the plight of the Third World. American military intervention in Vietnam made anti-imperialists of an entire generation who recoiled at the horrors of napalm and rejoiced at victories of a Third-World David against the Yankee Goliath.[15] At the same time Socialists like Gaston Defferre warned of American imperialism encroaching on Europe via foreign investment and preventing the emergence of either an independent or a socialist Europe.[16] A notable example of this neoimperialist critique came from a reporter who covered America for *Le Monde*, Claude Julien. The latter spoke less for student radicals than he did for much of *Le Monde*'s readership.

Julien had studied at a Midwestern university and written extensively about the United States before publishing his celebrated book in 1968 entitled *L'Empire américain*. In an earlier study, relying on C. Wright Mills, Julien had analyzed the American power elite and emphasized the shadows that fell over the American way of life—racism and poverty, waste and consumerism, megalopolis and suburbia.[17] In his 1968 book Julien predicted the demise of this "American empire," noting its internal turmoil and the contradiction between skimming off the resources of the globe while preaching the American way to the Third World. If Americans accounted for only 6 percent of the world's population, they consumed the bulk of such resources as oil and metals. The gap between the rich and poor nations was growing and the United States had come to rely on dictators and military force to protect its access to raw materials. Increasingly, internal and external reality contradicted the American dream.

To Julien the American model was inappropriate for Europe. Adopting American techniques such as management or mass advertising, as some urged, would be insufficient to give Europe a standard of living similar to that of the United States. For Europeans to attain American prosperity, they would need access to a comparable volume of raw materials imported from the Third World at prices profitable to the industrialized north and ruinous to the underdeveloped south. Europe following America's strategy would end up with a puny version of the American dream and help precipitate a confrontation between the rich and poor nations. Imitating America would make Europeans accomplices in neoimperialism and earn them the wrath of the Third World—just what the United States faced in Vietnam.

Le Monde's reporter thus took issue with Gaullist economic strategy, which appeared to be fostering American consumerism, and tried to design a leftist alternative. "It is not indispensable to enter into the frenetic circle of consumer society to assure economic expansion," he wrote.[18] We do not need a new car every two years; and we do not need to consume a kilogram of newsprint every Sunday. Julien urged Europeans to develop sectors that Americans seemed to neglect such as leisure, culture, public works, and education. Economic growth need not come from expanded internal consumption alone—instead of manufacturing cars for the French, the automobile industry could build tractors and farm machinery to sell to the Third World.

L'Empire américain thus linked economic imperialism to consumer society. "Consumer society does not exist without empire and it will collapse with it" (507). Julien resisted the American model of consumer society because it gave prosperity to the privileged few at the expense of three billion other human beings. He also rejected the American model because it transformed society into what David Riesman called the "lonely crowd."

Presented as a paradise, consumer society carries in itself its own hell, with its areas of poverty, its expressions of racism, its injustices, its sometimes unbearable tensions, its hypocrisies, its neuroses, and its explosions of violence (510).

Fatally linked, consumer society and neoimperialism faced a violent end.

Such neoimperialist analysts, among whom were the Communists, continued to contend that America was guilty of exporting its benighted capitalist model to the rest of the world.[19] While these theorists ascribed American expansiveness to a need for cheap resources, other leftist critics attributed it to American arrogance—to Americans' sense of being the chosen people who exported their consumerism because they assumed they were making others happy.[20] Here was the thesis that America imposed its system on the rest of the world under the cover of a universal mission to make others free and prosperous. For most French critics the big American ego was difficult to accept.

....

In general leftist-inspired anti-Americanism modulated during the 1960s despite the anti-imperialist demonstrations of student radicals and the attacks of writers like Julien. This occurred in part because of Gaullist usurpation of the terrain. If de Gaulle was anti-American, then the left had to reconsider its position.

Le Monde, the anti-American voice of St-Germain-des-Prés, no longer systematically criticized Washington's foreign policy and refused, as we have seen, to give de Gaulle's anti-American policies its unqualified support. The newspaper shifted to reporting rather than editorializing about American society and politics. There were ironic, even caustic, comments about America, and an air of disapproval still informed its pages—Beuve-Méry after all remained editor and Julien was one of its authorities on America—but the newspaper was gradually exchanging Cold War antipathy for a more nuanced stance.

At the same time *Les Temps modernes,* Sartre's review that had once devoted considerable space to unmasking America, came to discount the United States as an unredeemable society. Where the review once carried long critical studies like those by Simone de Beauvoir and Claude Alphandéry, it now published occasional pieces on subjects like the John Birch society, the Weathermen, or black revolutionaries as it took note of the emergence of American fascism or its opposite, leftist militancy. Otherwise *Les Temps modernes* ignored America.

Far more significant for the evolution of the left's perception of American society than the contemptuous neglect of Sartre's review was the mellowing of *Esprit,* the other major interpreter of America for the intelligentsia. One might even speak of the conversion of its editor, Jean-Marie Domenach.

Domenach's review of Julien's *Empire américain,* in which he found Julien's reasoning mistaken—calling it a kind of mechanistic, Leninist interpretation of imperialism—but approved his conclusions, is illustrative.[21] To Domenach the underdevelopment of the Third World was not, as Julien believed, simply the result of American imperialism. Europeans were also responsible. Nor did the United States, given the Soviet invasion of Prague, monopolize imperialism. Julien was correct, however, in concluding that Europeans should reject an imperialism that resorted to violence, destroyed Third-World cultures, and endangered world peace. The danger of the American empire for Europeans was more subtle than Julien realized. It was not, like the Vietnamese conflict, a matter of open combat. Resistance took another form. To resist being enveloped, Domenach counseled, Europeans must strengthen themselves culturally and morally.

Julien's crude anti-Americanism, in the view of *Esprit*'s editor, led him mistakenly to condemn all Americans. Universities in the United States, which Domenach came to know from his frequent visits during the 1960s, were havens of anti-imperialism. Moreover, America was Europe's daughter and carried many of the parent's values. And Domenach applauded America for its new voices of dissent, whose "style of life is opposed to everything that we detest in the United States"; its social experimentation; and its capacity for self-correction.[22] Americans, for example, would probably face problems like pollution before Europeans did.

Despite his new sympathy for America and his comprehension of its diversity, the editor of *Esprit* remained an irreconcilable critic of America's frenetic pursuit of production and consumption. He reproached consumer society for "debasing human beings and human relations by systematically exploiting every element of covetousness." He evoked Heidegger to liken consumerism to the "descent of being and its submersion in things."[23] It sterilized man's creative and emotional powers; it divided mankind into races, classes, and developed as opposed to underdeveloped countries; it brought waste, overcrowding, and pollution; and it formed a "society of domination" in which a social order based on affluence served ruling elites. Pollution, crime, and drugs evoked not a Marxist economic crisis but a moral and spiritual crisis. "A society oriented toward material enjoyment and increasing the standard of living secretes such poisons."[24] It is no surprise that Domenach applauded the students' protests of 1968 and hailed them as victories for free speech and imagination and for what he saw as a rejection of consumer society. He proclaimed that "the critique of consumer society has moved into the streets." Domenach construed 1968 as "the first post-Marxist revolution in Western Europe." "Europe . . . has sketched the first response to the fascination with Americanism."[25]

Yet for all these misgivings, to the editor of *Esprit*, America announced Europe's future. In fact, "American society is already half installed in our future." He pleaded:

As long as our society does not show that it has chosen a path different from the one already chosen by the United States, all the sad truths that one must tell about the United States will concern us equally. We shall have their crimes. Could we also have their universities?[26]

Just as Domenach became more receptive to America, various of his colleagues on the left discovered the "other" or "good America" at the end of the decade. For leftists an "imperialist" America was even more hateful than an anti-Communist America, but a "revolutionary" America, especially one attacked by the Gaullists, made them question their assumptions about the fortress-of-world reaction. The left's stereotype of America, along with its Marxist dogma, concealed this discovery from some who continued to dwell on America's underprivileged and exploited—the victims of capitalism and affluence. But others found a new revolutionary camaraderie across the Atlantic. The radicals of the 1960s discerned an ideological fellowship with the civil-rights movement, antiwar militants, radical ideologues, feminists, black liberationists, hippies, dropouts, and other members of the new American counterculture. French students borrowed what they believed represented American counterculture—including jeans and the music of Bob Dylan and Joan Baez—and honored blacks as victims of the system.

Perhaps the most acclaimed examples of this new discourse from the left were Edgar Morin's *Journal de Californie* and Jean-François Revel's *Ni Marx, ni Jésus,* which appeared simultaneously in 1970.

Morin, a prominent sociologist of contemporary culture, held solid leftist credentials even though he had long since broken with Marxism. Despite his preconceptions Morin discovered during his 1969 stay in California that he liked America, or elements of it, though he continued to profess the standard list of grievances about imperialism, racism, materialism, gadgets, and vulgarity—for example, the pet boutique in San Francisco that sold pearl necklaces for dogs. America was "the most barbarous of civilized countries, but also the most civilized of barbarous countries (all countries being barbarous)."[27] In Morin's eyes, Americans seemed obsessed with organization and function to the point that the disorder of an Italian grocery in La Jolla seemed like an "oasis in this geometric desert" (50). If he once had no sympathy or interest in America, Morin's visit to California made him confess, "I love America" (76).

America, according to Morin, faced internal rupture. The most advanced country in the world was also confronting "the first symptoms of civilization's inevitable crisis" (136). In Morin's view it was precisely because America was the most advanced bourgeois, bureaucratic, capitalist society that it was also fostering real revolution (162). The Apollo astronauts watching Los Angeles strangle in its own smog became a metaphor for America's social contradictions. Similarly Morin stressed that the nation fighting an imperialist war in Vietnam was also generating a powerful peace movement. And if Americans massacred civilians at My Lai, *Time* magazine also published an examination of conscience about the massacre that, in Morin's view, had no parallel in any French journal during the Algerian war. For "America is not only the country of imperialism, it is also the country of the adolescent crusade" (262).

This "adolescent crusade" captivated Morin, who plunged into California's counterculture by attending peace demonstrations and rock concerts and by visiting communes. Young people attracted his admiration because of their social and cultural experimentation that aimed at inventing a new way of life. The French sociologist perceived that this revolt grew out of individualistic, bourgeois consumer society; but it also broke with this society because it opposed an individualism of sensation, joy, and exaltation to an individualism of property and acquisition—"the hedonism of being (the cultural revolution) radically opposes the hedonism of having (bourgeois society)" (134).

He realized that this revolt against the American way of life was American too—for it emerged from an American sense of brotherly and sisterly goodness and openness. Morin reveled in the hedonism of California of the 1960s, the commingling of the races, the free and easy ways of the "flower children," while sensing a tragic naivete and even destructive introversion in their reliance on drugs. And repression seemed imminent to him in 1969 because what once appeared as social deviance now loomed in the eyes of the majority as a threat to the American way of life. "These Anglo-Americans devote themselves with industry and seriousness to efficiency: they are the leaders in technologizing the world, but they don't know how to live, and the art of living will come from those they despise" (149).

What America's young rebels disliked about their society, in Morin's analysis, were those features of America that the French left had habitually scorned. Yet their dissent was more cultural and existential in character and aimed at revolutionizing a way of life, whereas the rebellion of French student radicals was more ideological. Morin hoped American youth could shun the suffocating dogma of Marxism and maintain their innocence. "The young are saving or killing American society. Or rather they are saving and killing it at the same time" (231).

When another prominent intellectual from the left went a step beyond Morin and proposed America as the prototype of the only truly revolutionary society, as did Jean-François Revel in *Ni Marx, ni Jésus,* then one might conclude anti-Americanism was fading within St-Germain-des-Prés itself—that Parisian quartier most associated with Yankee-baiting.

To be sure, Revel was something of an *enfant terrible* known for his pugnacious attacks on the establishment. Still he was a respected man of letters and a well-known journalist writing for *L'Express*. In *Ni Marx, ni Jésus* he provocatively hailed America as the land of revolution in order to display what was wrong with France. Revel regarded the left's anti-Americanism as a symptom of its own paralysis. The French left was committed to ideological purity, not action. "The Holy Grail of socialism has attained a state of such ineffable purity that there is no place for it anywhere in the present social situation."[28] Revolution could not come from those who also took pride in being antiscientific and antitechnological as well as anti-American. Gaullism fared no better in Revel's view—he found it archaic and authoritarian. Left and right, according to Revel, kept France from advancing.

As Morin did, Revel contested the left's stereotype of America as fascist, racist, and conformist. Europe killed twice as many Jews as those now living in the United States, Revel observed, yet the left dared to label America as anti-Semitic. And Europe, not America, gave the world Hitler, Mussolini, Franco, and Pétain. Revel criticized the left for its doctrinaire anti-Americanism and cited *Le Monde* for its slanted reporting. At the anecdotal level he recalled a conversation with a friend who said Americans were uncultivated and prudish; Revel had taken exception to his remark, citing data that Americans read more books than the French. His friend's only response: that was because most of the books Americans read were obscene.

But in America there was hope. For in the New World the voices of dissent were far stronger than anywhere in Europe, and America possessed the economic and technical leadership to support revolutionary change, as well as the freedom and respect for law to permit it.

The United States is the country most eligible for the role of prototype nation for the following reasons: it enjoys continuing economic prosperity and rate of growth, without which no revolutionary project can succeed; it has technological competence and a high level of basic research; culturally it is oriented toward the future rather than toward the past, and it is undergoing a revolution in behavioral standards, and in the affirmation of individual freedom and equality; it rejects authoritarian control, and multiplies creative initiative in all domains—especially in art, life-style, and sense experience—and allows the coexistence of a diversity of mutually complementary alternative subcultures (183).

Revel asserted that "the American left is probably the world's only hope for a revolution that will save it from destruction" (127). For in America there was the black revolt, the feminist attack on masculine

domination, the youthful rejection of exclusively economic and technological goals, concern about poverty and the environment, a movement
for consumer protection, and a radical new approach to moral values.
And, most important, the antiwar movement was destroying imperialism
from within. The common basis for this dissent, according to Revel, was
rejection of a society dominated exclusively by profit and ruled by
competition. In the American counterculture human beings were once
again an end and a value in themselves. Revel's version of Montesquieu's
Persian Letters found in America the prototype of the good modern
society. He concluded, provocatively, that Europeans' self-esteem made
it impossible for them to admit that Americans were more civilized,
democratic, and revolutionary than they themselves were (188).

In retrospect we can see that this discovery of the "other America"
by leftist intellectuals like Domenach, Morin, and Revel, as well as
Gaullist usurpation of Yankee-baiting and the Soviet's waning star,
initiated the gradual retreat of anti-Americanism among those who had
been the strongest source of criticism. The magnitude of this shift can
be seen in Morin's preface to a translation of David Riesman's *Lonely
Crowd*.

American society has ceased to be an "impossible" society for us, a society
without political parties and structured ideologies, without any revolutionary
protest, containing only technocrats in "human relations" and "public relations." . . . We sense that, from the point of view of civilization, America not
only preserves the present of Western civilization, but also the future of the
human race.[29]

America was receding as a target for the leftist intelligentsia.

· · · · · · · · · ·

Along with the mellowing of the left, of equal significance for the
future was the growing enthusiasm for the American model. I employ
the term "Americanizer" for this perspective without implying that its
proponents intended to meet *le défi américain* by indiscriminate imitation. To a striking extent these enthusiasts were drawn from the ranks of
public officials, managers, and social scientists rather than the literati.

For the Americanizers there was an alternative to resistance. Americanization, they contended, was essentially a global imperative and, on
the whole, a beneficial process that could be tamed and adapted to
preserve the French way. Selectivity and lucidity were the keys.

These self-styled realists recognized that Americanization might be
accompanied by various afflictions: the fetishism of products; a constant

escalation of unsatisfied desires; cultural homogenization; a pampered but restless youth; dependence on alcohol, drugs, and psychoanalysis; and impending ecological disaster. But the analysts believed that these assorted pestilences could be avoided or mitigated and that the benefits outweighed such troubles.

An author of a college text on American civilization, for example, rejected extreme interpretations of Americanization.[30] It was not an apocalypse, according to this expert, and the accounts of theorists like Simone de Beauvoir and Cyrille Arnavon were distorted by passion and politics. He debunked the notion that the French were any less materialistic than the Americans and scoffed at the Gallic rationalization of a richer spiritual or inner life. Like it or not, America was the model of global development; Europeans could either accept and adapt to it or passively submit and sacrifice their identity.

The national economic planning agency, founded by the ardent Americanizer Jean Monnet, championed the modernist stance. Officials in the agency who in the early 1960s were trying to map out the future shape of France had to address the imminent confrontation with America. One such expert, Bernard Cazes, pointed out that it was unfair to trivialize consumerism as the pursuit of artificial needs. The family of the 1960s might be not only comfortable but also happy in its dreamlike world of consumer products. Cazes stripped away the irrelevant moralizing about consumer society in order to present it as an economic mechanism constructed around rational human choice.[31]

These planners, taking their cue from the Gaullist government, insisted that in order to be competitive France would have "to imitate an economy that surpasses Europe in growth." At the same time they also wanted to design "an original society" different from that of the challenger.[32] They believed that the richness of Europe's traditions and its different scale of values would virtually "guarantee that the structure of consumption" in France would be different from what existed across the Atlantic. In order to reach "a new civilization" and ward off the American menace, the planners sketched a social-economic future based on growth, high consumption, and competitiveness that also paid attention to public goods and services, the quality of life, aesthetics, and the participation of citizens in the collective effort of remodeling the nation. Pierre Massé, who headed the planning agency at the time, took issue with the consumer society and tried to define "a less partial idea of human beings."[33] Many social scientists, who on balance saw more virtue than vice in the New World, also contributed to what was both a "modernist" affirmation of America and a critique of French institutions.

During the 1960s publishers like Seuil and Gallimard made available translations of the work of such American social scientists as David Riesman, John Kenneth Galbraith, and William A. Whyte, which offered a critical arsenal to assess contemporary society. Translations also appeared of studies about France written by American or European-born social scientists living in America. Publication of *A la recherche de la France*, for example, made available the critical assessments of French institutions by experts like Stanley Hoffmann, Charles Kindleberger, and Laurence Wylie.[34] Indeed the very concept of France as a "blocked" or "stalemate society" with its internal rigidities, compartments, privileges, and hierarchies that impeded "modernization"—a term that connoted a dose of American-style decentralization, self-reliance, and mobility— was a contribution of authorities like Hoffmann and Michel Crozier. Crozier, who was the sociologist most closely associated with this critique, largely drew his conception of French resistance to modernity from his experience in the United States and his knowledge of American social science.

By the 1960s Crozier had earned a reputation as a gadfly of St-Germain-des-Prés. He was one of the principal interpreters of both America and its social science to the Parisian intelligentsia. Writing about a foreign country in order to critique one's own society became a French literary genre even before Montesquieu's *Persian Letters;* Crozier, like Revel, made good use of this literary technique.

Examining the intellectual climate of America in early 1968, Crozier chided French leftists who pictured the United States as a "brave new world" run by trusts and technocrats and smothered by comfort and conformity. "Nothing is more false," he wrote, than to conceive of contemporary America in the mode of William Whyte's *Organization Man*. "Men of action in modern America have never been less conformist."[35] What was striking in 1968 was not complacency, as in Eisenhower's America, but "the aggressive confidence in human reason and in the American capacity to use it to solve all problems" (7). The French sociologist cited the heightened rationality of American managers to calculate and adjust means to ends. The hero of this new managerial rationalism was Robert McNamara, who brought to government techniques developed in private industry. It was Europeans who suffered from the timidity of "the organization man"—weighed down by the closed world of the administrative corps and elite schools. It was America that was run by young Turks—for example, the innovative scientist who, blocked by his employer, found venture capital to build his own firm.

After criticizing both the intelligentsia and the managerial and bureaucratic elites of France, Crozier turned to American counterculture to demonstrate that America was advancing in still another way. The progress of hyperrationality, the "harsh sun" of calculating cost-efficiency, the French sociologist acknowledged, disturbed America's youth. He recommended to Americans that they allow more room for inefficiency and spontaneity so that participants could tolerate the rigors of the new managerial rationality. The psychedelic bohemia that captivated the young proved not that America was sick, but that it was "in the process of a profound shift" (5). America was once again on the move. Conversely, France was not.

That Crozier's essay appeared in *Esprit,* as did excerpts of Morin's journal, suggests the extent to which the intelligentsia had evolved in its thinking about America. An even more prominent spokesman for this cautiously affirmative position was yet another social scientist, Raymond Aron, who did not address America directly but treated it as the most advanced example of "industrial society"—a category that embraced all Western societies.

Industrial societies, according to Aron, were all caught up in the same dynamism of economic growth, technology, and scientific research; they consumed the same products, used similar management techniques, and mixed state intervention with market forces. Differentiation within this class of societies was essentially cultural. The basic choices within these Western societies over such questions as private consumption versus public service were not polar opposites but decisions about shares. Europeans, Aron believed, would, as they had in the past, continue to choose different alternatives than Americans did. "Whether successful or not, resistance to certain aspects of American commercialism will continue in Europe, at least verbally."[36] Aron himself awarded high priority to these cultural differences: "What must remain inviolate is not progress or the rate of growth, but culture—that is, the totality of works of the mind" (204). He refused to predict to what extent technology was going to dilute cultural diversity, but he was skeptical about the prospect of a coming universal civilization, since the goal of culture was a unique way of life and a singular expression of creative freedom.

Like the other "realists," Aron reflected on both the promise and the penalties of economic development. If material well-being was a prerequisite for the good life, he asked, "in what does the good life consist?"

and "who defines it?" The ultimate source of disillusionment with economic progress was the continuing conflict over modern values—equality, personality, and universality. Expanding production did not automatically solve social problems or give individuals a reason to live. It often made things worse. It created new losers—the young and old, the unskilled and the disadvantaged—all those who could not compete and who went unrewarded. And the consumer was bombarded by the media as ever rising targets of consumption evoked envy and even anger from those who felt deprived. Even the richest nations like America had not satisfied people's wants because desires escalated along with rising productivity. And the whole system devalued personality. "Just as each individual aspires to equality he also aspires to individuality," Aron wrote (xv). "The world in which industrial man must live has lost its enchantment," he concluded (203).

A measure of the shifting mood was the growing popularity of Aron—whom Domenach had once debunked as "the sociologist of *Le Figaro,*" a conservative paper. Aron's book on industrial society appeared in Gallimard's paperback series and sold over 50,000 copies. And his success was greeted with approval from some quarters on the left. Pierre Nora, for example, wrote in 1963: "Aron has surpassed Camus. Does industrial society interest the public today more than Sisyphus? Let's accept the omen."[37]

Within the ranks of the Americanizers, in contrast to Aron's subtle and almost tortured assessment, was the rooting section of unabashed enthusiasts. These included familiar names like the influential Jean Monnet and the prolific Jean Fourastié.[38] Since the days of the productivity missions, the former had been preaching the American way to public officials. "The French," Monnet lectured, must learn to accept "the psychology of Americans," that is, "the disposition to change constantly."[39] And in his popular books the economist Fourastié had been telling the French about the promise of the coming postindustrial society. If the leap to the future required a stage of turmoil and confusion, Fourastié predicted a new stability would be reached when people would enjoy brief work days and more leisure and education. He believed that as time went by the novelty of consumer goods would fade and individuals would choose to consume less and do more. The "tertiary civilization will be brilliant, the machine letting human beings specialize in things human."[40]

Equally sanguine about the future were prominent managers from both the private and public sectors like Jean St-Geours and Louis

Armand. Here we encounter a veritable celebration of Americanization—but a celebration that also recognized risks. St-Geours, who made
his career in public finance, wrote a personal testament, *Vive la société de
consommation*, that charted the progress of industrial society in lifting
humanity from its present needs and fears by providing a high standard
of living and greater freedom to address its problems.[41] We shall pass
through the materialistic phase, he wrote, and in the postindustrial future
the modern individual will be freer, better informed, more confident,
and thus better able to fulfill higher personal, and even spiritual, goals.
At the same time St-Geours rhapsodized about such consumer products
as television and the automobile. He expressed his delight about a
Sunday drive to the Loire valley with his car radio playing Beethoven.
Armand, who had modernized the French railways after the war, pointed
out that no one was forcing Europeans to Americanize.[42] We adopt
American technology—typewriters, television, home appliances, nylon,
computers, and ballpoint pens—because we find them beneficial. We do
so, he said, because we welcome technology and ignore the costs in
congestion, pollution, and upheaval. To Armand the world, whether or
not the French approved, was living in the "American era."

The 1960s also witnessed the Americanization of French business
management. Executives like Jacques Maisonrouge of IBM-France,
consulting organizations like CEGOS (Centre d'études générales d'organisation scientifique), and business journals like *L'Expansion* proselytized American managerial techniques—but that is a subject unto itself.[43]

For the growing contingent of "yes-sayers," America was a source of
inspiration.[44] It had not turned out to be Duhamel's nightmare. The
way forward, from this managerial perspective, lay neither in servile
imitation nor in systematic criticism but in learning from the American
model. Jean-Jacques Servan-Schreiber, the editor of the newsweekly
L'Express, issued this perspective's most widely discussed invitation to
Americanization. His book, *Le Défi américain*, has already appeared in
the context of American investment (in chapter 7) but also bears on this
discussion because it synthesized and popularized the realist or modernist position.

Servan-Schreiber saw the American challenge emerging from economic dynamism—a dynamism generated by tapping human creativity
through organization and education and by rewarding initiative and
mastering change. Modern power derived, not from natural resources
or capital, but from "the capacity for innovation, which is research, and
the capacity to transform inventions into finished products, which is

technology."[45] He praised American management and called the close association of business, university, and government the "basic secret" of American success (168). Servan-Schreiber, citing Michel Crozier, asserted: "The Americans know how to work in our countries better than we do ourselves" (182).

Le Défi américain was a "call to action." Not much time remained for Europe to "counterattack" before it became an American satellite. "If America is the place where decisions are made, and Europe where they are later put into application, within a single generation we will no longer belong to the same civilization" (44). The United States, Canada, Japan, and Sweden would enter postindustrial society, but Europe would not. The choice for Europeans was either to remain passive before the American challenge and become an economic backwater and an "annex of the United States" or to imitate the American way and thus join the race to the postindustrial future.

The stakes were higher than merely maintaining a comparable standard of living. If the day came when American subsidiaries called the tune and Europe's drive for freedom and independence flagged, then "the spirit of our civilization will have broken." "Without suffering from poverty, we would nevertheless soon submit to fatalism and depression that would end in impotence and abdication" (191). American business would one day cross "the threshold of the European sanctuary" and take control of publishing, newspapers, recordings, and television.

[Then the] channels of communication by which customs are transmitted and ways of life and thought formulated—would be controlled from outside. Cairo and Venice were able to keep their social and cultural identities during centuries of economic decline. But it was not such a small world then, and the pace of change was infinitely slower. A dying civilization can linger for a long time on the fragrance left in an empty vase. We will not have that consolation (192).

In order to meet the American challenge France had to compete with the United States in all the essential areas of technology and science. If the French were content with being a big Switzerland, highly specialized in a few areas, he argued, they could eventually have a high standard of living but without developing an autonomous civilization.[46] A European counterattack meant mobilizing the continent's creativity by pooling the region's resources and talent, establishing European-wide multinationals, and creating a truly federal Europe that could formulate, fund, and direct an industrial and scientific policy. Ultimately the counterattack was a matter of political will or ambition rather than economics. Europeans could meet the challenge if they willed it, if they federated and embarked on internal reforms to democratize and open their societies.

The way forward to postindustrial society required massive social and cultural, as well as economic, overhaul. Servan-Schreiber's notion of France as a blocked society owed much to the work of other social critics such as Michel Crozier and Stanley Hoffmann. The journalist argued that the secret of America's success lay in the confidence it placed in its citizens—in their ability to decide for themselves and in their intelligence. He inverted the Gallic cliché about the gadget society by stating that "American society wagers much more on human intelligence than it wastes on gadgets . . . this wager on man is the origin of America's new dynamism" (253). His message was that the French needed to encourage initiative and delegate authority, for example, to decentralize management and local government. Once their energy and creativity were released, they could "produce phenomenally."

The message of Le Défi was perplexing. Europe must Americanize in order to escape being run by Americans. That is, Europeans must selectively imitate American ways, for example, in the scale of enterprise, management techniques, research and development, education, and, above all, individual initiative. But for Servan-Schreiber such borrowing did not mean the continent should duplicate America. He held out Sweden and Japan as alternative ways to postindustrial society.[47]

When asked if he were anti-American he answered, "It's not a question of being anti-American, but it's not necessary for us to become 'pseudo-Americans.'"[48] Nor did he blame Americanization on America. Europe would have followed the same path even if the United States were lagging rather than leading:

The contempt and distrust of America felt by many Europeans is really their own fear of a future that was chosen by their fathers when they launched the first industrial revolution, and which they themselves reaffirmed by starting the second (193).

Thus he urged Europeans to study and imitate America without offering it as a model.

Virtually every review of Servan-Schreiber's book agreed that there was a dangerous American challenge and that he had correctly formulated it as a lag in technology, management, and research rather than capital.[49] The disagreement came over solutions. The most common response was to accept some measure of Americanizing therapy. Among those who at least nominally endorsed *Le Défi*'s thesis were managers like Louis Armand and Marcel Dassault; public officials like Jean Monnet, François Bloch-Lainé, and Albin Chalandon; and journalists or economic experts like Michel Drancourt, Raymond Cartier, Jean Fourastié, and Pierre Lazareff. Giscard d'Estaing, the former minister of finance (and future president of France) who had once forcefully resisted American investment, had only praise for Servan-Schreiber's analysis and his solutions.[50] A few prominent Socialists, among them Gaston Defferre, who had been the candidate of *L'Express* for president in 1965, praised the book. Spokesmen for corporations like IBM-France, however, preferred to let existing multinationals lead the way rather than create new Eurocompanies.[51] Just as Servan-Schreiber took exception to the Gaullists' handling of the problem, others, mainly on the left, disapproved his remedies.

Such critics, including Claude Julien, were quick to fault *Le Défi* for preaching Americanization as the way to resist America.[52] François Mitterrand, then head of the Fédération de la gauche démocrate et socialiste, echoed the alarm *Le Défi* sounded, but objected to finding a solution in a liberal rather than a socialist Europe.[53] Others argued that Servan-Schreiber's conception of Europe was too "capitalist" to assure either independence from America or a social democratic future. His rejection of nationalization, his neglect of class analysis, and his disregard for the Soviet Union, from this perspective, seemed wrongheaded. The Communists likened Servan-Schreiber's notion of a European community to a capitalist club and saw no solution in merging French monopolies with other European monopolies.[54] The proper response, for the Communists, was to build socialism on a national basis.

It should be no surprise that many of those who responded to *Le Défi* found French civilization at risk. The emphasis was, borrow if we must; but find another path to development than the one blazed by America. Thierry Maulnier of the Académie française, for example, acknowledged that the United States had become a global model, even for Socialist countries, but he contended that Europeans should use their values to chart an alternative to the Americans' endless pursuit of consumption.[55] *Le Monde,* true to form, saw Americanization as cultural self-destruction:

It's not sinning by chauvinism or traditionalism to think . . . that European culture still has a word to say, that it, more than ever, has its values to express, in a civilization that risks becoming, for the first time perhaps in the history of the world, a *civilization without culture.*[56]

Even a technocrat like Michel Drancourt argued that the French and the Europeans could not ward off America by submission but must somehow give Europe its own personality.[57] Servan-Schreiber had made much the same argument—that transfers from America need not mean duplication of the American model but that some imitation was necessary if Europe were to survive as an independent civilization.

The controversy stirred by *Le Défi américain* in 1967–68 expressed Gallic alarm over American expansion, especially over a threatened economic independence and an endangered national identity. Response to the best-seller suggests growing acceptance of a measure of Americanization as the necessary therapy.

....

During the 1960s while de Gaulle was correcting the imbalance in Franco-American relations, America lost its centrality in the domestic debate about socioeconomic modernity. The way the intelligentsia construed the issue was to make it more diffuse, as discussion moved away from America toward reflection on subjects like postindustrial society or indigenous problems that accompanied abundance. America had become more a fellow victim of a universal process than the agent of some international disaster. Indeed, Americanization in the form of American products and fads had progressed so far—from McDonald's and jeans to franglais and pop singers with American names like Johnny Hallyday—that familiarity seemed to dampen anxiety. There were those, to be sure, on the left and the right, from Claude Julien to René Etiemble, who continued to blame the United States for exporting its economy or its culture. But most of those who interpreted the coming modernity excused America or made it merely the most advanced example of a general development. Thus Raymond Aron's judicious and cautious assent became representative of the new discourse. Most believed France could adapt to American ways and some welcomed a healthy dose of Americanization to open French society and its economy.

On the left, where a new sympathy for America emerged, dogmatic Marxists might continue to rail about monopoly capitalism, but others like Domenach, Morin, and Revel found a common camaraderie of dissent in the two countries. If there was still a "bad America" of technocrats, dollars, and the Pentagon, there was another America—the one associated with the civil rights movement, Berkeley, the Black Panthers, hippies, communes, and Herbert Marcuse—which the left found appealing. Soviet misbehavior in invading Czechoslovakia assisted this turnabout by causing a loss of faith among the faithful. The next

decade would bring the long march of the left away from its revolutionary past and from affiliation with Marxism and would bring it closer to
Western democracy and the United States.

The 1960s were an example of historical serendipity. A decade that
saw some of the most virulent expressions of anti-Americanism since the
early 1950s also reduced acrimony. The 1960s ushered in an era of
détente, and not only among the intelligentsia: at the very end of his
presidency even de Gaulle softened his tone toward Washington. The
decade eased antagonism and nuanced perceptions, opening the way for
the new, more affirmative, mood of the 1970s and 1980s.

CHAPTER 9

Vive l'Amérique

*An Epilogue from 1970
to Euro Disneyland*

By the mid-1980s outsiders were saying, and with some astonishment, that France had become the most pro-American country in Western Europe. The French had apparently replaced anti-Americanism with unqualified enthusiasm for all things associated with America. "Made in America" suddenly held the same cachet that Americans have always awarded to products coming from Paris. Shoppers or strollers on the Champs-Elysées could eat at McDonald's; students at the Sorbonne dressed like American preppies; and the smart set at St-Tropez sported T-shirts with such fractured phrases as "International Best Country Club." America and American ways had become à la mode (see fig. 22). Many speculated that Gallic anti-Americanism had vanished. The change was obviously less sweeping than some outsiders thought; yet a considerable, even dramatic, turnabout had occurred. The French had been seduced.

A study of the postwar response to the American way requires at least a brief sketch of the evolution of attitudes since 1970. Not only will such an epilogue complete the story, but it will strengthen conclusions we might draw about this phenomenon.

The 1970s marked a transition toward the philo-Americanism of the 1980s. Despite continuing expressions of anti-Americanism, especially in economic policy and culture, the tide was shifting. The 1970s accelerated what was already evident in the 1960s. The wave of anti-Americanism under de Gaulle's presidency had concealed the longer

22. French cowgirls. (Courtesy AP/Wide World Photos)

trend away from animus; in the first post-Gaullist decade, momentum developed for the conversion that would be so complete by the 1980s that one could speak of a Gallic "American mania."

In a political sense the scaffolding for anti-Americanism began to come apart during the 1970s. Control of policy shifted from one anti-American group on the right, the Gaullists; they also modified their position. De Gaulle resigned from the presidency in 1969 and died a year later. His successor, Georges Pompidou (1969–74), took a less aggressive stance toward Washington, though friction remained; the subsequent head of state, Valéry Giscard d'Estaing (1974–81), who was conservative but not a Gaullist, was even more pliant. A former minister under de Gaulle, Alain Peyrefitte, published *Le Mal français* in 1976, a best-seller attacking the nation's stifling bureaucratic centralism and urging a more open society and more competitive practices in fields like education and the economy. Peyrefitte's therapy gave some observers the impression that even the Gaullists were preaching Americanization.[1]

In international affairs during the 1970s, French preoccupation with American hegemony began to fade. Détente, or a general relaxation of tensions, came to characterize East-West relations. Washington under Presidents Nixon, Ford, and Carter pursued a less ideological and more accommodating policy toward Moscow, and their efforts brought such accomplishments as agreements on strategic arms limitations and on European security and cooperation.

Within the context of détente, French perceptions of the superpowers changed markedly from what they had been under de Gaulle, when freeing France from American tutelage took priority. Soviet misbehavior aroused growing awareness of a Soviet menace. The publication in 1974 of Aleksandr Solzhenitsyn's revelations about the Soviet labor camps, the so-called Gulag, marked the belated discovery, at least among the French left, of Soviet totalitarianism. Confidence in the Soviet model, already badly shaken by the armed invasion of Czechoslovakia in 1968, ebbed rapidly especially for those who had retained faith in the Soviets as a progressive society. Russian military intervention in Afghanistan in 1979 only confirmed suspicions that the threat to French independence lay more to the East than the West.

Events in the United States contributed to altering Western Europeans' perception of vulnerability to the Soviet superpower. Washington began to appear weak and indecisive: first came the defeat in Vietnam, then the near impeachment of President Nixon, followed by the vacillations in American policy under Presidents Ford and Carter; yet another humiliation in Iran gave the French more concern about Washington's firmness than its hegemony. American "arrogance," which had seemed so oppressive in the 1960s, faded in the diplomatic defeats and political turmoil of the 1970s. A majority of the French in 1976, for example, expressed a lack of confidence in Washington's leadership.[2]

Under Giscard, French policy appeared more Atlanticist than it had been under either of his Gaullist predecessors. He adopted a more conciliatory outlook toward the United States, made some gestures toward French reintegration into NATO, and, in general, accepted the growing détente between the superpowers. But tension persisted between Paris and Washington. There were differences over the Middle East and the economic crisis initiated by the international oil cartel (OPEC). Giscard pursued détente even after the Soviet invasion of Afghanistan and long after Washington believed the West was being duped by Moscow. If in essence Giscard continued Gaullist policy of French independence, he was perceived by some as being soft on America. He also adopted a personal political style, for example in his campaign tactics, that prompted one newspaper to call him "the first Americanized president."[3]

The old issues that had prompted anti-Americanism, however, remained alive in the 1970s. There was the envy of a superpower by a nation that had not quite fully accepted its relative decline in world affairs. And American economic and technological leadership, made apparent by the continuing influx of American-based multinationals, was a constant reminder that, no matter how they tried, the French could not catch up. Above all else was the vexing suspicion that French cultural eminence was in eclipse. More than ever, anti-Americanism focused on these threats of economic subordination and cultural degradation.

Giscard's efforts at opening the French economy to world trade stirred opposition from both right and left. Gaullists, Socialists, and Communists protested against his internationalism and urged a more protectionist stance.[4] They perceived a growing French dependence on the United States. A case in point was the end of a project initiated by de Gaulle to build a national computer industry, the *Plan calcul*. In 1975 the government accepted a merger with Honeywell-Bull that seemed to represent surrender to an American-run firm. Gaullists warned that American multinationals and American banks were taking control of the dynamic sectors of the French economy and relegating France to a specialized, but subordinate, place in a global economy dominated by the United States.[5] "Multinationalization" of the economy, from this perspective, was a trap. Subordination to American multinationals was only one aspect of Giscard's economic posture that roused such prominent Gaullists as former ministers Jean-Marcel Jeanneney, Michel Debré, and Michel Jobert. Jobert, who had been Pompidou's foreign minister, denounced Giscard's liberalism as an abdication and described America's loose monetary policy as plunder and its waste of resources as profligacy.[6]

On the left a revived Socialist party under François Mitterrand sought an alliance with the Communists and remained committed to a hard-edged Marxist analysis of capitalism. The left promised, once elected, a rupture with the conservatism of the Gaullists and Giscardiens who had controlled the Fifth Republic since its birth. The Socialists denounced American imperialism and the injustices of American society, announced their sympathies with the Third World, and adopted a Jacobin (read: nationalist) posture on cultural issues. Fearing that Giscard's liberal policies risked foreign takeover of vital industrial sectors and jeopardized French social welfare accomplishments, the Socialists, like the Gaullists, sought a "reconquest" of the domestic economy. Those on the left of the party labeled their colleagues, in particular the followers of Michel Rocard who criticized this Jacobin line, as "the American left."[7] The presence of the Rocardian faction, however, indicates the party's division over an American policy.

Georges Marchais, the head of the Communist party, leveled similar protests against Giscard's alleged capitulation to American business.[8] And the PCF continued to denounce the arrogance of American imperialism. But détente between East and West served to mute the tones of this formerly shrill source of anti-Americanism. In 1972, for example, L'Humanité published a series of articles on America complimenting its workers on their efficiency and industry and acknowledging that the American people had the highest standard of living in the world.[9] Yet the party maintained that the quality of an American worker's life, marked by insecurity and anxiety, was no better than that of a French worker. The Communists also acknowledged that Americans enjoyed considerable personal freedom, yet claimed these freedoms were often illusory. The Communists asserted that the class struggle persisted in spite of the ideology of "Americanism" that appeared to offer opportunity and tolerance. But the message of these former Yankee-baiters was now mildly flattering and far less polemical than ever before.

The danger of cultural assimilation, like the fear of American economic and technological domination, also roused the anti-Americans during the 1970s. And this issue was available to both left and right. Jacobin tendencies among the Socialists were to lead them, once they attained power, toward an aggressive and protective nationalist cultural policy. Taking up the struggle for the right were both Gaullists and certain young intellectuals who formed the New Right. Among the

Gaullists, Michel Jobert juxtaposed the words "COBOL" and "Kabul" to strike a parallel between American and Soviet imperialism. To Jobert the computer language of COBOL was more insidious, because it went unnoticed, than was Kabul, referring to the Soviet takeover in Afghanistan.[10] Another Gaullist, Jacques Thibau, contributed a book, *La France colonisée,* which warned against the Americanization of the "French soul." Thibau observed that one of the most advanced forms of cultural dominance occurred when the colonized themselves shared the idea the colonizers had of them. This was happening to the French, he claimed. For now they believed the American caricature of France as a backward, provincial society. Thibau reserved special scorn for intellectuals like Michel Crozier, Raymond Aron, and Alain Peyrefitte for their advocacy of Americanization. He warned that the French might commit *ethnocide*—ethnic suicide—if they continued to submit to American cultural manipulation.[11] In a similar book titled *La Guerre culturelle,* a professor of literature warned that if the French continued to imitate the Americans, they would become "Gallo-Ricains" (Ricains = *amé-ricains*) living in a "ZOA" (Zone of American Occupation). Americanization, in this view, was not the victory of one culture over another, but the invasion of a commercialized culture based on the negation of culture that mixed the arts, styles, and religions of all countries into an "undefined hamburger that was not American but simply *usaïque.*"[12] Another conservative academic at the Collège de France, Jean-Marie Benoist, drew a parallel between the two tyrannies of uniformity, the Soviet Gulags and the American media:

The police brutality of the Gulag, whose operation has been laid bare by Solzhenitsyn in his explanation of how the cancer spreads throughout the social organism . . . is the counterpart, albeit asymmetrical, of course, of the way the media and opinion polls are used as channels of propaganda by Atlantic imperialism in order to condition the people of Western Europe and the Mediterranean basin.[13]

On the extreme right some younger writers seized on the old theme that America's rootlessness and egalitarianism made it the enemy of Western civilization. Employing some rather tortured logic, intellectuals like Alain de Benoist argued that the United States posed a greater danger than did the Soviet Union. Western American-Atlanticism was the principal enemy because it came closer to the universalism, cosmopolitanism, and egalitarianism that destroyed all cultures. The New Right preferred "peoples" and "cultures" to the individualism of Western democracy. Because of American civilization's Judaic and Puritan past it was, these conservatives alleged, indifferent to beauty. Americanization killed all cultures. In his anti-American fervor Alain de Benoist wrote:

It's not true that there is, on one side, a socialist, totalitarian world and, on the other, a "free world" in the shape of Disneyland, of which American society would be the natural leader. That's a fable in which the Soviet foil serves as an alibi for the introduction of a "new domestic order" equally disquieting. The truth is that there are two distinct forms of totalitarianism, very different in their effects but both formidable. The first, in the East, imprisons, persecutes, and physically bruises; but at least it leaves hope intact. The other, in the West, leads to the creation of happy robots. It air-conditions hell. It kills the soul.[14]

If forced to choose between the two evils, Benoist wrote that he would wear "the Red army cap" rather than "eat hamburgers in Brooklyn."[15] While the vocabulary may be different, the substance of this charge belongs in the mainstream of cultural anti-Americanism dating from Georges Duhamel.

At the level of popular perceptions, the Gallic stereotype of Americans survived the arrival of consumer society. If the French continued to say they liked Americans, the caricature of *les grands enfants* also remained. Americans were seen as optimistic, wealthy, informal, and dynamic. Opinion in the 1970s affirmed the Gallic perception that no matter what the Americans possessed in power and prosperity, the French still lived better and were more civilized. According to texts read by French schoolchildren, Americans lived in a consumer paradise yet were slaves to comfort, beholden to business, and had little culture in a European sense.[16] American society was marked by conformity, rootlessness, and violence. Polls recorded French disapproval of many aspects of America—from an alleged lack of family togetherness to a lack of fresh food.[17] An informal survey of Parisian high-school students revealed that at a manifest level the students were anti-American. But the latent content of their responses showed that these young people were deeply impregnated with American values and attitudes— including their preferences for films and clothes, their attitudes toward family traditions, and their vocabulary.[18] Anti-American posturing seemed, in this instance, to be an expression of youthful conformity or a ritualistic reflex. Similarly, apparent expressions of anti-Americanism were sometimes not what they seemed. Thus a popular song of the time whose title, "Les Ricains," suggested sarcasm, in fact told of a GI who had died for the liberation of France during the landings at Normandy.[19]

Times were changing. In 1977 *Le Canard Enchaîné,* the satirical political journal, proclaimed that America had become chic. Speaking English and praising the dynamism of the United States was now de rigueur among the upper classes who supposedly wanted to Americanize everyone. In a mocking tone the journal described how American television programs dominated prime time; how music companies preferred English titles to sell records; and how the newspaper *Libération,* with its young leftist audience, expressed itself in "French-américain." For all its preening about Gaullist grandeur, the country depended on America for everything from its security to its mass culture. *Le Canard* concluded:

To be modern is to imitate the Americans. That's the French trouble: there is no modern way of being French. France, once the "mother of arts, letters, and science," has become a little copycat. Yesterday, we were the locomotive, today, the caboose.[20]

....

The appearance of Gallic *américanomanie* in the 1980s was accompanied by a momentary defensive reaction. Yet, compared to the waves of anti-Americanism of the early 1950s and the mid-1960s, what occurred in the early 1980s was a mere ripple. This time some Socialist politicians tried to trigger the familiar reflex—but, significantly, with little success. The French, including the leftist intelligentsia, had become indifferent to such appeals.

In 1981 the Socialists and their Communist allies came to power for the first time since the birth of the Fifth Republic. Led by their new president, François Mitterrand, the Socialists launched a vigorous program of domestic renovation to bring the nation closer to a socialist future. Such a coalition and such an agenda were not well received by the conservative American government. And Mitterrand's stance on certain international issues, such as relations with the Third World, gave Washington further pause. Under its new conservative president, Ronald Reagan, the United States seemed to be taking the opposite direction in both domestic and foreign affairs. Reagan's reputation as a Hollywood actor also contributed to an initial coolness by the Socialist government and the French people toward the Republican administration.

Jack Lang, the minister of cultural affairs, ignited controversy in 1982 by denouncing an unspecified (read: American) financial and cultural imperialism that appropriated consciences, ways of thought, and ways of living.[21] Not long afterwards another Socialist minister, Jean-Pierre Chevènement, warned about the danger of cultural Americanization:

Never since the Hundred Years' War has our people known such an identity crisis. Our language is threatened with extinction for the first time in history. America has become the last horizon of our young because we have not offered them a great democratic design.[22]

This Socialist outburst led nowhere. It was not long before Lang swallowed his words and professed an interest in closer Franco-American cultural exchange. What surprised the Socialists was that there was so little response from the intellectual community to their cultural Jacobinism. A major shift had been occurring among the intellectuals that put them at odds with their hereditary allies, the Socialists. This complex story of the intelligentsia's migration away from the Soviet promised land toward America can only be sketched here.

As late as 1976, Pierre Nora wrote of an "impossible dialogue" between French and American intellectuals.[23] This incommensurability derived, according to Nora, less from French affinity for Marxism than from differing conceptions of revolution. Whereas the American revolution established a consensus and made leftism marginal, the French revolution destroyed consensus and made revolution the *mater et magistra* of the French intelligentsia. "Whereas in France, revolution is the eternal future of a country with a long memory, in America it is the eternal past of a nation that has no memory."[24] Stewards of the revolution, the French intellectuals remained locked in their own social stratum impervious to America.

But the "impossible dialogue" became possible not long after Nora's essay. Perhaps the best analysis of why St-Germain-des-Prés discarded its anti-Americanism belongs to Diana Pinto, who argues that anti-Americanism was linked to the historic role of revolutionary, engagé intellectuals.[25] Once the promised land of the revolution, the Soviet Union, looked more like a Gulag and once the United States lost its invincibility, the intelligentsia was cast adrift. Setting out to revise its own national past, the group discovered traces of the Gulag in its revolutionary tradition. The star of French culture, which had continued to shine so brightly through the 1960s, began to dim as the intelligentsia searched for a new cultural identity based on democratic, pluralistic, and libertarian values. Simultaneously the negative stereotype of America collapsed in the turmoil of the 1960s and French intellectuals discovered that American universities were cultural oases.[26] While Parisian intellectuals did not necessarily become Americanophiles in the late 1970s, they did become open to America. A kind of reunion with America occurred when the intelligentsia decided to place itself within the tradition of the democratic revolutions of the eighteenth century rather than claim inspiration for the totalitarian revolution of 1917. We can round off this analysis by noting that the Parisian infatuation first with structuralism and then with deconstruction also diminished interest in such engagé subjects as American society.

Other analysts of the conversion of the postwar intelligentsia call attention to social and economic changes.[27] As the number of university graduates soared, an enlarged and diluted class of intelligentsia appeared, its tastes better served by journals like *Libération* than by the old leftist party publications. The professionalization of intellectual enterprise and its specialization also denied intellectuals the grand scope of earlier years. Meanwhile, television and the media changed incentives and messages. And the culture of the mass media undermined the elite's control over cultural products. Culture was being redefined at the expense of those who had traditionally monopolized it. Such changes eroded the global, universalist vocation of the intelligentsia and moved the generation of the 1980s toward greater modesty and a centrist, modernist position that was no longer anti-American.

Whatever the reasons for this so-called crisis of the intelligentsia, the results were striking. There was a disaggregation of its traditional role. Some intellectuals became academic specialists and relinquished their right to speak for humanity; others discovered a shared community of values with all of Europe, in particular Central and Eastern Europe; and still others fell silent. The Sartrian model was obsolescent. One example of this migration was the switch of onetime admirers of Maoist China, Philippe Sollers and Julia Kristeva. They turned toward America to discover alternative solutions to the European impasse over political and social injustice.[28] And a spate of books and essays about America in 1983–84 suggested the new affirmative mood.[29] What best marked this change of heart was the enthusiastic reception awarded to the publication of Raymond Aron's *Mémoires* in 1983. An academic who had been castigated by the left for his Atlanticism during the Cold War was now honored.

In the place of the engagés stepped the "media intellectuals" to preach the American way in the 1980s. Among the new Americanophiles were former *gauchistes* who, in reviews or newspapers like the *Nouvel Observateur* or *Libération,* promoted everything American either as a means of escape or as a way of enhancing social status. Another group of more pragmatic intellectuals sought to borrow American technology and remake France in the image of Silicon Valley. And a third group of more ideological Americanophiles projected their own market beliefs on Reagan's America. Yet none of these Americanophiles, according to Pinto, tried to understand America in its complexity and contradictions. America remained, in their eyes, what it had always been—a storehouse of objects, technologies, and dreams that they would, from time to time, borrow or reject. America in 1985 still did not occupy the center of the French intellectual landscape or fill the role of a model in the way that the dream of the Soviet Union once did. In this way the "impossible dialogue" survived the new mania for America.

The eclipse of the revolutionary tradition, the redefinition of culture and its disaggregation, and the end of the intelligentsia's monopoly, combined in the 1980s to dry up a historic source of anti-Americanism. This conversion meant that for the first time the views of St-Germain-des-Prés about America and popular opinion converged. The historic split over America between much of the intellectual elite and the average population, if not closed, had at least been narrowed.

One consequence of this transformation was the indifference with which the leftist intelligentsia greeted the Socialists' attacks on American culture in the early 1980s. The former had moved away from Marxism and zealous Third Worldism toward liberal-democratic values and a new appreciation of America as a source of dynamism and freedom. When Jack Lang tried to enlist their support by attacking the cultural destruction wrought by American popular culture, the intellectuals were outraged because Lang made no reference to Soviet violations of human rights.[30] Lang's crusade against American cultural imperialism seemed ridiculous to those who were concentrating their attention on Soviet totalitarianism and the liberation of Eastern Europe. For example, Jean-Marie Domenach, who had made a career of chastising America, took exception to the government's chauvinist and defensive tone. Domenach recommended less denigration of other cultures and more attention to restoring the prestige of French culture.[31] Georges Suffert, a prominent journalist, ridiculed Lang and the Socialists for their vulgar anti-Americanism.[32] The Socialist government could not attract the intelligentsia to its cultural barricades and openly complained about the silence of the intellectuals. An era that reached back at least to the 1930s had closed.

This did not mean that the intelligentsia endorsed America or ended its attacks. Jean Baudrillard, for example, in a dyspeptic study entitled *Amérique* still inveighed against the falseness and artificiality of the New World and reiterated, though in a postmodernist vocabulary, condescending clichés about the cultural wasteland.[33] But even Baudrillard wistfully observed, "America is the original version of modernity. We are the dubbed or subtitled version."[34] Other prominent men and women of letters signed a manifesto against the Americanization of French radio and television.[35] But the intellectuals' attention was no longer riveted on the American menace.

Among the ruling Socialists there was also a historic change. Faced with economic disaster in 1982–83, the Socialists dropped their attempt to find their own way to socialism and forgot their pledge to break with capitalism. Entrepreneurship and the market were back in style. State intervention and economic planning were passé. President Mitterrand made a personal pilgrimage to Silicon Valley in 1984—reminiscent of the productivity missions of the 1950s—to discover the secret of American venture capitalism and high technology. His ministers shelved the cultural crusade against American popular culture.

At the same time as the intelligentsia and the Socialists deserted the cause, the unnatural alliance of Communists and Gaullists that had tilted French attitudes against the United States lost its political edge. The Communist party broke with the Socialists and suffered severe electoral losses. The Communists' critique, which had abated anyway, counted for less and less. Meanwhile the Gaullists became less irascible. According to a 1984 poll, of all the political parties, the Gaullists most closely aligned themselves with American positions in foreign affairs and domestic economic policy.[36] And in 1986 when the Socialist government gave way to conservatives under Prime Minister Jacques Chirac, the head of the Gaullist party, there was an even more avid courting of the American market model. Now Ronald Reagan, the "cowboy president," became a French hero because he had led the United States and the West out of a decade of "stagflation." Apparently the French confirmed the Gaullist flirtation with Reaganism since they, far more than the British or the West Germans, would have voted for Reagan's reelection in 1984.[37] Free enterprise à l'américaine was in style. As if to crown the American fad, the Chirac government completed negotiations with the Disney corporation to build its European version of the Disneyland amusement park outside Paris.

The Socialist-inspired wavelet of anti-Americanism during the early 1980s was engulfed in a flood of American mania. By the mid-1980s it was obvious to any visitor that French attitudes toward America were more friendly than ever before. Everywhere America took on the appearance of a fad. The trendiest restaurant in Paris became a grill serving

23. A trendy French youth emulates Americans, 1986. (Courtesy William T. Coulter)

California cuisine and Napa Valley wines. Fashionable youth sported American college sweatshirts, such as "University New Jersey" [*sic*] (see fig. 23); the quintessential American designer, Ralph Lauren, opened a boutique on the place de la Madeleine.[38] By this time over three hundred thousand French tourists per year were traveling to the United States. And if Gallic visitors no longer found glamour in Hollywood, they continued their fascination with *El Lay* (L.A.).

Ordinary citizens, who had always been more or less sympathetic, now voiced almost unqualified approval. Polls taken between 1982 and 1988 suggest that only a tiny fraction of the French felt antipathy for the United States.[39] More of the French people considered themselves pro-American than did British or Germans.[40] With respect to the media, free enterprise, political institutions, and education, America now set a "good example" (though the French public believed the United States also set a "bad example" for the problem of integrating minorities).[41] Meanwhile, the Gallic stereotype of Americans remained largely intact. Americans continued to convey an image of power, dynamism, wealth, and freedom.[42] But, to a lesser extent, Americans also appeared violent, racist, nonegalitarian, and morally lax. Far fewer than ever before thought of Americans as young, generous, and naive. Thus an essential element of the stereotype, that of American immaturity, seems to have vanished.

A measure of the new affinity appeared in French attitudes toward American business and culture. In contrast to the 1960s, a slight majority now wanted to see American firms increase their investments in France.[43] With respect to American cultural influence, the French in 1988 did not find it excessive in such fields as literature, cuisine, or clothes.[44] And, pace M. Etiemble, very few were shocked by franglais. The only areas where they considered American influence excessive were television, cinema, and, to a lesser extent, music and advertising. But a majority still professed to be poorly informed about the United States.[45]

Perhaps the most important cause for this gradual realignment— besides what has already been presented about the shifting agendas of political parties, especially those of the Gaullists and the Socialists, and the transformation of the leftist intelligentsia—derives from the growing similarity of the two nations' socioeconomic orders. Economic development did effect a certain uniformity. And the move toward a consumer society, so visible in the 1960s, formed part of the French way by the 1980s. It is not without some irony that American visitors to France began to complain of a loss of Frenchness. A faculty couple from California, for example, lamented that France had become "civilized," pointing out that while Americans were rediscovering cotton handkerchiefs, grandmother's jam, homemade bread, wood stoves, and small cars, the French had been converted to frozen food, carpeted bathrooms, dishwashers, Kleenex, and shopping centers.[46] By 1984 *Le Monde* could proclaim, in an survey entitled "Uncle Sam's French," that anti-Americanism made little sense because France was Americanized. American ways were so much a part of France that they no longer provoked either fascination or rejection. America was *banalisée* or commonplace. Capping the historic turnabout, the author of the inquiry announced, "*Le Monde* itself seems to have given up its anti-American cult."[47]

The French themselves contributed to the dilution of anti-Americanism by adopting a more modest assessment of their nation's place in world affairs. De Gaulle had provided the needed boost to self-esteem in the 1960s, but Gaullist calls to *grandeur* disappeared from the agenda of more pragmatic presidents like Pompidou and Giscard as well as from Mitterrand's goals. If during the general's presidency a substantial element of public opinion believed that France was one of the world's leading powers, there had also been doubts. And without de Gaulle's leadership, aspirations adjusted to the realities of a global distribution of power that relegated France to a lesser place. By the early 1980s almost two out of three French citizens believed France was a middle-rank power. Fewer than one-fourth still held to the notion that it was a great power.[48] One winegrower in Bordeaux insisted that his children watch the morning broadcast of an American news program to show them how little news about France was televised—demonstrating how unimportant France had become in the eyes of the rest of the world.[49] Increasingly de Gaulle's vague, but grandiose, aspirations, which had led to jousting with Washington, seemed illusory. Yet the sense of a French global vocation and a gritty determination for independence survived.

There are two final reasons for the French change of heart. It was probably no coincidence that anti-Americanism diminished as new dangers emerged. These came from immigration and from European integration. It may be impossible to prove, but it seems likely that the supposed threat to French identity posed by Arab and Islamic immigration distracted attention from America. By the early 1980s, among the most disruptive domestic political issues was how France should treat its growing cultural diversity—especially its large Arabic population. On the extreme right, a xenophobic political party whose program centered on curbing, if not expelling, Arabic immigrants quickly gained prominence by attracting sizable numbers of votes in elections. These initial electoral successes of the Front national occurred in 1983–84 precisely at the moment when anxiety about the American cultural challenge waned. Perhaps at some deep unarticulated psychological level the Arab and Islamic presence seemed to the French public equally, or even more, menacing than the American.

Finally the movement for European unity, which gathered momentum after the mid-1980s, also posed a clear and present danger. The proximate opening of economic, and even political, frontiers among the twelve nations of the European community could be construed as undermining national independence and cultural uniqueness. To right-wing nationalists, in particular, Frenchness faced external immersion in Europe as well as internal subversion from immigration. Americanization no longer had exclusive rights to the charge of endangering national identity: it had to share space in the dock with Europeanization and immigration.

By the end of the 1980s only traces of what once seemed like hereditary Gallic anti-Americanism survived. The political, ideological, social, and economic bases of the phenomenon had eroded. What remained was essentially the cultural danger, even though that was much diminished. And the mood of France was decidedly pro-American.

One should not conclude, however, that we have seen the end of anti-Americanism, because much of what caused it survives today in American geopolitical hegemony and technological-scientific leadership, prickly Gallic pride, the stereotype of *les grands enfants*, and French cultural snobbery. We can expect a certain ambivalence even today.

Ambivalence about America and consumer society should come as no surprise because the very language of the French expresses such ambiguity. The word *affluence* evokes not only "abundance" but also a "crowd"; "les heures d'affluence" refer to rush hours. Whereas Americans conceive of affluence as an indication of wealth and happiness, the French also glimpse in the term a teeming conformity. When an international group of scholars assembled in the mid-1980s to examine the recent history of French attitudes toward America, they discerned equivocation. They noted, despite a rampant mania for all things American, persistent ambivalence about America. "As model or foil," they concluded, "America has never ceased to fascinate and exasperate the French, as well as, on occasion, inspire all sorts of fantasies."[50] Appropriately the cover of their anthology depicted the Statue of Liberty against an orange sunrise swarming with helicopters reminiscent of the film *Apocalypse Now*.[51]

··········

The opening of Euro Disneyland outside Paris (at Marne-la-Vallée) in the spring of 1992 has once again raised the issue of the American danger. This controversy reveals not only the current French attitudes toward Americanization but also confirms the analysis of this study.

Even before the opening the Walt Disney Company, like American corporations of the 1950s and 1960s, encountered trouble of all sorts. There were charges that the French government had given away land, money, and services to attract the park. Local residents complained of everything from increased traffic to noise from the nightly fireworks. Then there was the employee dress code proscribing beards and moustaches for men, and requiring natural hair color as well as "appropriate underclothing" for women. Labor unions protested that Disney's regulations about appearance were an attack on the French sense of individual liberty and dignity. One spokesperson from the Communist-controlled CGT complained that the government, by allowing the company to impose such discipline, had awarded Disney extraterritorial rights and that the region was becoming "the fifty-first American state."[52] But, above all, there was the cultural menace.

It should come as no surprise that the inauguration of the park provoked some intellectuals, especially on the left, to attack. Alain Finkielkraut said Euro Disneyland was "a terrifying giant step toward world homogenization." The Socialist deputy Max Gallo predicted Disney would "bombard France with uprooted creations that are to culture what fast food is to gastronomy." One journalist recalling "the American challenge" of the 1960s warned of the coming "Disneylandi-zation" of French châteaux, museums, and historic sites. Unless people resisted, he argued, France would follow America toward "the industri-alization of leisure."[53] *Le Monde* called the park a "slice of the American dream" affordable only for the well-heeled visitor. It evoked images of abundance and antiseptic happiness—which were "a long way from the real America."[54] Others criticized the park from the perspective of myth making, aesthetics, values, creativity, and spectator participation.[55] The most quoted comment was that made by theatrical director Ariane Mnouchkine, who denounced the park as "a cultural Chernobyl." Jacques Julliard, an editor for *Le Nouvel Observateur,* hoped a fire might destroy it![56]

But there was ambivalence and evasiveness on the left. And 1992 was not 1962. One writer for *Le Nouvel Observateur,* after noting that "Euro Disneyland, like hell, is paved with soft caramel," admitted that he enjoyed visiting the park, wearing Mickey Mouse ears, eating popcorn, and touring its attractions.[57] Jack Lang, the Socialist minister of culture who a decade earlier had warned against American cultural imperialism, snubbed Euro Disney—he explained that he was too busy to attend the opening. Lang expressed his regret that Euro Disneyland afforded little place for attractions representing European countries. While admiring the technical prowess of Disney (Lang visited Disneyworld in Florida and found it "quite fascinating"), he worried that Euro Disneyland might mark the beginning of an American takeover of the leisure industry in France. Yet the minister denied he was hostile to American culture and said he was one of "the principal promoters of modern American culture. I hold dear the America of bold and inventive ideas. The question is different when speaking of standardized culture. . . . This is less a question of American culture than of marketing."[58] In the name of diversity Lang called for vigilance against the massive diffusion of the "subproducts" of American culture. Thus he applauded artists like Jack Nicholson and Ella Fitzgerald but deplored those who mer-chandised "subproducts." Lang's distinction seems rather arbitrary, since he decorated an American actor associated with the cinema of violence, Sylvester Stallone, with the award of *chevalier* of arts and letters. One spectator who observed Lang posturing before the television cameras with Stallone commented caustically, "Envy and snobbery often go together."[59]

Equally reminiscent of the past was the astonishment of the Americans at Gallic criticism. Representatives of the Disney corporation defended the park by saying, "It's not America, it's Disney." One employee responded more truculently: "Who are these Frenchmen anyway? We offer them the dream of a lifetime and lots of jobs. They treat us like invaders."[60] The president of Euro Disney, Robert Fitzpatrick, said he nearly fell off his chair when he heard about Ariane Mnouchkine's comment. After all, she had accepted his invitation to visit the California park where she had posed with Mickey Mouse. The French scrutinized the amusement center as an important cultural phenomenon while the Disney corporation defended it as mere entertainment. Fitzpatrick refuted the argument of a Parisian museum director who claimed no visitor to the museum would also tour Marne-la-Vallée. "Diversion is also a form of culture," Fitzpatrick responded; "the French know it well. Have they forgotten?"[61] To those like Lang, who criticized the park for not being more European, the Disney people replied that they believed Europeans wanted a real Disneyland, that is, an American park featuring attractions like Frontierland and Mainstreet U.S.A.

Given the current fascination with America, it is to be expected that the French response to Euro Disneyland would not be dominated by the critics. The cover of one newsweekly announced, "Culture: Let's not fear America." The philosopher Michel Serres said that he was indifferent to Euro Disneyland except for the fact that the park was going to make his commute to Paris more crowded since his train linked the capital with Marne-la-Vallée. Jean-François Revel refuted the leftist critics of America as he had twenty years earlier (in *Ni Marx, ni Jésus*). "If French culture can be squashed by Mickey Mouse," he wrote, "or more exactly by simply moving Mickey geographically, it would have to be disturbingly fragile." Moreover, Revel argued, culture always circulates and, in the case of Euro Disneyland, California was merely repackaging for Europeans such European stories as Cinderella and Pinocchio. According to Revel, French culture was not being colonized and if any culture was in crisis, he contended, it was that of America with its fad for political correctness and other forms of "neoprovincialism."[62]

An American expert on popular culture put the debate about Euro Disney in perspective when he observed, "American popular culture doesn't erase all vernacular alternatives. The new semiculture coexists with local cultures more than it replaces them." American popular culture was becoming "everyone's second culture."[63]

In the 1990s the dilemma about Americanization focuses, now more than ever, on the issue of culture. Some purists dread the inroads of American popular culture, yet the opening-day crowd at Euro Disneyland included such intellectual celebrities as Bernard Henri-Lévy. Or as one writer remarked, the French "remain fascinated by America. . . . I am convinced [the ideas of] Merleau-Ponty are still of value, but tomorrow I am going to Euro Disneyland."[64] Meanwhile thousands of French men, women, and children ignore the dangers of the cultural Chernobyl and join the daily throng at Marne-la-Vallée. And if the arrival of Mickey Mouse to the Paris region represents an incursion similar to those we have seen and a further step toward Americanization, this American animal has also adapted to the land—at least he speaks French.

CHAPTER 10

Reflections

The French Face Americanization

As we look back at the French response to Americanization in the postwar era, a few general questions invite our further
attention. What still needs answering is why there was such determined
resistance to the American way. What did the French perceive was at risk
if the American model crossed the Atlantic? To raise this question is not
to assume some intrinsic superiority for the American way. Far from it.
Rather it assumes that the latter part of the twentieth century produced
a universal imperative—the pursuit of abundance—that captivated the
French, as it has almost everyone else. A second question focuses on the
discussion in France about American society. Has the debate over the
American model fundamentally changed since the war—or has it ceased
altogether? A related, and equally difficult, topic is Americanization. Has
a French identity been preserved despite Americanization? I begin my
reflections with this last issue.

Americanization, in a sense, did occur. That France took an American
path toward consumer society is hardly a surprise, since the French acted
like everyone else in this respect. They began their rush toward consumer
society during the 1950s and quickly adopted most of the products,
mores, and values that accompanied this revolution. They realized, for
example, one of the dreams of the Marshall Plan missionaries—personal
ownership of an automobile. Contemporary France is a different society
because of the changes associated with Americanization. France engaged
in the pursuit of abundance and in so doing developed, among other

things, a more productive and more service-oriented economy, a high standard of living, a social status dependent on levels of consumption, a more commercialized culture, a comfortable habitat—even suburbias and a youth culture.

In retrospect the enormity of such changes makes the resistance of the early Cold War years seem hidebound. Louis Aragon's outrage over a "bathtub civilization" seems to us like little more than the spasm of a cantankerous ideologue. Similarly Jacques Tati's film satires about modernism seem quaint today. But this does not mean that the totality of Americanization has occurred or that it was, or is, accepted. There has been both an incompleteness and a resistance to the process that leads me to conclude that France has not been Americanized.

In many ways the French did not succumb to Americanization. The deluge of consumer products, the new life-style centered on the act of purchase, and the profusion of mass culture did not sweep away French differences. French kitchens were electrified and McDonald's sold hamburgers on the Champs-Elysées, but French cuisine did not disappear. Indeed, fast food represents only a small fraction of commercial meals prepared in France compared with those consumed in Britain and the United States today.[1] Or American management, including Harvard MBAs, may have attained a certain cachet in French business circles, but this did not mean that enlightened French managerial practice was identical to that of corporate America. As for *la France profonde,* what modernizers consider the most backward regions of the countryside, it has fought a rearguard action to adapt and thus preserve some traditional ways. In stores, American products share shelf space with French products and a host of others drawn from around the world. And if American films occupy an increasingly large share of cinema viewing, part of the market has remained a French preserve.

The Americanization process was not akin to a foreign invasion or colonization that swept away all in its path. It was more a change brought about by selection and adaptation. In the early 1950s the returning missionaries from the productivity program, for example, discarded much of what their Yankee hosts promoted, such as the human-relations approach to industrial management, and borrowed only those techniques they deemed transferable. The French response was as much adaptive as it was imitative. Often what appeared to be Americanized was still quite French. Many industrial mergers of the 1960s, designed to heighten the scale of enterprise, resembled traditional French holding companies more than they did integrated American corporations.

Similarly, le Drugstore on the boulevard St-Germain is more a Parisian boutique than its name suggests. And if Coca-Cola is available in cafés, it is served in such a way that it seems more like an aperitif than a soft drink. Indeed one might want to consider the "Frenchification" of America as well as the Americanization of France. At least for young and fashionable Americans it has become chic to wear Vernet sunglasses and Dior ready-made clothes, to ski with Rossignol equipment, and to drink Evian water. If anything, we have learned that modern culture is eclectic and porous.

In retrospect the apprehension about Americanization seems unnecessary. Wasn't it puerile, perhaps even paranoid, to believe, as some did, that the process would destroy French identity? It seems naive to have worried that, once equipped with automobiles and electric kitchens, the French would no longer be French. And the charge that America was imposing its crass ways on the French seems equally unwarranted. Gallic accusations of materialism, social conformity, and status seeking were a caricature of America. More important, these faults were as inherently French as they were native to America. The mere mention of Balzac or Flaubert should suffice to attest to these French vices. They were not American imports. As we look back, the threat of Americanization seems much less foreign and monstrous than the anti-Americans supposed.

Americanization neither obliterated French independence nor smothered French identity. France did change, but it remained the same. Nevertheless, for the French, anxiety about Americanization, and thus debate, persists. The stakes of the contest, as perceived from France, were, and are, monumental. National identity and independence often seem at risk; to succumb totally means to forfeit Frenchness. The French continue to perceive differences that they want to protect and maintain. They still want the benefits of Americanization without paying all the costs. They want, for example, Euro Disneyland with a French accent. So the dilemma remains and the debate goes on.

Although discussion of the American model continues, it has changed. Perhaps the major shift in this exchange, one that emerged between the wars, is that the French no longer blame the United States for the introduction of consumer society and its alleged adverse consequences. To most it is evident that the Americans and the French are all victims of a global process. America has not committed some international crime by forcing its ways on the inhabitants of the hexagon. We are all caught up in the same imperative, whether we call it consumer society or postindustrial society or just modern society. Over the years the tendency to hold America responsible for this modernity has diminished. Nevertheless, there will be those—most certainly fewer than in the past—who continue to urge resistance to modernity by attacking America. It has become both a tradition and a reflex, even if the charge is unjustified.

A second major change has been the capping of major sources of anti-Americanism. We have seen the eclipse of the Communists, the muting of the Gaullists, the reversal of the Socialists, the recovery of national pride under de Gaulle, and the new realism about French status in world affairs. We have seen, above all, the *banalisation* of America as the two socioeconomic systems grew more similar and as American products and ways became commonplace. And we have seen the conversion of the leftist intelligentsia as the "good America" appeared and the "good Soviet experiment" disappeared. During the Cold War the Parisian literati "ideologized" America into a capitalist-imperialist menace. Inversely, from this leftist perspective America was also a menace because it represented the end of ideology. As ideological thinking declined after 1968, along with the traditional cultural role of the intelligentsia, so did anti-Americanism. It may be objected that St-Germain-des-Prés never spoke for *la France profonde*. Even if this were true, the intelligentsia's influence among the country's elite has been indisputable. *Le Monde* may not have been the voice of France, but its pronouncements mattered to leaders in politics, business, and high culture.

Today the debate is also, far more than before, focused on American mass culture. Political issues receive less attention than they did in the testy 1950s and 1960s. Economic and trade issues recur with varying intensity, yet certain problems from the past such as the invasion of multinationals that disturbed relations in the 1960s and 1970s are absent. Now the quarrel is over problems like the Americanization of the media.

Do these changes mean then that the dragon of anti-Americanism has been slain? I think not. For certain issues and forces that account for the hostility during the postwar years persist and could easily renew tension. An unfavorable conjuncture in the future could provoke a repetition of events in the 1950s and 1960s—though probably with less fervor and perhaps in a different form. In part these latent sources of trouble are endemic to Franco-American international relations. A perennial tension arises from a superpower's hegemonic position over an ally that insists with punctilio on its independence within the alliance. Moreover, French and American interests and strategies have never been identical and will, inevitably, cause friction. There is a further complication. Gallic confidence in the superiority of French culture does not easily fit the dictates of political and economic reality, which remind the French they should accept a secondary position in the world economy and in international affairs—whatever their cultural pretensions. Such humility is difficult.

Finally there remains the fundamental question of why the French have been so wary of being seduced by Americanization. Resistance stemmed from a perception that their national identity was at risk. They expressed their resistance as a contest over safeguarding *civilisation*. Thus the peak of anti-Americanism came during the first postwar decades, a period of sinking self-confidence about the nation's status, when the American other seemed on the verge of eradicating Frenchness. A parallel defensiveness has extended to other groups, for example, the Muslim immigrants who are seen to pose a similar danger to national identity.

The French perception of self has been, and is, at odds with the conception of an American other. We can discern this construction of national identity through French perceptions of the New World. It was as much, if not more, a projection of French sensibility than it was a description of American social reality. The American model was a kind of mirror in which the French viewed themselves or, perhaps, before which they preened. By inventing an America that reeked of materialism and vulgarity, wallowed in conformity and naive optimism, the French separated themselves from the New World, asserted their superiority, and defined Gallic identity and virtue. The French hoped they were, in fact, the mirror image of their caricature of the Americans. That is why so often French self-assessment seemed to be the inverse of what was American. That is why Frenchness meant individualism, humanism, good taste, skepticism, and, above all, *civilisation*—the very virtues denied to Americans.

In the final analysis, understanding the French response to Americanization in all its ambivalence turns on the notion of *civilisation*. For this was, and is, how the French defined the distance between the two societies. It was the holy grail that had to be protected from Yankee barbarism and that held the twentieth-century notion of Frenchness. The meaning of *civilisation* and thus of the stakes in this rivalry has been elusive: there was no consensus about why the American challenge had to be resisted, except that Frenchness—a way of life, in other words, *civilisation*—was at risk. As employed by its postwar advocates, *civilisation* connoted a humanistic or classical education; a style of life that sometimes equated with *bon goût, flânerie,* wine, and haute cuisine; a philosophical stance—skeptical, tragic, and realistic; and a language of great intrinsic merit. Again and again, and on both right and left, not only intellectuals but also politicians, business leaders, trade unionists, and (according to opinion polls) the public at large presented these as the stakes of the contest, the heart of a sensibility that had to be protected against Americanization.

A cynic might argue that Gallic cultural hubris became the best salve for damaged national pride and the apt expression of unacknowledged national jealousy. Another interpreter of the Franco-American cultural rivalry might contend that the New World represented the Old World's hopes for a heaven on earth. The fact that American reality did not measure up to these aspirations was a source of frustration and disappointment to Europeans. When Americans permitted racism, justified gross inequalities, and behaved as base materialists or cultural philistines, they betrayed French desires for a new humanity.

Whatever the claims for hubris, to belittle this sensibility would be an error. I would be loathe to dismiss as trivial what the French accord to *civilisation* because it is, in many ways, what Americans respect and enjoy most about France and the French.

The basis of anti-Americanism is cultural and pivots on the notion of protecting and disseminating *civilisation.* Though differences over international relations, trade, and economics will continue to stir criticism of the hegemonic Western power, the core of resistance derives from a sense of French difference, superiority, and universal mission—all bound up in the term *civilisation.* I see little evidence that this sensibility has dulled since the last war. It has spurred every generation, since those French travelers to the New World in the 1920s and 1930s, to attack America. The criticism may have quieted by the 1990s, but the rivalry is latent and potent.

The implied universality of *civilisation* inevitably breeds competition with the United States because America has its own sense of universal mission. Americans like to think they stand for elevating humankind by advancing freedom and prosperity. The French feel culturally superior and destined to enlighten the globe. Despite the greater economic and political weight of the Americans that seems to legitimate their claims to universality, the French will continue to express cultural superiority and thus we should expect continued rivalry.

The history of Americanization confirms the resilience and absorptive capacity of French *civilisation*. The French seem to have won the struggle of how to change and yet remain the same. The contest and the debate continue. But, as of the present, Americanization has transformed France—has made it more like America—without a proportionate loss of identity. France remains France, and the French remain French.

Notes

Unless otherwise stated, all French publications were published in Paris, all English-language publications in New York. In most cases where French and English editions are available, I cite the latter.

Some frequently cited abbreviations in endnotes:

AFAP	Association française pour l'accroissement de la productivité
AN	Archives nationales (Paris)
AP	Archives privées (in the Archives nationales)
CCCA	Coca-Cola Company Archives (Atlanta, Ga.)
CNP	Comité national de productivité
CNPF	Conseil national du patronat français
ECA	Economic Cooperation Administration
FRUS	*Foreign Relations of the United States*
IFOP	Institut français d'opinion publique
JO	*Journal officiel de la République française*
MAE	Ministère des affaires étrangères
MFAE	Ministère des finances et des affaires économiques
NARA	National Archives and Records Administration (Washington, D.C., and Suitland, Md.)
RG	Record Group

Notes from ECA archives: The abbreviations used in endnotes to chapter 4 from the ECA archives, NARA, record group 469, Records of Foreign Assistance Agencies, are:

OSR/E	Office of the Special Representative in Europe
MF	Mission to France
OD	Office of the Director
CRU	Communications and Records Unit
GSF	General Subject Files
CSF	Country Subject Files
P/TAD	Productivity and Technical Assistance Division
LID	Labor Information Division

Preface

---

1. Charles de Gaulle, *War Memoirs,* trans. J. Griffin (1955), 1:104.

Chapter 1. Anti-Americanism
and National Identity

---

1. Georges Duhamel, *America the Menace: Scenes from the Life of the Future,* trans. Charles Miner Thompson (Boston, 1931).

2. Alain Touraine, "Existe-t-il encore une société française?", *The Tocqueville Review* 11 (1990): 143–71. Fernand Braudel, *The Identity of France,* 2 vols. (London, 1988). Or see the essay by the editor of *Le Point,* Claude Imbert: "The End of French Exceptionalism," *Foreign Affairs* 68 (Fall 1989): 48–60; and the volume of conference papers entitled *Searching for the New France,* eds. James Hollifield and George Ross (1991).

3. Jean-Pierre Rioux, "Twentieth-Century Historiography: Clio in a Phrygian Bonnet," in *Contemporary France,* eds. Jolyon Howorth and George Ross (London, 1987), 204.

4. A sample of this voluminous literature includes Pierre Nora, ed., *Les Lieux de mémoire,* 4 vols. (to be 7 vols.), 1984–; Colette Beaune, *Naissance de la nation de la France* (1986); Maurice Agulhon, *Marianne au combat* (1979); Peter Sahlins, *Boundaries: The Making of France and Spain in the Pyrenees* (Berkeley, 1989); Gérard Noiriel, *Le Creuset français, histoire de l'immigration, XIXe–XXe siècles* (1988); Herman Lebovics, *True France: The Wars over Cultural Identity in France, 1900–1945* (Ithaca, 1992); Eugen Weber, *Peasants into Frenchmen: The Modernization of Rural France, 1870–1914* (Stanford, 1976); and Susan Carol Rogers, *Shaping Modern Times in Rural France* (Princeton, 1991). Where Weber, among other historians, sees a process of cultural diffusion in the late nineteenth century from urban to rural France, Rogers doubts that modernization brings cultural uniformity. She finds that local adaptability to processes like economic globalization sustains sociocultural diversity within France. For the debate among historians over conceptualizing the nation and for further bibliography see Steven Englund's review of *Les Lieux de mémoire:* "The Ghost of Nation Past," *Journal of Modern History* 64, no. 2 (June 1992): 299–320.

5. Benedict Anderson, *Imagined Communities: Reflections on the Origin and Spread of Nationalism* (1983). Ernest Gellner (*Nations and Nationalism* [Oxford, 1983]) argues that nationalism is not simply invention but corresponds to a stage of socioeconomic development. A critical review of the literature on national identity is Philip Schlesinger, "On National Identity: Some Conceptions and Misconceptions Criticized," *Social Science Information* 26, no. 2 (1987): 219–64. For the oppositional character of nation-building

and further bibliography see R. D. Grillo's introduction to a volume of essays he has edited: *"Nation" and "State" in Europe: Anthropological Perspectives* (London, 1980), 1–30.

6. Marie-France Toinet, "Does Anti-Americanism Exist?", in *The Rise and Fall of Anti-Americanism: A Century of French Perception,* eds. Denis Lacorne, Jacques Rupnik, and Marie-France Toinet, trans. Gerry Turner (1990), 225; this anthology contains papers presented at a 1984 conference by French and American scholars. A succinct historical survey of anti-Americanism is Michel Winock, "'US Go Home': l'antiaméricanisme français," *L'Histoire* no. 50 (1982): 7–20. For a survey of relations there is Jean-Baptiste Duroselle, *France and the United States from the Beginnings to the Present,* trans. Derek Coltman (Chicago, 1976).

7. Marie-France Toinet, "French Pique and *Piques Françaises,*" *Annals of the American Academy of Political and Social Science* no. 497 (1988): 135.

8. *New York Herald Tribune,* 20 November 1946, European edition (further cites refer to this Paris edition unless otherwise noted).

9. *New York Herald Tribune,* 19 and 20 August 1957.

10. Charles W. Brooks, *America in France's Hopes and Fears, 1890–1920,* 2 vols. (1987). A recent poll published in *Le Figaro* (4 November 1988) revealed that the French still perceived Americans as powerful, dynamic, and rich. But the youthful, generous, naive image has faded.

11. Laurence Wylie, *Chanzeaux: A Village in Anjou* (Cambridge, Mass., 1966), 361.

12. French textbooks used during the 1960s and 1970s are analyzed by Laurence Wylie and Sarella Henriquez in "French Images of American Life," *The Tocqueville Review* 4 (Fall–Winter 1982): 176–274.

13. Bernadette Galloux-Fournier, "Voyageurs français aux Etats-Unis, 1919–1939: contribution à l'étude d'une image de l'Amérique" (thèse de 3e cycle, Institut d'études politiques, Paris, 1986); Paul A. Gagnon, "French Views of Postwar America, 1919–1932" (Ph.D. diss., Harvard University, 1960); Donald Allen, *French Views of America in the 1930s* (1979). Galloux-Fournier published a summary of her thesis: "Un Regard sur l'Amérique: voyageurs français aux Etats-Unis, 1919–1939," *Revue d'histoire moderne et contemporaine* 37 (April–June 1990): 297–307. During the 1920s the skyscraper became the architectural stereotype of America and the object of fascination for the French according to Isabelle Jeanne Gournay, "France Discovers America, 1917–1939: French Writings on American Architecture" (Ph.D. diss., Yale University, 1989). Some of the twentieth-century images of America, e.g., materialism, mechanization, imperialism, and cultural backwardness, had been sketched even before 1914 according to Jacques Portes, *Une Fascination réticente: Les Etats-Unis dans l'opinion française, 1870–1914* (Nancy, 1990).

14. Brooks, *America in France's Hopes,* 776 ff.

15. Quoted by Paul A. Gagnon, "French Views of the Second American Revolution," *French Historical Studies* 2 (Fall 1962): 444.

16. Allen, *French Views,* 112.

17. Marguerite Yerta-Melera, quoted in Gérard de Catalogne, *Dialogue entre deux mondes* (1931), 129.

18. Georges Duhamel, quoted in Gagnon, "French Views," 437.

19. Duhamel, *America the Menace,* 194.

20. Ibid., 51.

21. Allen, *French Views,* 90.

22. René Rémond's comment on Mounier from *Le Personnalisme d'Emmanuel Mounier hier et demain* (1985), 23. This paragraph is dependent on Marc Simard, "Intellectuels, fascisme et antimodernité dans la France des années trente," *Vingtième Siècle* no. 18 (1988): 60; and Michel Winock, *Histoire politique de la revue "Esprit," 1930–1950* (1975).

23. Emile Baumann, quoted in de Catalogne, *Dialogue,* 181.

Chapter 2. The New American Hegemony

1. Even casual French tourists noted that Americans seemed unusually sensitive to criticism and anxious to be liked. "How do you like America?" was the query that almost every French visitor faced. In contrast, the French never asked this question of their visitors. Given Americans' passion to be admired, it should be no surprise that Americans listened closely to the attacks from Paris.

2. Julian G. Hurstfield, *America and the French Nation, 1939–1945* (Chapel Hill, 1986).

3. Robert O. Paxton, "Anti-Americanism in the Years of Collaboration and Resistance," in *The Rise and Fall of Anti-Americanism,* eds. Lacorne et al., 55–66.

4. Pierre Nora, "America and the French Intellectuals," *Daedalus* 107 (Winter 1978): 325.

5. The best treatment of Franco-American relations in the Cold War is Irwin M. Wall, *The United States and the Making of Postwar France, 1945–1954* (New York, 1991).

6. Patricia Hubert-Lacombe, "La Guerre froide et le cinéma français, 1946–53" (thèse de 3e cycle, Institut d'études politiques, Paris, 1981).

7. Michel Margairaz, "Autour des accords Blum-Byrnes," *Histoire, économie, société* 3 (1982): 439–70.

8. Chief of ECA France to ECA Washington, 21 November 1949, *Foreign Relations of the United States,* 1949 (Washington, D.C., 1975), 4:678–80 (hereafter cited as *FRUS*); the minister of finance was Maurice Petsche. The story of counterpart funding is ably told in Chiarella Esposito, "The Marshall Plan in France and Italy, 1948–50: Counterpart Fund Negotiations" (Ph.D. diss., State University of New York, Stony Brook, 1985).

9. AN F60bis 378, Bonnet to CIQEE (Paris), 24 November 1949. The CIQEE or Comité interministériel pour les questions de coopération économique européenne handled American aid, and its records are housed in the Archives nationales (hereafter AN) in record group F60bis.

10. Department of State, External Research Staff, *French Attitudes on Selected National and International Issues,* 30 September 1950, 31. This report is in the ECA archives (National Archives and Records Administration, hereafter NARA), RG286, Mission to France, General Subject Files, 1946–53, box 44.

11. Wall, *Making of Postwar France,* 63–157; Annie Lacroix-Riz, *La CGT de la libération à la scission de 1944–1947* (1983); Edward Rice-Maximin, "The United States and the French Left, 1945–49: The View from the State Department," *Journal of Contemporary History* 19 (October 1984): 729–47; Stephen Burwood, "American Labor and Industrial Unrest in France, 1947–52" (Ph.D. diss., State University of New York, Binghamton, 1990).

12. On French anti-Americanism circa 1952 see Raymond Cartier, "Ce que la France reproche aux Américains," *Paris-Match,* 25 October–1 November 1952, 19–21; Arnold M. Rose, "Anti-Americanism in France," *Antioch Review* 12 (December 1952): 468–84.

13. Janet Flanner, *Paris Journal, 1944–1965* (1966), 182.

14. Ambassador Dunn to State Dept., 3 November 1952, *FRUS,* 1952–54, vol. 6, pt. 2 (1986), 1270. For Franco-American quarrels over Indochina and the EDC in the early 1950s see Wall, *Making of Postwar France,* 233–96.

15. Ambassador Dunn to State Dept., 11 October 1952, *FRUS,* 1952–54, vol. 6, pt. 2, 1259.

16. From Vincent Auriol, *Journal du Septennat* (1952), quoted in Pierre Mélandri, "France and the Atlantic Alliance 1950–53," in *Western Security: The Formative Years, European and Atlantic Defense, 1947–53,* ed. Olav Riste (1985), 266. The date of Auriol's letter is 12 November 1952.

17. Douglas MacArthur II to Asst. Sec. of State, 19 October 1952, *FRUS,* 1952–54, vol. 6, pt. 2, 1259–60.

18. Ambassador Dunn to State Dept., 8 October 1952, *FRUS,* 1952–54, vol. 6, pt. 2, 1251–52.

19. The State Department believed Pinay was making "domestic political capital" by his show of defiance and by blaming French difficulties in Indochina on alleged reductions in American military aid. Sec. of State's daily meeting, 10 October 1952, *FRUS,* 1952–54, vol. 6, pt. 2, 1256.

20. Ambassador Dillon to State Dept., 4 August 1953, and Special Assistant Hanes to Sec. of State, 3 April 1954, *FRUS,* 1952–54, vol. 6, pt. 2, 1372–75 and 1405–7.

21. *New York Times,* 15 December 1953.

22. Wall, *Making of Postwar France,* 296.

23. Ambassador Dillon tried, unsuccessfully, to alleviate such resentment in his speech to the diplomatic press (NARA, 611.51/3–2056, 20 March 1956). One French economist accused the United States of hypocrisy for "colonizing" the Indians yet adopting a "holier-than-thou" attitude toward the French in Algeria (NARA, 611.51/5–1556, 15 May 1956).

24. NARA, 751.00/7–1558, U.S. Consul in Marseilles to State Dept., 15 July 1958. Within six months the consulate reported a marked improvement in attitudes toward the United States in the Midi (NARA, 751.00/2–2059, 20 February 1959).

25. *The Gallup International Public Opinion Polls: France, 1939, 1944–75,* 2 vols. (1976), 1:191 (henceforth cited as *Gallup Polls* followed by year of poll).

26. Marie-France Briguet, "L'Anti-américanisme en France de 1956 à 1958" (mémoire de maîtrise, Université de Grenoble, 1978). For the earlier period, see Mary M. Benyamin, "Fluctuations in the Prestige of the U.S. in France . . . French Attitudes towards the U.S. and Its Policies, 1945–55" (Ph.D. diss., Columbia University, 1959).

27. Reported in NARA, 611.51/12–456, 4 December 1956.

28. NARA, 611.51/11–2956, Dillon to State Dept., 29 November 1956.

29. NARA, 711.51/9–1546, "France, Policy, and Information Statement," 15 September 1946, Department of State.

30. Steven P. Sapp, "The United States, France, and the Cold War: Jefferson Caffery and American-French Relations, 1944–1949" (Ph.D. diss., Kent State University, 1978).

31. Yves-Henri Nouailhat, "Aspects de la politique culturelle des Etats-Unis à l'égard de la France de 1945 à 1950," *Relations internationales* no. 25 (1981): 87–111. Howard Rice, a director of the U.S. Information Library in Paris, recorded his experience in "Seeing Ourselves as the French See Us," *French Review* 21 (1948): 432–41.

32. From a memorandum of 22 October 1952 by Harold Kaplan found in the ECA archives (NARA), RG286, Mission to France, Office of the Director, General Subject Files, box 51. Kaplan argued that the information program had confused aims: "We do not carry on cultural relations primarily for political ends. It is more correct, I should think, to turn things around and say that we wage our political struggle in Europe in order that we may be able to maintain and intensify our cultural (and economic) relations with the European peoples."

33. Caffery to Sec. of State, 3 March 1949, and Bruce to Sec. of State, 7 October 1949, *FRUS,* 1949, vol. 4, 633, 668–69; René Sommer, "La France dans la guerre froide: Paix et Liberté, 1950–1956" (mémoire de maîtrise, Institut d'études politiques, Paris, 1980). For American propaganda efforts in 1951–52, especially contributions to Paix et Liberté, see Wall, *Making of Postwar France,* 149–51, 213–18.

34. French reaction to the festival is conveyed in reports from the Paris embassy (NARA, 511.51/5–952, 9 May 1952 and 511.51/5–2952, 29 May 1952) and in Herbert Luethy's article, "Selling Paris on Western Culture," *Commentary* 14 (July 1952): 70–75.

35. Serge Lifar, in *Le Combat,* 30 April 1950. Lifar was a Russian and a wartime collaborator.

36. *Le Combat,* 15 May 1952.

37. Quoted in Peter Coleman, *The Liberal Conspiracy: The Congress for Cultural Freedom and the Struggle for the Mind of Postwar Europe* (1989), 56.

38. Thoughtful reflections on how historians should approach the study of public opinion are in Pierre Laborie, "De l'opinion publique à l'imaginaire social," *Vingtième Siècle* no. 18 (1988): 101–17.

39. "Les Etats-Unis, les Américains, et la France, 1945–1953," *Sondages* no. 2 (1953): 3–78 (henceforth cited as *Sondages* 1953). The basic poll, taken by the Institut français d'opinion publique (IFOP) in early 1953, interviewed nearly two thousand respondents, including rural and small-town inhabitants

and all social and professional groups. This poll was secretly funded by the Americans and some of its findings were published under the title "Ce que les Français pensent des Américains" in *Réalités* no. 91 (1953): 18–22.

40. From Gordon Wright, "Sometimes a Great Nation," *The Stanford Magazine* 8, no. 1 (1980): 18.

41. Martine Soete, "Visions des Américains dans la presse du Nord, 1944–1947" (mémoire de maîtrise, Université de Lille III, 1979), 62 ff.

42. *Sondages* 1953, 18.

43. *Sondages* 1953, 20–22, reporting a UNESCO poll of 1948 that the IFOP repeated in 1953 with similar results.

44. *Sondages* 1953, 17; "Ce que les Français pensent des Américains," 21.

45. "Ce que les Français pensent des Américains: un sondage par l'UNESCO," *Perspectives,* 10 September 1955, 3–6.

46. *Sondages* 1953, 28–32.

47. *Sondages* 1953, 40.

48. *Sondages* 1953, 8.

49. *Sondages* 1953, 25.

50. *Gallup Polls* 1947, 1:94.

51. Dept. of State, *French Attitudes on Selected Issues,* 35.

52. *Sondages* 1953, 27–28.

53. Laurence Wylie, *Village in the Vaucluse* (Cambridge, Mass., 1964 ed.), 364.

54. *Rapports France-Etats-Unis* no. 49 (1951): 1.

55. Dept. of State, *French Attitudes on Selected Issues,* 43.

56. *Gallup Polls* 1952, 1:162–63.

57. *Sondages* 1953, 42. A study of opinion on NATO up to 1950 concludes that the French were uneasy about the pact and American hegemony and looked for a more independent or European solution for their security. See Thérèse Boisclair-Sultana, "La France et le pacte Atlantique, février 1948-octobre 1950: aspects de l'opinion" (thèse de 3e cycle, Université Paul Valéry, Montpellier, 1977).

58. *Gallup Polls* 1959, 1:269 and 1960, 1:280.

59. *Sondages* 1953, 32–33, 45.

60. François Jarraud, *Les Américains à Châteauroux, 1951–1967* (Arthon, 1981).

61. *Sondages* 1953, 39.

62. *Sondages* 1953, 44.

63. *Sondages* 1953, 40.

64. *Sondages* 1953, 46. Only 6 percent liked American films *beaucoup,* while 38 percent said *assez,* and 43 percent said *pas du tout.* Also see Hubert-Lacombe, "La Guerre froide et le cinéma français."

65. The 1953 *Sondages* is verified by a Gallup Poll on this count. The Gallup finding was that, for example, 58 percent of Communist voters believed the United States was preparing an aggressive war while only 1 to 3 percent of voters in all other parties voiced this opinion (*Gallup Polls* 1952, 1:162–63).

66. *Sondages* 1953, 71.

67. *Gallup Polls* 1959, 1:269 and 1960, 1:274, 280.

Chapter 3. Yankee Go Home

1. Marianne Amar, "Instantanés américains; les Français aux Etats-Unis, 1947–1953" (mémoire de maîtrise, Institut d'études politiques, Paris, 1980). According to Amar, visitors avoided politics other than discussion of the American political structure and regarded such phenomena as McCarthyism as passing bouts of political fever in an otherwise healthy constitutional body.

2. Louis Aragon, "Victor Hugo," *Les Lettres françaises,* 28 June 1951.

3. For Communist strategy see Jean Baby, "L'Impérialisme américain et la France," *Cahiers du communisme,* January 1948, 83–97; the series of articles on the Marshall Plan in *L'Humanité,* 7–17 November 1949; Jean-Pierre Plantier, "La Vision de l'Amérique à travers la presse et la littérature communistes françaises de 1945 à 1953" (mémoire de maîtrise, Institut d'études politiques, Paris, 1972).

4. Edward Rice-Maximin, "The French Communists, the United States, and the Peace Offensive of the Cold War, 1948–52," *Proceedings of the Twelfth Annual Meeting of the Western Society for French History . . . 1984,* ed. John Sweets (Lawrence, Kans., 1985), 283; Bernard Legendre, "Quand les intellectuels partaient en guerre froide," *L'Histoire* no. 11 (1979): 79–80.

5. Pierre Hervé, "L'Oncle d'Amérique," article of 19 February 1948 in *L'Humanité* quoted in Plantier, "La Vision," 33.

6. Bernard Legendre, ed., *Le Stalinisme français: qui a dit quoi? 1944–1956* (1980), 242.

7. *The New York Times,* 23 March 1948.

8. Roger Vailland, article of 14 March 1952 in *La Tribune des nations,* reprinted in Legendre, ed., *Le Stalinisme,* 301–2.

9. Ariane Chebel d'Appollonia, *Histoire politique des intellectuels en France, 1944–1954* (Brussels, 1991), 2:11–53.

10. Daniel Guerin, *Où va le peuple américain?,* 2 vols. (1950–51). Excerpts of Guerin's book appeared in *Les Temps modernes* during 1950–51.

11. Claude Roy, *Clefs pour l'Amérique* (Geneva, 1947).

12. Aragon, "Victor Hugo."

13. Edgar Morin, "Abêtisseur de poche," *Les Lettres françaises,* 25 December 1947.

14. Quoted in Plantier, "La Vision," 108.

15. "Les Etats-Unis, les Américains et la France, 1945–53," *Sondages* 1953, 59–60.

16. For a discussion of the neutralists see Chebel d'Appollonia, *Histoire politique,* 2:121–41.

17. Author's interviews with Jean-Marie Domenach and Edgar Morin, June 1989.

18. To these progressive Catholics the United States, engaged in the Korean War, was the principal enemy of world peace. They attacked the Marshall Plan for assisting an American takeover of French industries and inflating military spending. In the mid-1950s the Vatican condemned both this review and the

missionary worker movement (Yvon Tranvouez, "Guerre froide et progressisme chrétien, *La Quinzaine,* 1950–53," *Vingtième Siècle* no. 13 [1987], 83–94).

19. Quoted in Winock, *Histoire politique de la revue "Esprit,"* 272.

20. From a 1948 manifesto by Camus quoted in Herbert R. Lottman, *Albert Camus, A Biography* (1979), 460.

21. Laurent Greilsamer, *Hubert Beuve-Méry, 1902–1989* (1990); Jean-Noël Jeanneney and Jacques Julliard, *"Le Monde" de Beuve-Méry ou le métier d'Alceste* (1979); Jacques Thibau, *"Le Monde," histoire d'un journal, un journal dans l'histoire* (1978).

22. *Le Monde,* 14 and 15 September 1948 quoted in Greilsamer, *Beuve-Méry,* 339.

23. *Une Semaine dans le Monde,* 9 May 1949, quoted in ibid., 334.

24. *Le Monde,* 2 March 1949.

25. Emmanuel's articles on America are in *Le Monde,* 25, 26, and 28 October 1949.

26. Greilsamer (*Beuve-Méry,* 278–83) has an account of Beuve-Méry's trip to the United States.

27. *Le Monde,* 9 August 1948.

28. Raymond Aron, *Les Guerres en chaîne* (1951), 422.

29. *Le Monde,* 28 October 1949.

30. Courtin's critique of Beuve-Méry's position is cited in Jeanneney and Julliard, *"Le Monde" de Beuve-Méry,* 104. In private, Courtin unfairly accused the editor of preferring Soviet totalitarianism to American capitalism.

31. *Le Monde,* 31 January 1951, quoted in Greilsamer, *Beuve-Méry,* 340.

32. *Le Monde,* 6 April 1949.

33. Claude Bourdet, "Letter to America," *Nation,* 6 December 1952, 510–11.

34. Pierre Grémion, "*Preuves* dans la Paris de guerre froide," *Vingtième Siècle* no. 13 (1987): 63–82; the author's interview with M. Grémion, June 1989; and Coleman, *The Liberal Conspiracy,* 53–55, 83–84, 187.

35. André Malraux's speech of 5 March 1948, published as an appendix to an edition of his novel *Les Conquérants,* cited in Nora, "America and the French Intellectuals," 326.

36. Claude Mauriac quoted in Thibau, *"Le Monde,"* 243–44.

37. This account relies on the essay by Pierre Milza, "La Guerre froide à Paris," *L'Histoire* no. 25 (1980): 38–47.

38. *La Marseillaise,* 20 May 1952 (quoted in NARA, 751.001/5–2052, 20 May 1952).

39. *L'Humanité,* 19 May 1952.

40. Pinay told the American ambassador that the suppression of these disorders marked the beginning of repressive measures against the PCF (Ambassador Dunn to State Dept., 29 May 1952, *FRUS,* 1952–54, vol. 6, pt. 2, 1214–15).

41. Marie-Christine Granjon, "Sartre, Beauvoir, Aron: An Ambiguous Affair," in *The Rise and Fall of Anti-Americanism,* eds. Lacorne et al. (1990), 116–33. Annie Cohen-Solal, *Sartre, A Life* (1987), 223–44, 269–79, 290–359.

42. *New York Herald Tribune,* 20 November 1946.

43. Cited in Michel Contat and Michel Rybalka, eds., *Les Ecrits de Sartre* (1970), 706–8.

44. *New York Herald Tribune,* 20 November 1946.

45. Jean-Marie Domenach, "L'Antisémitisme rest logique," *Esprit,* January 1953, 149. Also Jean-Marie Domenach, "L'Exécution des Rosenberg," *Esprit,* July 1953, 58–60.

46. Henri Pierre, *Le Monde,* 17 January 1953.

47. *Le Monde,* 21–22 June 1953.

48. E. J. Kahn, *The Big Drink: the Story of Coca-Cola* (1960), 4–5. Histories of the company are Pat Watters, *Coca-Cola: An Illustrated History* (Garden City, N.Y., 1978), and Julie Patou-Senez and Robert Beauvillain, *Coca-Cola Story: l'épopée d'une grande star* (1978).

49. Watters, *Coca-Cola,* 162.

50. Kahn, *The Big Drink,* 13.

51. *Time,* 15 May 1950.

52. Farley's statements are from J. C. Louis and Harvey Z. Yazijian, *The Cola Wars* (1980), 75–76.

53. Coca-Cola Company Archives, Makinsky to Ladas, 23 January 1950 (henceforth these archives will be cited as CCCA).

54. *L'Humanité,* 8 November 1949.

55. *Le Monde,* 24 September 1949.

56. *Climats,* 25 March 1950.

57. *Libération paysanne,* 1 December 1949.

58. Cited in *French-American Commerce* no. 3 (1950): 2. Also see J. F. Gravier, "Champignons et Coca-Cola," *La Vie française,* 31 March 1950.

59. AN 363AP12, René Mayer papers, "Note sur l'introduction en France de la boisson Coca-Cola," 19 August 1949. This well-informed and critical report based on investigation into Coca-Cola's current operations in Belgium and elsewhere also contains copies of the company's franchise contracts. It is apparently the work of a treasury official. This official investigation is mentioned in the archives of the Ministry of Finance: Secrétariat d'état aux affaires économiques, B16.022, 18 January 1950. Officials doubted that the Marseilles plant, as the multinational claimed, would bring dollars to France via exporting its concentrate to other European nations; they worried that dollars would be spent importing ingredients and paying the mother company for advertising. Moreover, from the treasury's perspective, profits were sure to be repatriated. The Ministry of Finance told an American banker that the ministry's main objection was Coca-Cola's "lack of visible investments" and the repatriation of profits (CCCA, Makinsky to Ladas, 23 January 1950). Ambassador Henri Bonnet confirmed these objections to company officials (CCCA, Memorandum on visit to French Embassy of Mr. Farley and Dr. Ladas, 19 March 1950).

60. CCCA, Farley to Bonnet, attached memorandum, 24 March 1950.

61. AN 363AP12, "Note sur l'introduction."

62. CCCA, Makinsky to Ladas, 23 January 1950. Makinsky also recognized that the administration was subject to pressure from the beverage interests.

63. CCCA, Farley to Bonnet, attached memorandum, 24 March 1950.

64. CCCA, Makinsky to Talley, 31 December 1949. The Coca-Cola Company blamed the Ministry of Finance for this new round of legal battles (CCCA, "Memorandum Concerning the Coca-Cola Product in France," March 1950).

65. An account of the legal actions to 1951 can be found in AN 363AP12. The charges by the Service de la repression des fraudes are in Albert Bonn, "La Question du jour: 'Coca-Cola,'" *Revue des produits purs et d'origine et des fraudes* nos. 13–14 (1949): 67–72.

66. CCCA, Makinsky to Ladas, 23 January 1950.

67. Farley claimed to have "positive written evidence" that proved the government's responsibility for initiating proceedings against the sale of the soft drink (CCCA, Farley to Bonnet, 24 March 1950).

68. *Journal officiel de la République française, débats parlementaires, Assemblée nationale,* séance du 28 février 1950, 1528 (henceforth cited as *JO, débats, Assemblée nationale*).

69. The debate is in *JO, débats, Assemblée nationale,* séance du 28 février 1950, 1525–36.

70. *JO, débats, Assemblée nationale,* séance du 28 février 1950, 1536.

71. CCCA, Makinksy to Ladas, 23 January 1950.

72. CCCA, Makinsky to Talley, attached memoranda, 5 January 1950.

73. CCCA, Farley to Bonnet, 24 March 1950.

74. CCCA, Makinsky to Smith (U.S. embassy), 28 April 1950.

75. NARA, 851.316/3–1550, 15 March 1950; 851.316/4–350, 3 April 1950; 451.11174/2–2550, February 25, 1950. All these telegrams are nominally from Bruce to the State Dept. Bruce met with Bidault in December 1949 and with Foreign Minister Schuman in February and March 1950.

76. NARA, 451.11174/2–2550, 25 February 1950.

77. Farley's comments appeared in *The New York Times,* 2 March 1950.

78. *New York Enquirer,* 6 March 1950.

79. Quoted in Louis and Yazijian, *The Cola Wars,* 78.

80. Reported in *Le Monde,* 4 March 1950.

81. *France-Amérique,* 12 March 1950.

82. Ministère des affaires étrangères (hereafter MAE), B Amérique, Etats-Unis, carton 253, H. Bonnet to MAE, 14 March 1950.

83. AN 363AP12, Clappier to Mayer, 5 December 1950.

84. MAE, B Amérique, Etats-Unis, 253, 17 March 1950.

85. CCCA, O'Shaughnessy (State Dept.) to Curtis, 20 April 1950.

86. "Bienfaits et méfaits du Plan Marshall" and "Alerte au Coca-Cola" in *Témoignage chrétien,* 10 February and 3 March 1950.

87. *Le Monde,* 23 November 1949.

88. *Le Monde,* 30 December 1949.

89. *Le Monde,* 29 March 1950.

90. Quotes in this paragraph are from *JO, débats, Conseil de la République,* séance du 6 juin 1950, 1581–82.

91. CCCA, Farley to Webb (State Dept.), 11 January 1952.

92. CCCA, Makinsky to Farley, 3 October 1952.

93. CCCA, Carl West, memorandum, 8 December 1953.

94. "Les Etats-Unis, les Américains, et la France, 1945–53," *Sondages* no. 2 (1953): 46.

95. Recent data show that the French consume far less per capita than the Germans, Spanish, British, or Italians (*New York Times,* 21 November 1991).

96. *Témoignage chrétien,* 3 March 1950.

Chapter 4. The Missionaries of the Marshall Plan

1. International Cooperation Administration, *European Productivity and Technical Assistance Programs, A Summing Up, 1948–58* (Paris, 1959), 139.

2. For formal definitions of the various conceptions of productivity that French experts formulated, see Comité national de productivité (hereafter CNP), *Actions et problèmes de productivité: premier rapport, 1950–53* (1953), 118–23. By 1953 productivity was no longer a synonym for output or efficiency of labor—an earlier crude notion suggesting "anti-human timing" that had aroused labor's resentment and fear—but became a broader synthetic notion of efficiency, a result of a complex combination of factors including equipment, materials, and organization.

3. For a general interpretation of American postwar international economic strategy see Charles S. Maier, "The Politics of Productivity" in *Between Power and Plenty,* ed. P. J. K. Katzenstein (Madison, Wis., 1978), 23–49. Maier's focus is not the productivity drive itself, but how the United States used international monetary and trade policy and foreign aid to promote economic efficiency and affluence as a way of resolving political and class conflict, especially in Europe and Japan. An introduction to the U.S. productivity effort is William A. Brown and Redvers Opie, *American Foreign Assistance* (Washington, D.C., 1953). A recent critical analysis, based on archival research, is Anthony Carew, *Labour under the Marshall Plan* (Detroit, 1987).

4. I have analyzed the technical assistance program more fully in Richard F. Kuisel, "The Marshall Plan in Action: Politics, Labor, Industry and the Program of Technical Assistance in France," that will be published in the collected papers of the colloquium entitled *Le Plan Marshall et le relèvement économique de l'Europe.* An introduction to the productivity drive in France is Jean Fourastié, *La Productivité,* 3d ed. (1957). The drive's official report is CNP, *Actions et problèmes,* of which there is an English version: French Embassy, *Productivity in France: Problems and Progress: An Abstract of the First Report of the French National Productivity Committee,* Commercial Counselor's Office (Washington, D.C., 1954).

5. The ECA had allocated only 34 million dollars; by the end of 1951 no more than half this sum had been actually expended, according to Immanuel Wexler, *The Marshall Plan Revisted* (Westport, Conn., 1983), 93.

6. AN, F60ter 517, Bingham (MF/ECA) to de Margerie, 31 January 1950. Those individuals prominent in negotiating the productivity program who are mentioned in these notes include (among the Americans): Averell Harriman, the special representative in Europe; Richard Bissell, assistant deputy ECA

administrator; Barry Bingham, head of ECA/France; Clinton Gordon and Bert Jewell, chief labor advisers to ECA/Washington, D.C.; Henry Martin, director of labor information/OSR; Harry Turtledove, labor information officer/OSR; Kenneth Douty, chief labor adviser ECA/France; and James Silbermann, head of productivity studies in the Labor Dept., Washington, D.C. On the French side: Jean Monnet, commissioner for economic planning; Henry Bonnet, ambassador, and R. Donn, commercial counselor, in the Washington embassy; P.-P. Schweitzer and Bernard de Margerie, successive heads of the Interministerial Committee on Questions of European Economic Cooperation; Pierre Girmanelli, director of economic programs at the Ministry of Finance; and Robert Buron, head of the CNP.

7. MF, OD, CRU, GSF, box 60, Bingham to ECA/Wash., 8 May 1950. Citations using this form are from the archives of the ECA housed by NARA in record group 469. The abbreviations for these citations are identified at the beginning of the notes.

8. OSR/E, LID, OD, CSF/France, box 8, Desser to Timmons (ECA/France), 19 July 1950.

9. OSR/E, LID, OD, CSF/France, box 6, Douty to Bingham, 7 February 1950. Also OSR/E, LID, OD, CSF/France, box 8, Turtledove to Martin, 31 January 1950.

10. OSR/E, LID, OD, CSF/France, box 6, Bissell to Gordon and Jewell, 27 March 1950.

11. AN, F60ter 518, MAE, "Conversations de Washington sur l'Assistance technique à l'Europe," December 1951. ECA position reported in *Le Monde,* 28 July 1951, and the *New York Times,* 25 July 1951.

12. Richard M. Bissell, "The Impact of Rearmament on the Free World Economy," *Foreign Affairs* 29 (April 1951): 404–5.

13. William Joyce, ECA productivity chief, made this comment in a speech. French press reaction is summarized in MF, OD, CRU, GSF, box 61, ECA/France to ECA/Wash., 16 August 1951.

14. MF, OD, CRU, GSF, box 61, Timmons to Sec. of State, 10 August 1951.

15. Barry Bingham, ECA chief in France, thought Buron and Monnet "displayed more interest in and understanding of productivity than any other persons in public or private life that we have met in France" (MF, OD, CRU, box 60, Bingham to ECA/Wash., 11 April 1950). Yet Buron wondered whether the French could ever accept the rules of American production. Even those people of French stock who lived in North America, Buron noted, the Québécois of Canada and the Cajuns of Louisiana, seemed to prefer their traditional ways to progress. He concluded, "There is a psychological, perhaps a metaphysical, problem here. The Frenchman distrusts progress. He doesn't adopt it with the enthusiasm of the American" (Robert Buron, *Dynamisme des Etats-Unis* [1957], 87).

16. Ministère des finances et des affaires économiques (hereafter MFAE), archives, B16.023, Grimanelli, 24 April 1951.

17. AN, 80AJ80, Donn to Monnet, 17 February 1949.

18. Joint Committee on Foreign Economic Cooperation, *Knowledge of the Marshall Plan in Europe,* 19 October 1949 (Washington, D.C., 1949).

19. AN, F60ter 381, Secrétaire d'état de l'information to Président du Conseil, 12 November 1948.

20. MF, OD, CRU, GSF, box 60, Bingham to ECA/Wash., 22 July 1949.

21. Michel Hincker, "L'Opération 'Productivité,'" *Cahiers internationaux* no. 29 (1951): 51–58.

22. Auguste Lecoeur, *Les Dessous de la campagne américaine sur la productivité*, conférence prononcée . . . 14 mars 1952 (1952). Also Comité central du Parti communiste français, *La Productivité du travail*, Documents économiques, no. 3, May 1951.

23. MF, OD, CRU, GSF, box 62, Taff to Pioda (OSR), 25 September 1951.

24. AN, F60ter 394, Préfet du Cher to Ministre de l'intérieur, "Manifestation à Vierzon", 29 February 1952.

25. For example see *Force ouvrière*, 27 July 1950; *Le Monde*, 21 June 1950.

26. Each syndicate specified different conditions for joining the CNP, according to CNP, procès-verbal, séance du 10 octobre 1950, AN, Fourastié papers, box 15.

27. MF, OD, CRU, GSF, box 61, Desser to Bingham, 15 March 1950.

28. OSR/E, LID, OD, CSF/France, box 8, Turtledove to Martin, 31 June 1950.

29. See, for example, the criticism leveled against the CNP by a prominent CNPF official: René Norguet, "Rapport sur les travaux de la commission de la productivité," *CNPF: Bulletin* no. 84 (1952): 40–42.

30. MF, OD, CRU, GSF, box 61, Gingembre to Carmody, 12 September 1951. Excerpt published in *Le Monde*, 15 September 1951.

31. OSR/E, LID, OD, CSF/France, box 8, Cony to Martin, November 1950. Jean-Roger Herrenschmidt, "La Préparation des missions de productivité en France," *Productivité française*, May 1952, 26–27; Pierre Bize, "L'Assistance technique au service de la productivité française," *Productivité française*, February 1952, 6–10.

32. The French government paid for the teams' cross-Atlantic journey; French employers covered the salaries of team members during the trip, and the ECA covered the dollar expenses (per diem, travel in the United States). See the convention of 5 October 1949 (ECA, P/TA, OD, CSF, box 6).

33. MF, OD, CRU, GSF, box 59, Bingham to Schweitzer, 26 July 1949.

34. ECA, P/TA, OD, CSF, box 6, Harris, "Comment on the Productivity Program," 1949.

35. AN, F60ter 517, Schweitzer to Bingham, 7 October 1949; and MFAE archives, B16.022, Grimanelli to MFAE, 25 May 1950.

36. AFAP, *Missions de productivité aux Etats-Unis, annuaire, 1949–53*, (1953), 7. An extensive report on the CNP's activities, including the missions, is CNP, Memorandum sur la politique française de productivité et l'assistance technique, 18 July 1951, AN, F30ter 518.

37. Of 4000 team members surveyed, 45 percent were employers, managers, or technicians; 25 percent were workers or foremen; and the remainder were mostly *fonctionnaires*: see P.-L. Mathieu and Philippe Leduc, "La Politique française de productivité depuis la guerre" (mémoire de maîtrise, Institut d'études politiques, Paris, 1961), 64–65.

38. M. Lemarsquier, "L'Action de l'AFAP et du Comité national de la productivité" in CEGOS (Centre d'études générales d'organisation scientifique), *Les Facteurs humains de la productivité américaine* 1 (1951): 4.

39. Such records are post-mission interviews with AFAP staff; policy debates within the CNP/AFAP; and follow-up evaluations of the drive's success. See AN, Fourastié papers, boxes 14–17, and notes 85 and 86.

40. Carew, *Labour,* 139–57; Pier Paolo d'Attore, "ERP Aid and the Politics of Productivity in Italy during the 1950s" (paper, European University Institute, 1985).

41. Pierre Baruzy, "Compte rendu des sessions . . . d'industriels américains," *CNOF* (Comité national de l'organisation française): *Revue* (February 1952): 26–29.

42. Bernard Pigoreaux, *Cinq Semaines aux Etats-Unis avec une mission de productivité* (n.d.), 41.

43. See, for example, the analysis of the metallurgists' trade association: Albert Metral, "La Productivité américaine," *Les Etudes américaines* no. 32 (1952): 18–20.

44. French electronics companies could not readily import America's huge markets, easy credit, or industrial relations. But they could specialize production lines, undertake market studies, and simplify work. This report is AFAP, *Les Industries de l'électronique aux Etats-Unis,* rapport de la sixième mission de la construction électrique (1952).

45. Quoted in Pierre Badin, *Aux sources de la productivité américaine: premier bilan des missions françaises* (1953), 57.

46. Ibid., 37.

47. Luc Boltanski, "America, America . . . Le Plan Marshall et l'importation du 'management,' " *Actes de la recherche en sciences sociales* 38 (May 1981): 19–41.

48. Among the differences between the terms is their scope: "management" encompassed far more staff personnel than the more narrow French term *direction.* For management see AFAP, *Productivité . . . problème de direction* (1954); Jean-Michel de Lattre, "Vue cavalière de l'entreprise américaine," *Productivité française,* March 1953, 39–54; AFAP, *Productivité aux Etats-Unis, essai de synthèse, rapport de la cinquième mission française d'experts* (1953), 35–62; AFAP, *La Comptabilité mesure et facteur de productivité: rapport de la mission française des experts-comptables aux Etats-Unis* (1952); Jean Milhaud, "Aspects humains de l'Amérique au travail," *Hommes et techniques* nos. 78 (1951): 15–19, and 79–80 (1951): 19–34.

49. Report of management consultants' mission in *Le Monde,* 30 September 1950.

50. "Défauts de l'industrie française . . . chefs d'entreprise américaines," *Productivité française,* February 1953, 53. American managers' critique is also in CNP, *Actions et problèmes,* 81–82.

51. James Silbermann, *La Faiblesse de la productivité française vue par les Américains* (1952), 8.

52. De Lattre, "Vue cavalière," 49.

53. AFAP, *Productivité aux Etats-Unis, essai de synthèse,* 31.

54. Badin, *Aux sources,* 32.

55. R. Donn, "Les Etats-Unis tirent leur génie et leur puissance de la productivité," *Productivité française,* December 1952, 24.

56. Badin, *Aux sources,* 58.

57. CNPF views reported in MAE archives, B Amérique, Etats-Unis, rélations commerciales franco-américaines, 253, Seydoux to Bonnet, 14 December 1951. For lag in French advertising see Marc Martin, *L'Histoire de la publicité en France* (1992).

58. AFAP, *Le Marketing, conférences, discussions, octobre–novembre 1956* (1958), 7–8.

59. Claude Foussé, *Traits caractéristiques de la prospérité américaine* (1953), 88.

60. AFAP, *Rapport de la mission d'étude du marché et publicité* (1954), 8.

61. Foussé, *Traits caractéristiques,* 63–64.

62. Badin, *Aux sources,* 35.

63. AFAP, *Intégration du travailleur dans l'entreprise* (1953), 81.

64. J. Gouin, "Le Climat social d'une entreprise américaine: Barber-Greene company" in CEGOS, *Les Facteurs humaines de la productivité américaine* 3 (1951): 1–3.

65. AFAP, *Les Relations humaines aux Etats-Unis,* rapport de la mission de productivité T.A. 38–395 . . . octobre 1954 (1955), 25.

66. De Lattre, "Vue cavalière," 45.

67. AFAP, *Productivité . . . problème de direction,* 58.

68. Badin, *Aux sources,* 25–26.

69. One technical adviser analyzed the costs of France's imperfect markets, that is, the waste caused by manufacturers' lack of information about consumers or by consumers' ignorance about products—all of which drove up costs, created uncertainty, and undermined the optimal exchange that a market was supposed to bring. See Jean Dayre, "Productivité et organisation des marchés," in AFAP, *Productivité d'une nation, productivité d'une industrie* (1951), 30.

70. M. P. Weinbach, "Emploi des statistiques dans les entreprises privées américaines," *CNOF,* October 1954, 21.

71. De Lattre, "Vue cavalière," 54.

72. *Quatre Syndicalistes français aux Etats-Unis* (n.d.), 10. This report is in AN, 81AJ69.

73. André Blanchet, *Le Monde,* 14 October 1950. Blanchet wrote a series on "Les Leçons de la productivité américaine" for *Le Monde,* on 11, 12, 14, and 17 October 1950.

74. A FO delegate observed the respect for "the human personality at work. Men of all types, organized labor in the lead, seek to maximize workers' freedom by making more comprehensible and less exacting the indispensable discipline of production and by providing workers with a growing part of this production. In France we quibble about the idea, we examine it closely and touch it up. In the U.S.A. they seriously try to implement it" (*Quatre Syndicalistes,* 11, 19).

75. *Quatre Syndicalistes,* 21.

76. AFAP, *Quelques Aspects de l'organisation et du fonctionnement des syndicats ouvriers américains, par une mission syndicale française, octobre–novembre 1951* (n.d.), 44.

77. MF, OD, CRU, GSF, box 58, Max Rolland's letter relayed to A. Harriman by J. Hutchison, 11 May 1950.

78. Lucienne Rey, "Le Syndicalisme américain vu par des militants français," *Rapports France-Etats-Unis* no. 46 (1951): 52–56.

79. Blanchet, *Le Monde*, 14 October 1950.

80. *Quatre Syndicalistes*, 20.

81. *Quatre Syndicalistes*, 21.

82. *Quelques Aspects . . . des syndicats ouvriers américains*, 47.

83. Badin, *Aux sources*, 58.

84. I make such an assessment in Kuisel, "The Marshall Plan in Action."

85. ECA follow-up surveys of individual enterprises are in MF, OD, CRU, GSF, box 62.

86. AN, Fourastié papers, box 14, AFAP, "Projet spécial de 'follow-up' des missions," March 1955; and AN, 81AJ42, AFAP, "Enquêtes sur l'exploitation des missions de productivité, première partie: chefs d'entreprises et cadres, 1er semestre 1956.

87. AFAP, "Projet spécial," 3.

88. AFAP, "Enquêtes sur l'exploitation," 15.

89. Ibid., 18.

90. AN, Fourastié papers, box 16, Henri Migeon to Grimanelli, 27 November 1952, annex to: CNP, commission exécutive, procès-verbal, séance du 27 novembre 1952.

91. AN, Fourastié papers, box 16, CNP, commission exécutive, procès-verbaux, séances du 13 octobre, 22, 27 novembre 1952.

92. René Richard, "Productivity and the Trade Unions in France," *International Labour Review* 68 (September 1953): 290.

93. AN, Fourastié papers, box 16, CNP, Commission "productivité" et coopération du personnel des entreprises: Groupe de travail spécial, compte-rendu de la réunion du 22 novembre 1952. See also address of Georges Villiers in *CNPF: Bulletin* no. 87 (1952): 1–2.

94. MF, OD, OFD, box 7, Labouisse to Sec. of State, 1 December 1952.

95. For such examples see *Le Monde*, 31 October 1954; *La Vie française*, 11 December 1953; *Le Figaro*, 18 May 1953; and French Embassy, *Recent Developments of the Productivity Drive in France: An Abstract of the Third Report of the French Productivity Agency*, Commercial Counselor's Office, Industry and Productivity Division (Washington, D.C., 1956).

96. Commissariat général à la productivité, *Objectifs et réalisations, 1955–56* (1956), xvi.

97. MFAE archives, 16.027, Ardant, Note, 27 November 1956.

98. In most of these respects the Italian productivity experience parallels the French (see d'Attore, "ERP Aid"). Carew (*Labour*, 180) concludes that from the perspective of integrating organized labor the productivity drive was "pretty much a disaster" in France, Italy, and Germany.

99. See, for example, Bernard Jarrier, "La Croisade pour la productivité," *Esprit*, February 1952, 285–308.

100. De Lattre, "Vue cavalière," 45.

101. AFAP, *Productivité aux Etats-Unis, essai de synthèse*, 15.

102. Ibid., 14.

103. AN, Fourastié papers, box 14, AFAP, "Réunions d'exploitation des missions de productivité: mission 'produits amylacés', 17 juin 1954," 16–17.

104. Foussé, *Traits caractéristiques*, 13.

105. Robert Buron, "Les Eléments de la productivité américaine," *Productivité française*, January 1953, 2.

Chapter 5. The American Temptation

1. NARA, 611.51/3–1656, 16 March 1956, Memo on Franco-American conference at Arden House. Among the French guests at the Arden House conference were Jean-Marie Domenach, Raymond Aron, Alfred Grosser, Stanley Hoffmann, Jacques Fauvet, and Michel Debré. Domenach was detained by immigration authorities at Ellis Island because he had signed the Stockholm peace appeal and was released only when his political adversary Debré threatened to take the whole delegation home if Domenach were not allowed to rejoin the group (letter from Stanley Hoffmann, 20 October 1989).

2. *Le Monde*, 22 July 1954.

3. Jean-Pierre Rioux, *The Fourth Republic, 1944–1958*, trans. Godfrey Rogers (1987), 322–27, 358–74.

4. Ibid., 369. Still the average French consumer contracted less private debt than his European neighbors or the Americans.

5. Ibid., 370–72.

6. Those most rewarded were top managers and professionals. Workers maintained a middling rank though they missed improvements in leisure and culture. Those most left out of the new prosperity were farmers, rural laborers, and those not actively employed. Yet from these groups also came the best customers for new television sets and refrigerators; they were the most eager to improve their material comforts. At the other end of the social scale top managers and professionals only modestly accelerated such purchases because they were already well equipped.

7. Wylie, *Village in the Vaucluse*, 143.

8. Rioux, *Fourth Republic*, 374.

9. At one point, in order to appear to be fair, *Le Monde* published a series by an American entitled "Soyons juste même pour les Américains" (27–28, 30 December 1950).

10. Alain Bosquet, ed., *Les Américains* (1958). Bosquet, a poet and authority on American literature, added a most unflattering commentary to these photographs.

11. Jean-Marie Domenach, "Le Modèle américain," *Esprit*, July–August 1960, 1221. Subsequent articles in this series appeared in September and October 1960.

12. Jean Cocteau, *Lettre aux américains* (1949), 81–82. Another reactionary polemic against "la civilisation des machines" is Georges Bernanos, *La France contre les robots* (1947).

13. Duhamel joined Raymond Aron, André Siegfried, and others to debate the American danger in "L'Amérique et nous," *Le Figaro,* 11 May 1956.

14. Diana Pinto, "Sociology as a Cultural Phenomenon in France and Italy, 1950–1972" (Ph.D. diss., Harvard University, 1977), 167. Also Alain Drouard, "Réflexions sur une chronologie: le développement des sciences sociales en France de 1945 à la fin des années soixante," *Revue française de sociologie* 23 (January–March 1982): 62. Pierre Nora ("America and the French Intellectuals," 327) observed that French social scientists were blind to American social science in the 1950s because the work of thinkers like Talcott Parsons, Walt Rostow, Daniel Bell, and Seymour Martin Lipset was grounded in American uniqueness and consensus; the French viewed it as a kind of self-justification, even an "insidious tool of Yankee imperialism." Thus Bell's *End of Ideology* was never translated into French.

15. Guerin, *Où va le peuple américain?*

16. Michel Crozier, "Les Intellectuels et la stagnation française," *Esprit,* December 1953, 771–82.

17. Jean Fourastié, *Le grand Espoir du XXe siècle; progrès technique, progrès économique, progrès social* (first published in 1949); Jean Fourastié and André Laleuf, *Révolution à l'ouest* (1957).

18. See the insightful study by Amar, "Instantanés américains"; also useful are the studies by Kornel Huvos (*Cinq Mirages américains,* 1972) and David Strauss (*Menace in the West: The Rise of French Anti-Americanism in Modern Times* [Westport, Conn., 1978]).

19. Pierre and Renée Gosset, "The U.S.A. Through a French Looking Glass," *Reader's Digest,* December 1953, 36. The Gossets described their travels in *L'Amérique aux américains,* 2 vols. (1953–54).

20. Examples of Maurois's many studies, some of which date from between the wars, are *Histoire du peuple américain,* 2 vols (1955–56); *Histoire des Etats-Unis* (1954); and *Journal: Etats-Unis 1946* (1946). For Maurois's views also see Huvos, *Cinq Mirages,* 280–81.

21. Words of Alexandre Koyré in UNESCO, *The Old World and the New: Their Cultural and Moral Relations,* International Forums of Sao Paulo and Geneva, 1954 (Paris: UNESCO, 1956), 240.

22. Domenach, "Le Modèle américain," September 1960, 1368.

23. From Domenach's review of a book by L.-L. Matthias (*Autopsie des Etats-Unis*) in *Esprit,* April 1955, 731. *Esprit* mockingly published an "American lexicon" that explained "credit," for example: "every honorable citizen has to pay for most of his purchases on credit, savings being a depraved virtue of decadent countries" ("Petit Lexique américain," *Esprit,* May 1953, 749).

24. Claude Alphandéry, *L'Amérique est-elle trop riche?* (1960). *Les Temps modernes* published an excerpt of this title in its 19 December 1959 issue.

25. Ibid., 100.

26. Ibid., 113.

27. André Fontaine, "Les Etats-Unis vus de l'intérieur," *Le Monde,* 4 February 1955. Georges Friedmann, "De Boston au Mississipi [*sic*]," *Esprit,* June 1949, 785.

28. Aron, in "L'Amérique et nous."

29. Siegfried, in "L'Amérique et nous."

30. André Siegfried, *America at Mid-Century* (1955), 172–75.

31. Raymond Aron, "From France," in *As Others See Us: The United States through Foreign Eyes*, ed. Franz M. Joseph (Princeton, 1959), 60.

32. William Rappard in UNESCO, *Old World and the New*, 195.

33. UNESCO, *Old World and the New*, 198. Cushing Strout, "America, the Menace of the Future: A European Fantasy," *The Virginia Quarterly Review* (Autumn 1957): 569–81.

34. Friedmann, "De Boston," 794.

35. Simone de Beauvoir (*L'Amérique au jour le jour* [1948]) quoted in Strauss, *Menace*, 260.

36. Roy, *Clefs pour l'Amérique*, 134.

37. Michel Crozier, "'Human Engineering': Les nouvelles techniques 'humaines' du Big Business américain," *Les Temps modernes* no. 69 (1951): 72–73.

38. Julien, *Le Monde*, 19 March 1959. Also Claude Julien, *Le nouveau nouveau Monde* (1960).

39. Sidney Lens, "L'Homme standard," *Esprit*, March 1959, 385–400.

40. Albert Béguin, "Réflexions sur l'Amérique, l'Europe, la neutralité . . . ", *Esprit*, June 1951, 886.

41. Domenach, "Le Modèle américain," October 1960, 1525, 1523, 1529.

42. Jean-Marie Domenach, "Les Diplodocus et les fourmis," *Esprit*, March 1959, 431–32.

43. Raymond Bruckberger (*L'Amérique des Pyramides* [1952]) quoted in Amar, "Instantanés américains," 49.

44. Jean Planchais, "Instantanés américains," *Le Monde*, 3 May 1952.

45. Fontaine, "Les Etats-Unis vus de l'intérieur," *Le Monde*, 3 February 1955.

46. Planchais, *Le Monde*, 2 May 1952.

47. Béguin, "Réflexions sur l'Amérique," June 1951, 887.

48. Domenach, "Le Modèle américain," September 1960, 1364.

49. Julien, *Le nouveau nouveau Monde*, 169.

50. Raymond Bruckberger quoted in Amar, "Instantanés américains," 53.

51. Charles Brindillac, "Promenade aux Etats-Unis," *Esprit*, September 1959, 234–35.

52. Maurois in UNESCO, *Old World and the New*, 313.

53. Roy, *Clefs pour l'Amérique*, 306.

54. Aron, "From France," 69.

55. Alphandéry, *L'Amérique est-elle trop riche?*, 52–53.

56. Quotations are from Ernest van den Haag, "Sur la Culture populaire américaine," *Les Temps modernes*, October 1958, 690, 699.

57. Siegfried, *America at Mid-Century*, 352.

58. Aron, "From France," 70.

59. "Petit Lexique américain," 749.

60. Aron, "From France," 70.

61. Serge Groussard, "L'Amérique et nous."

62. Winock, " 'US Go Home,' " 20.

63. Edgar Morin, *L'Esprit du temps* (1962), 15.

64. Lens, "L'Homme standard," March 1959, 394.

65. Maurois in UNESCO, *Old World and the New*, 321–25.

66. Robert Escarpit, *Le Monde,* 14 February 1951.

67. *Le Monde,* 23 October 1957.

68. Philippe Labro, *The Foreign Student,* trans. William Byron (1988), 249.

69. Jacques Maritain, *Reflections on America* (1958), 29. Europeans, Maritain contended, were equally acquisitive and gadget-minded, but they were less open about it.

70. Maritain, *Reflections,* 188.

71. Julien, *Le Monde,* 19 March 1959.

72. Domenach, "Le Modèle américain," October 1960, 1531.

73. Quotes in this paragraph are from excerpts of Simone de Beauvoir's *L'Amérique au jour le jour* published in *Les Temps modernes* no. 10 (1948): 1836–44.

74. Jean-Paul Sartre, *Situations III* (1949), 126. Quoted by Jean-Philippe Mathny, "L''Américanisme,' est-il un humanisme? Sartre aux Etats-Unis, 1945–46," *The French Review* 62 (February 1989): 458. My interpretation relies on Mathny's essay.

75. Sartre, *Situations III,* 129–30.

76. Béguin's quotes from "Réflexions sur l'Amérique," 887, 890.

77. Domenach, "Le Modèle américain," July-August 1960, 1231.

78. Aron, "From France," 71.

79. Ibid.

80. Cyrille Arnavon, *L'Américanisme et nous* (1958), 341, 345, 370.

81. Reporting from the United States in the months of soul searching that followed the launch of Sputnik, Claude Julien explained how America's faults, e.g., its obsession with consumerism and profits, had caused its loss of technological-scientific leadership to the Russians (*Le Monde,* 23 October 1957). Another correspondent, Jean Schwoebel, used the occasion of Sputnik to reproach the United States for its misplaced priorities ("Les Etats-Unis à l'heure de la recession," *Le Monde,* 1–7 April 1958).

82. Domenach, "Le Modèle américain," October 1960, 1534, 1530.

83. In the wake of 1956 several former PCF militants like Edgar Morin who had broken with Stalinism, along with other leftist intelligentsia, founded the review *Arguments.* See Sandrine Treiner, "La revue 'Arguments,' 1956–62" (mémoire de maîtrise, Institut d'études politiques, Paris, 1987). For the impact of 1956 on Communist intellectuals and *compagnons de route,* see Jean-François Sirinelli, *Intellectuels et passions françaises* (1990), 167–91.

84. Quotes in this paragraph are from Albert Béguin, "Les Flammes de Budapest," *Esprit,* December 1956, 771–78.

85. Harold Rosenberg, "Fantaisie orgaméricaine," *Les Temps modernes* no. 152 (1958): 583. This issue of *Temps modernes* was devoted to new aspects of American society.

86. Pierre Nora ("America and the French Intellectuals," 329–30) locates the turning point for America's image in the years 1956–58 for a series of reasons that include the Communist "diaspora"; Gaullist anti-Americanism; the rise in the standard of living; the Algerian war; and the shift to a new language of social science.

87. For example, see G. Rottier, "Nourriture, logement ou télévision?" *Esprit,* December 1957, 737–46.

88. Pierre Emmanuel, "Is France Being Americanized?", *The Atlantic Monthly* 201 (June 1958): 35–38.

89. *Le Monde* closely followed this shift. See, for example, André Fontaine's series in the 31 July and the 1, 2 August 1957 issues.

90. Domenach, "Le Modèle américain," July–August 1960, 1231, and October 1960, 1534.

91. Pinto, "Sociology as a Cultural Phenomenon," 157 ff.

92. Aron's course was later published as *Dix-huit leçons sur la société industrielle* (1962). In 1955 he published his celebrated attack, *L'Opium des intellectuels,* against the Marxists.

93. Geneviève d'Haucourt, *La Vie américaine* (1958).

94. Julien, *Le nouveau nouveau Monde,* 268–69.

95. "Les Sciences sociales aux Etats-Unis," *Esprit,* January 1959.

96. Brindillac, "Promenade aux Etats-Unis."

Chapter 6. The Gaullist Exorcism

1. Philippe de St-Robert, *Le Jeu de la France* (1967), 157.

2. My interpretation of Gaullist foreign policy relies mainly on the following works: Stanley Hoffmann's two essays in his collection *Decline or Renewal? France since the 1930s* (1974), 283–331, 332–62; Michael Harrison, *The Reluctant Ally: France and Atlantic Security* (Baltimore, 1981); Alfred Grosser, *Affaires extérieures. La politique de la France 1944–1984* (1984); Edward Kolodziej, *French International Policy under de Gaulle and Pompidou* (Ithaca, 1974); and the articles, especially Anton De Porte's "De Gaulle's Europe: Playing the Russian Card," in the issue of *French Politics and Society* 8 (Fall 1990) devoted to de Gaulle. I also used the papers prepared for conferences on de Gaulle held during 1989 and 1990, especially those of Frank Costigliola (on John Kennedy), Richard Challener (on John Foster Dulles), and Lloyd Gardner (on Lyndon Johnson) that will appear in *De Gaulle and the United States, 1930–1970: A Centennial Reappraisal,* ed. Nicholas Wahl and Robert Paxton (1993). Another important source is Jean Lacouture, *De Gaulle,* vol. 3, *Le Souverain* (1986). The abridged translation of the three-volume Lacouture biography is Jean Lacouture, *De Gaulle,* vol. 1, *The Rebel, 1890–1944,* trans. Patrick O'Brian (1990); and vol. 2, *The Ruler, 1945–1970,* trans. Alan Sheridan (1992). My citations will be from the English translation.

3. Charles de Gaulle, *Discours et messages: Avec le renouveau, mai 1958–juillet 1962* (1970), 3:198.

4. NARA, 611.51/8–1659, 16 August 1959, Ambassador Houghton to Sec. of State.

5. The American embassy reported that de Gaulle "knows that if we wanted to, we could give him far greater satisfaction than we have to date in meeting his requests. If we were willing to give France a status of real partnership in formulating world policies and military strategy, the other problems might be more readily solved. He undoubtedly realizes we are

unwilling to do this and has therefore embarked in rough poker playing tactics with us" (NARA, 611.51/5–559, 5 May 1959, Livingston Merchant to Sec. of State).

6. Evidence is not conclusive on this issue, but de Gaulle did speak privately about replacing the Atlantic alliance with bilateral pacts (Lacouture, *De Gaulle* 2:382). It is difficult to see how a complete separation from NATO would have benefited France.

7. Karl W. Deutsch et al., *France, Germany, and the Western Alliance: A Study of Elite Attitudes on European Integration and World Politics* (1967), 20–22, 60–69. Nearly 150 politicians, military officers, civil servants, business-men, and intellectuals were interviewed by American social scientists in the summer of 1964.

8. This group included Emmanuel d'Astier de la Vigerie, Pierre Emmanuel, David Rousset, and Jean-Marie Domenach (Sirinelli, *Intellectuels et passions françaises*, 241).

9. Stanley Hoffmann, "De Gaulle, l'Europe et l'Alliance," *Esprit*, June 1963, 1058–83.

10. Jean-Marie Domenach, "Les Contradictions de l'anti-américanisme de gauche," *Esprit*, July–August 1963, 100. Michel Winock (*Chronique des années soixante*, 1987, 155–56) recalls this "Gaullism" at *Esprit*.

11. Domenach, "Encore sur l'anti-américanisme," *Esprit*, October 1963, 458.

12. Serge Mallet, "Un certain antagonisme," in *Les Américains et nous* (1966), 139–49. This title was published separately but appeared originally as an issue (no. 26, 1966) of the journal *La Nef* (hereafter cited as *Les Américains et nous*). In *Esprit* also see Mallet's articles: "Le deuxième âge du gaullisme" (June 1963, 1041–57) and "L'Après-gaullisme et l'unité socialiste," (July–August 1963, 30–42).

13. Gaston Defferre, "L'Indispensable Europe," *Les Américains et nous*, 151–59.

14. Editorials by Beuve-Méry in *Le Monde*, 16 January and 31 July 1963, 25 July 1964, and 6 February 1965. Also see Jeanneney and Julliard, *"Le Monde" de Beuve-Méry*, 237–40.

15. *Le Monde*, 19 April 1966.

16. An Institut français d'opinion publique (IFOP) poll of late 1957 showed that 38 percent wanted American troops to leave "immediately" and only 26 percent wanted them to remain. By early 1960 58 percent were very hostile to the GIs while only 20 percent were favorable (IFOP, *Les Français et de Gaulle*, ed. Jean Charlot [1970], 77). A Gallup poll of 1966 showed that 41 percent believed U.S. military bases in France were a "bad thing" and that only 29 percent termed them a "good thing" for French security, with 30 percent saying they didn't know (*The Gallup International Public Opinion Polls: France, 1939, 1944–75* [1976], 1:530–31).

17. Under the Fourth Republic the proportion of those polled who rejected the integration of France into the Western bloc oscillated between 39 and 51 percent but reached a peak of 57 percent following the end of the war in Indochina. After 1958 an absolute majority chose nonalignment (IFOP, *Les Français*, 78).

18. "Pacte Atlantique: les Français désavouent de Gaulle," *Le Nouvel Observateur*, 18–24 October 1967, 26–29. Even 44 percent of those who voted Communist wanted to retain NATO. In 1966 to the question: "At the present time do you think NATO is essential to the security of France?", 46 percent said yes; 22 percent said no; and 32 percent said they didn't know (*Gallup Polls*, 1:519). To the query posed in March–April 1966 "Do you think it desirable that France withdraw from NATO?," 38 percent said no; 22 percent said yes; 40 percent abstained (IFOP, *Les Français*, 269). Interviews with members of the elite revealed a preference for reform, but not for withdrawal from NATO (Deutsch, *France, Germany, and the Western Alliance*, 78).

19. Polls from 1956 to 1968 in IFOP, *Les Français*, 264.

20. Ibid., 265–67.

21. Polls taken in 1964 and 1965 (ibid., 268).

22. Serge Berstein, *La France de l'expansion: La République gaullienne, 1958–1969* (1989), 1:271. Since the left opposed de Gaulle's regime and his policies, 29 percent disapproval does not seem like a high figure.

23. Those who estimated that independence was possible at the political level fell from 46 to 34 percent; at the economic level, from 41 to 26 percent; and on the military level, from 31 to 28 percent (IFOP, *Les Français*, 88).

24. Jean Charlot, "Les Elites et les masses devant l'indépendance nationale d'après les enquêtes d'opinion" in *Les Conditions de l'indépendance nationale dans le monde moderne*, Institut Charles de Gaulle (1977), 39–49.

25. De Gaulle, *Discours et messages: Pour l'effort, août 1962–décembre 1965* (1970), 4:341.

26. Ibid., 4:429.

27. Lacouture, *De Gaulle* 2:363–64.

28. From an article entitled "Mobilisation économique à l'étranger" that first appeared in 1934 and has been reprinted in Charles de Gaulle, *Trois Etudes précédées du mémorandum du 26 janvier 1940* (1971), 185.

29. Cited in Alfred Grosser, *The Western Alliance* (1982), 211.

30. Charles de Gaulle, *Memoirs of Hope: Renewal and Endeavor*, trans. Terence Kilmartin (1971), 35.

31. Charles de Gaulle, *Mémoires d'espoir: L'Effort* (1970–71), 119. My translation differs slightly for this quotation, as it does for the subsequent one, from that of the English translation (*Memoirs of Hope*, 342).

32. De Gaulle, *Mémoires d'espoir: Le Renouveau 1958–62* (1970–71), 115–17 (English version in *Memoirs of Hope*, 341). Although de Gaulle wrote these lines in 1970, he makes them appear in his memoirs as if they preceded 1968.

33. John Bovey, "Charles XI," *French Politics and Society* 9 (Spring 1991): 35.

34. Quoted in André Passeron, *De Gaulle parle: 1962–1966* (1966), 2:306.

35. Charles E. Bohlen, *Witness to History 1929–1969* (1973), 511.

36. Quoted in Lacouture (*De Gaulle* 1:334–35) from an interview the journalist had with Pleven.

37. Ambassade de France, *French Foreign Policy, 1968*, 103–4.

38. *Le Monde*, 29 November 1967.

39. Data on the growth of consumerism are found in Jean-Pierre Rioux, "Vive la consommation," *L'Histoire* no. 102 (1987): 90–100, and Jean Baudrillard, *La Société de consommation* (1970), 41–59.

40. Marc Cantrel, "Les Américains explorent un marché: France," *Direction* no. 97 (1963): 710.

41. Rioux, "Vive la consommation," 95–96.

42. Fernand Braudel and Ernest Labrousse, eds., *Histoire économique et sociale de la France*, vol. 4, pt. 3 (1982), 1289.

43. Edgar Morin, *The Red and the White: Report from a French Village* (1970), 58. Similar changes are reported by Wylie in *Village in the Vaucluse*.

44. Claude Krief, "La France dans dix ans," *L'Express*, 27 June 1963, 34.

45. Areas that were seemingly resistant to the New World included literature and theater; in some fields such as comics and popular music, American dominance actually retreated. For the later years see Pascal Ory, *L'Entre-deux mai: histoire culturelle de la France, mai 1968–mai 1981* (1983), 200–4.

46. Georges Perec, *Les Choses: A Story of the Sixties*, trans. Helen Lane (1967), 58.

47. John Ardagh, *The New French Revolution* (London, 1968), 264, 228–29, 458.

48. Polls taken in 1962 and 1967 (IFOP, *Les Français*, 299, 90–91).

49. Rioux, "Vive la consommation," 100.

50. IFOP, *Les Français*, 299.

Chapter 7. The American Challenge

1. The response to these layoffs is reported in Olivier Brault, "Indépendance nationale et investissements américains: la politique française à l'égard des investissements directs américains sous les présidences du général de Gaulle et de Georges Pompidou" (mémoire de maîtrise, Université de Lille III, 1986), 35–36.

2. *L'Express*, 30 May 1966, 45.

3. *Le Monde*, 1 February 1963.

4. This interpretation of the general's interest and responsibility can be found in the account of one of his closest financial advisers, Alain Prate (*Les Batailles économiques du général de Gaulle* [1978], 18).

5. As a condition of returning to power in the late spring of 1958, de Gaulle had promised to respect the treaty. Moreover, several members of his cabinet strongly supported the treaty—some had actually signed it. See Edmond Jouve, *Le Général de Gaulle et la construction de l'Europe, 1940–1966* (1967), 1:211–13. In part the general was keeping his word and honoring his nation's commitments. In addition de Gaulle acted to promote the Europe of the Six in order to eliminate the British-sponsored free-trade area. The Six

were in danger because the British hoped to derail the fledgling European community with their own scheme. With the help of Chancellor Adenauer in late 1958, de Gaulle opted for the Six and killed the British project. France's immediate entry into the Common Market strengthened its future and weakened pressures from outside the Six for a wider free trade area (NARA, 840.00/1–659, 6 January 1959, Butterworth to Sec. of State). Moreover, de Gaulle feared that France would be left behind should he delay France's entry. It seems likely that in 1958, despite certain misgivings about the Rome treaties, he entertained hope of constructing his kind of Europe—since in his words the community existed only "on paper"—and he did not want to start from an inferior position.

6. Television address of 30 January 1959 in de Gaulle, *Discours et messages* 3:78.

7. De Gaulle, *Memoirs of Hope*, 134–35.

8. Rainier Hellmann, *Puissance et limites des multinationales* (Tours, 1974), 72.

9. For one thing, it is difficult to ascertain the "nationality" of capital. A considerable fraction of American money arrived via Swiss or Belgian subsidiaries, which means that most estimates err by understating quantities. Only gross investments entered official figures, making calculations even less reliable. And how these estimates were made varied from one statistical agency to another. Nor is the distinction between "direct" and "portfolio" investment always clear.

10. Report of the Ministry of Industry in "Les Investissements étrangers dans l'industrie française," *Perspectives*, 9 October 1965, 2. Data on direct investment on a country basis can be found in the annual volumes U.S. Department of Commerce, Bureau of the Census, *Statistical Abstract of the United States* (Washington, D.C.).

11. Erick Schmill, *Les Investissements étrangers en France* (1966), 44.

12. Data on sectoral investment can be found in numerous studies. See for example Louis Manuali, *La France face à l'implantation étrangère* (1967); Gilles Y. Bertin, *L'Investissement des firmes étrangères en France 1945–1962* (1963); Jacques Gervais, *La France aux investissements étrangers* (1963); Erick Schmill, *Les Investissements étrangers en France*; Christopher Layton, *Trans-Atlantic Investments*, The Atlantic Institute (Boulogne-sur-Seine, 1968); Allan W. Johnstone, *United States Direct Investment in France* (Cambridge, Mass., 1965).

13. Hellmann, *Puissance et limites*, 75.

14. *New York Times*, 25 and 27 March 1963.

15. Quoted by Rosine Dusart, "The Impact of the French Government on American Investment in France," *Harvard International Law Club Journal* 7 (Winter 1965): 85.

16. Henri Nouyrit, "L'Implantation des capitaux américains dans la C.E.E. vue de Bruxelles," *L'Economie*, 22 January 1965, 11–12.

17. Press release published in *Agence France Presse économique*, 24 January 1963.

18. Quoted by Johnstone, *United States Direct Investment*, 27.

19. "Business en France," *Le Monde*, 15 June 1965.

20. Cited in Brault, "Indépendance nationale," 48.

21. Maurice-Bokanowski announced these criteria in the summer of 1965 (Hellmann, *Puissance et limites,* 77).

22. Paul Lemerle, an economist working for the plan, told *Fortune* that "France must not go so soft as to let important economic decisions be made on the other side of the Atlantic. . . . The U.S. already has responsibility for strategic decisions affecting the peace of the world; it is excessive for them to assume economic power of the same order" (Richard Austin Smith, "Nationalism Threatens U.S. Investment," *Fortune,* August 1965, 130).

23. Jonathan Wise Polier, "Indépendance nationale et investissement étranger, une étude de cas: la politique française à l'égard des investissements américains, 1945–1967" (mémoire de maîtrise, Fondation nationale des sciences politiques, 1967), 94–97.

24. Jean Meynaud and Dusan Sidjanski, *L'Europe des affaires* (1967), 75.

25. For opposition to Libaron and other American investments in agriculture, see *Le Monde,* 25 January and 5 March 1963. Richard Grenier, "U.S. Investments in France," *The Reporter,* 6 June 1963, 25; Ardagh, *The New French Revolution,* 93–95; Polier, "Indépendance nationale," 54–63.

26. *Le Monde,* 25 January 1963.

27. Ardagh, *The New French Revolution,* 95.

28. Polier, "Indépendance nationale," 97–103. Georges Vieillard, *"L'Affaire" Bull* (1969) is a collection of documents on the affair by the former director compiled in 1965. Henri Stern, *La Crise de la compagnie des Machines Bull* (1966), is a report drawn up by the local CFDT union. The legal aspects can be found in Robert D. W. Landon, "Franco-American Joint Ventures in France: Some Problems and Solutions; the Compagnie des Machines Bull-General Electric as an Illustrative Example, *Harvard International Law Club Journal* 7 (Spring 1966): 238–85.

29. Pierre Lelong, "Le Général de Gaulle et les industries de pointe" in *"L'Entourage" et de Gaulle,* ed. Gilbert Pilleul (1979), 191–95.

30. Brault, "Indépendance nationale," 44 n.4.

31. Bull's operations were divided into four new corporations. GE raised its offer to $43 million and won a majority equity interest in the new sales and service corporation as well as a 49 percent share in the manufacturing and in the market research and advertising corporations. A fourth corporation working for national defense remained entirely French, but it failed to develop.

32. Georges Villiers, "Le CNPF s'adresse aux industriels américains," *Patronat français* no. 253 (July 1965): 30. Also Georges Villiers, "Face à la concurrence américaine, les entreprises européennes devront souvent concentrer leurs moyens," *Patronat français* no. 243 (1964): 2–15.

33. "Pour ou contre les investissements américains en France?", *Entreprise* no. 472 (1964): 41–51.

34. Smith, "Nationalism Threatens," 131.

35. Jean Luc, "Les Investissements étrangers," *Le Journal des finances,* March 1963; "Faut-il refuser les investissements américains en Europe?", *Entreprise* no. 387 (1963): 13; Paul Deroin, "Les Investissements américains en France," *L'Economie,* 12 February 1965, 10–12. Also Manuali, *La France,* 67; Smith, "Nationalism Threatens," 128–29; *New York Herald Tribune,* 10 December 1964.

36. Pascal Arrighi, "La Puissance américaine et l'Europe," *Le Capital,* 2 December 1964. Among the experts who favorably assessed American investment yet counseled vigilance were Gervais (*Investissements étrangers*), Manuali (*Implantation étrangère*), and Bertin (*Investissement*); Schmill (*Investissements étrangers*) was far more critical of de Gaulle for politicizing the issue.

37. Maurice Duverger, "Le Grand Dessein," *Le Monde,* 10 January 1963.

38. Pierre Drouin, "Les Américains ont-ils les dents trop longues?", *Le Monde,* 13 May 1964; Alain Murcier, "Business en France," *Le Monde,* 15–18 June 1965. On the food industry see the issue of 23–24 April 1967.

39. *Le Monde,* 5 January 1967.

40. *L'Opinion,* 2 December 1966.

41. To the query, "In your opinion, everything considered, are American investments in France a good thing or a bad thing for our country?", 39 percent said they were good, 27 percent answered "bad," and 34 percent had no opinion in 1970. The principal nay-sayers were those identified with the Communist party as well as farmers and workers ("Investissements américains: les Français sont pour," *Les Informations industrielles et commerciales,* 9 March 1970). Opinion surveys from the mid-1970s indicate that French attitudes toward multinationals were similar to those of most other Western Europeans except that the French people expressed more anxiety—for political reasons—and declared themselves slightly less favorable. The French, more than other nationalities, also tended to identify multinationals with America and while praising them for their technical and managerial leadership also criticized them as "uncontrollable" (Jacques Attali et al., *L'Opinion européenne face aux multinationales* [1977], 47, 71, 75).

42. Brault, "Indépendance nationale," 158–63.

43. Quoted in Hellmann, *Puissance et limites,* 76.

44. Serge Mallet, "Un certain Antagonisme," *La Nef* no. 26 (1966): 148.

45. Gaston Defferre, *Un nouvel Horizon* (1965), 99.

46. *JO, débats, Assemblée nationale,* 26 November 1964, 5588. Another example in which the left criticizes the timidity of Gaullist anti-Americanism is L. Perceval, "Une Société américaine dans le Bas-Rhône-Languedoc," *Economie et politique* no. 104 (1963): 88–90. The Gaullists (Maurice-Bokanowski in *Le Monde,* 25 June 1965) chided Defferre for trying to outbid them on this issue. After failing to lead the left in the presidential campaign, Defferre continued to chastise de Gaulle for failing to protect France from American domination. According to Defferre, building European union rather than issuing Gaullist rodomontades was the answer (Defferre, "L'Indispensable Europe," 151–59).

47. In 1970, under Pompidou's presidency, American investment again became a political issue when Ford abruptly shifted the site of its new plant from Charleville (Ardennes) to Bordeaux where the prime minister, Jacques Chaban-Delmas, was a candidate in a legislative by-election. Servan-Schreiber, representing Nancy, led the attack on what seemed like a flagrant manipulation of foreign investment for political advantage. Chaban-Delmas's rival for the seat from Bordeaux wired a warning to the American Embassy that the United States risked losing its best friends if it continued to interfere in domestic French affairs. Chaban-Delmas won, but the affair lingered on for years (Brault, "Indépendance nationale," 156–57).

48. François Caron, who used the records of the Comité des investissements étrangers, states that in the chemical industry the search for a French partner was usually fruitless ("Foreign Investment and Technology Transfers: The Case of the French Chemical Industry in the 1950s and 1960s as Viewed by the Direction des industries chimiques" in *Overseas Business Activities: Proceedings of the Fuji Conference*, eds. Akio Okochi and Tadakatsu Inoue [Tokyo, 1984], 271). Also see Polier, "Indépendance nationale," 174.

49. "Business en France," *Le Monde,* 18 June 1965.

50. Polier, "Indépendance nationale," 106.

51. Conseil économique et social, "Investissements étrangers en France dans le cadre de la communauté européenne," report to committee on investments and planning by Louis Charvet, 10 May 1966.

52. For example, Jean Boissonnat, "L'Argent étranger," *La Croix,* 25 May 1966; Alain Murcier, "Business en France," *Le Monde,* 18 June 1965. Other experts who took this position are Schmill (*Investissements étrangers*), Bertin (*Investissement*), Jean-Jacques Servan-Schreiber (*Le Défi américain* or, in the English version, *The American Challenge,* trans. Ronald Steel [1968]), and C. Goux and J. F. Landeau, *Le Péril américain: le capital américain à l'étranger* (1971).

53. A summary of this report is "Les Investissements étrangers dans l'industrie française," *Perspectives,* 1–9. A commentary is Michel Herblay, "Investissements américains, la France sait-elle ce qu'elle veut?" *Direction* no. 123 (1965): 1134–37, 1164–73.

54. Maurice-Bokanowski in *Le Monde,* 11 June 1965.

55. Jacques Rueff, the economist and advocate of the gold standard, had written his views about monetary reform to de Gaulle in 1961. Views of de Gaulle's advisers on money matters can be found in Paul Fabra, "The Money Men of France," *Interplay,* January 1968, 37–40. The first ministerial discussions of the problem came in July 1963 (Prate, *Batailles économiques,* 208–9).

56. De Gaulle, *Discours et messages* 4:125. His comments came at his 29 July 1963 press conference.

57. De Gaulle, *Discours et messages* 4:332.

58. Interview with Rueff in *The Economist,* 13 February 1965, 662.

59. At a veritable summit meeting of French and American business leaders that included Georges Villiers, Wilfred Baumgartner (former minister of finance), Roger Blough (U.S. Steel), and Douglas Dillon (former secretary of the treasury), the French echoed the Gaullist arguments about inflation and asked the Americans to attend to their balance of payments deficit (*L'Express,* 16–22 May 1966, 53).

60. Prate (*Batailles économiques,* 221) presents data on dollar conversions from 1959 to 1967 when the Bank of France stopped such exchanges altogether because of shortages in the balance of payments.

61. Maurice Ferro, *De Gaulle et l'Amérique* (1973), 397–98.

62. Examples are *L'Aurore,* 11 January 1968, and *Le Nouvel Observateur,* 28 February 1968.

63. Prate, *Batailles économiques,* 213 n.

64. A former official at the quai d'Orsay, who later served as the governor of the Bank of France, observed that it was de Gaulle's foreign policy rather than

his assessment of financial problems that led him to intervene in monetary affairs (Olivier Wormser, "Le Général de Gaulle et la monnaie," *Etudes gaulliennes* nos. 3 and 4 [1973]: 148).

65. This section depends on the accounts of Edward L. Morse, *Foreign Policy and Interdependence in Gaullist France* (Princeton, 1973), 219–51; Prate, *Batailles économiques,* 201–35; and Kolodziej, *French International Policy under De Gaulle and Pompidou,* 183–210.

66. De Gaulle, *Discours et messages* 4:231. These remarks were made at his press conference on 27 November 1967.

67. De Gaulle instructed French negotiators at Stockholm that the conditions for approval of the SDRs were specific American commitments to solve their payments deficits; new voting procedures in the IMF that would give the Six veto powers; and maintenance of stringent rules on activating the drawing rights (Prate, *Batailles économiques,* 226). France secured only the veto powers for the Six (*The Economist,* 6 April 1968, 57–58).

68. Remark made in March 1968 (Prate, *Batailles économiques,* 229 n.).

69. Kolodziej, *French International Policy,* 205.

70. Morse, *Foreign Policy,* 250.

71. Direct annual investment in France between 1963 and 1966 (in millions of dollars), according to U.S. Department of Commerce figures (*Statistical Abstract of the United States*), fell from 210 to 149 while it rose from 304 to 646 in West Germany, from 114 to 169 in Italy, from 70 to 146 in Belgium and Luxembourg, and from 70 to 173 in the Netherlands.

72. *Le Monde,* 6 January 1966.

73. Prate, *Batailles économiques,* 215.

74. Cited by Brault, "Indépendance nationale," 68.

75. Interview with Debré in *Entreprise* no. 552 (1966): 27.

76. *Combat,* 24 May 1966.

77. A view expressed by the Direction des industries chimiques (Caron, "Foreign Investment," 274–75).

78. A thorough analysis of the new procedures adopted in 1966–67 is Charles Torem and William L. Craig, "Control of Foreign Investment in France," *Michigan Law Review* 66 (February 1968): 669–720.

79. According to Raymond Marcellin, the minister of industry, reported in *La Vie française,* 25 November 1966.

80. For example, Debré and Marcellin, the minister of industry, disagreed over the request of Mobil Oil, which intended to use by-products from its existing refinery, to build a fertilizer plant with a French associate in the Seine-Maritime. Marcellin echoed worries of the chemical industry about the financial and technical power of the giant American corporation. Debré was more receptive and Pompidou had to adjourn any decision for a year (*L'Indépendant,* 23 November 1966).

81. Robert B. Dickie, *Foreign Investment in France: A Case Study* (Dobbs Ferry, N.Y., 1970), 74–87; Brault, "Indépendance nationale," 126–53; Caron, "Foreign Investment," 270–73.

82. *New York Times,* 23 January 1967.

83. "M. Debré répond aux informations," *Informations industrielles et commerciales,* 18 November 1966, 30–35.

84. *Combat,* 24 May 1966.

85. Diana Pinto, in an unpublished paper of May 1983, has analyzed the commercial success of *Le Défi.*

86. Servan-Schreiber, *The American Challenge,* 30, 14.

87. Ibid., 277.

88. *Le Monde,* 29 November 1967.

89. French legislation adopted in 1967 on capital movements made no distinction between investments made by community-based companies and those from outside the Common Market. The European Commission started legal action in 1968 and the following year brought France before the European Court of Justice on the grounds that its legislation violated community rules on the right of establishment and the free movement of capital. The commission was not satisfied with explanations from Paris that French restrictions did not prohibit direct investment coming from companies in other community countries as long as these companies were truly European and not subsidiaries of non-European, i.e., American, firms. The commission pointed out that France was obligated to give nationals or companies of other member states identical treatment to that granted French citizens or French firms. It regarded any company as duly constituted within the European community if it had its administrative or legal headquarters within the territory of the Six. The Treaty of Rome, the commission held, made no distinction with respect to the origin of capital or nationality of shareholders—which the French considered essential for determining the legality of an investment. Thus according to the commission's interpretation most subsidiaries of American firms qualified for community protection under the Rome treaty.

In 1971, after years of maneuvering, the French government, in order to avoid a court decision that would have definitively established equality among European and non-European companies situated within the Common Market, modified its legislation to conform to community practice. Companies from outside the European community still had to give prior notification for investment but for insiders such notification was an automatic authorization (*Financial Times,* 24 April 1969; Hellmann, *Puissance et limites,* 79; Brault, "Indépendance nationale," 96–97).

90. *Paris-Presse l'Intransigeant,* 30 April 1969.

91. In early 1971 Prime Minister Chaban-Delmas claimed that in two years his government had rejected fewer than ten requests by American companies to make direct investments (Hellmann, *Puissance et limites,* 81–82).

92. *L'Express* (2–8 March 1970) and *Le Monde* (20 February 1970) report this survey.

93. Quoted in *La Croix,* 31 July 1970.

94. *Combat,* 26 February 1970.

95. Data presented to the interministerial committee on foreign investment stated the ratio between American and European requests for authorization as 45/64 in 1965 and 50/53 in 1966 ("Communiqué," Service de l'information du ministère de l'économie et des finances, 12 January 1967).

96. Service de l'information du ministère de l'économie et des finances, "Evolution des mouvements de capitaux privés entre la France et l'extérieur . . .

de 1968 à 1973," *Etudes et bilans,* February 1975, 11. Cf. Brault, "Indépendance nationale," 75.

97. According to Gilles Y. Bertin (*L'Industrie française face aux multinationales* [1975], 14–15) until 1972 the U.S. still contributed about half the total (direct and portfolio) of foreign investments in France, but America's share declined vis-à-vis the EC after 1966. From 1967 to 1969 the U.S. and the EC contributed about equal shares of total investment.

98. *Les Informations industrielles et commerciales,* 19 November 1965.

99. Smith, "Nationalism Threatens," 126–31, 228–36; Myra Wilkins, *The Maturing of Multinational Enterprise* (Cambridge, Mass., 1974), 345.

100. Meynaud and Sidjanski, *L'Europe des affaires,* 78–79; Layton, *Trans-Atlantic Investments,* 44–48.

101. Manuali, *Implantation étrangère,* 11–13.

102. Dickie, *Foreign Investment,* 20.

103. For example Benelux received $47, West Germany $37, France $30, and Italy $16, according to Meynaud and Sidjanski, *L'Europe des affaires,* 77.

104. Bertin, *L'Industrie française,* 50–51.

105. France's share fell in this decade from 28.7 to 21.2 percent. West Germany's share advanced from 35 to 41.7 percent (Hellmann, *Puissance et limites,* 41–42). See note 71.

106. There were other reasons such as a falling rate of return on investment, Washington's efforts at curbing the outflow of private capital, e.g., the Interest Equalization Tax adopted in 1963 and mandatory restraints enforced after 1967.

Chapter 8. Détente

1. An insightful survey of this problem is Paul Gagnon, "*La Vie future*: Some French Responses to the Technological Society," *Journal of European Studies* 6 (1976): 172–89.

2. For example, Jean Baudrillard, *Le Système des objets* (1968) and *La Société de consommation* (1970); Henri Lefebvre, *La Vie quotidienne dans le monde moderne* (1968); Bertrand de Jouvenel, *Arcadie: essais sur le mieux vivre* (1968); Alain Touraine, *La Société post-industrielle* (1969); Georges Elgozy, *Les Damnés de l'opulence* (1970).

3. Jean-Francis Held, "L'Homme-auto," in *La Nef* no. 37 (1969): 132. This issue of *La Nef* was devoted to essays on consumer society.

4. Philippe Bénéton and Jean Touchard, "Les Interprétations de la crise de mai–juin 1968," *Revue française de science politique* 20 (February 1970): 524–25. A few references to consumer society can be found in the documents reproduced in Alain Schnapp and Pierre Vidal-Naquet, *Journal de la commune étudiante: textes et documents* (1969), 356, 566–69, 595–98. The literature on the events of 1968 is voluminous, but a good recent interpretation is Henri Weber, *Mai 1968: vingt ans après* (1988).

5. Flanner, *Paris Journal,* 491.

6. Over half those polled in 1964 liked Americans, contrasted to only 11 percent who held a "bad opinion" (Gérard Vincent, *Les Jeux français* [1978], 326).

7. To the question, "Which people *least* resembled the French?", those polled said: the Americans (43 percent), the British (22 percent), the Italians (8 percent), and the Germans (7 percent) (Grosser, *The Western Alliance*, 217).

8. Alain Bosquet, *Les Américains sont-ils adultes?* (1969). A similar essay is Jacques Lusseyran, *Douce, trop douce Amérique* (1968).

9. Maurice Duverger, "Dans la carapace d'une automobile," *L'Express*, 5 March 1964, 39–40.

10. René Etiemble, *Parlez-vous franglais?* (1973 ed.), 37; the first edition was 1964. Page references for further quotations from this work are in the text.

11. Noting, for example, how the United Fruit company got the Pentagon's help to unseat Latin American rulers who interfered in its business, Etiemble wrote that one could understand "Washington's hate against the only European statesman who, since the 'Liberation,' dares resist the pretensions of the dollar. Since the OAS has not been able to get rid of him, and since they have not been able to buy him, American finance is out to get his hide" (234).

12. "As for the Yankee military who have automobiles baptized as *bus d'école* driving around the streets of Paris . . . I have to note that if the Nazis tortured and massacred members of the Resistance, they made the effort to draw up their atrocious *tableaux d'honneur* in good French" (239).

13. Philip H. Coombs, *The Fourth Dimension of Foreign Policy: Educational and Cultural Affairs*, Council on Foreign Relations (1964), 111–13.

14. St-Robert, *Le Jeu de la France*, 132–48.

15. Sirinelli, *Intellectuels et passions françaises*, 245–61.

16. Defferre, "L'Indispensable Europe," 152–53.

17. Claude Julien's earlier works include *Le nouveau nouveau Monde* (1960).

18. Claude Julien, *L'Empire américain* (1968), 502. Further page references for this work are in the text. There is a debate between Julien, Pierre Cot, and Jean-François Revel in "La Gauche face à l'empire américain," *Dire* no. 2 (1968): 12–27.

19. Employing a conventional Marxist approach Eric Gaument (*Le Mythe américain* [1970]) debunked America's economic achievement and ridiculed the French Americanizers. Real wages may have risen in the United States, but there was plenty of poverty and the middle class had difficulty making ends meet, according to this Communist critic. One could not speak of affluence in American education, housing, or medicine—not to mention the gross inequalities of wealth based on region, gender, and race. The Americanization of Europe would only bring the most noxious traits of unbridled capitalism. Marxist underconsumption theory led Gaument to predict, in the distant future, an intensification of the class struggle in America with the poor joining the working class and its white-collar allies.

20. Emmanuel Astier de la Vigerie, "Faut-il être anti-Américain?", *Réalités* no. 254 (1967): 40.

21. Domenach, "L'Empire américain," *Esprit*, April 1966, 650.

22. Domenach, "L'Explosion", *Esprit*, October 1970, 489.

23. Domenach, "Critique d'un éloge," *Esprit*, December 1969, 877.

24. Domenach, "Notes d'un retour en Amérique," *Esprit*, November 1969, 621.

25. Domenach's introduction in *Esprit*, June-July 1968, 968–69.

26. Domenach, "Notes d'un retour," 624–25.

27. Edgar Morin, *Journal de Californie* (1970), 209; further page references for this work are in the text. Extracts from his journal appeared under the title "La Mutation occidentale" in *Esprit* (October 1970, 515–48).

28. Jean-François Revel, *Without Marx or Jesus: The New American Revolution Has Begun*, trans. J. F. Bernard (1971), 47. Further page references for this work are in the text.

29. Quoted by Nora, "America and the French Intellectuals," 330.

30. Jean Guiget, *Aspects de la civilisation américaine*, 2d ed. (1971).

31. Bernard Cazes, "La Malaise dans la consommation," *La Nef* no. 37 (1969): 135–46.

32. *Réflexions pour 1985*, La Documentation française (1964), 12–13. A similar position was advocated by the former planner Lionel Stoleru in his study *L'Impératif industriel* (1969).

33. Pierre Massé, cited in Henry Rousso, ed., *De Monnet à Massé* (1986), 216.

34. Stanley Hoffmann et al., *A la recherche de la France* (1963) is a translation of *In Search of France* (Cambridge, Mass., 1961). Hoffmann had been interpreting American policy and Franco-American relations for years in such reviews as *Esprit*, and Wylie's work on rural France was well known.

35. Michel Crozier, "Le Climat intellectuel," *Esprit*, January 1968, 9; further page references for this work are in the text. In the early 1980s Crozier furnished a far more sober assessment in *Le Mal américain* (1980), in which he also charted his own intellectual itinerary in America since the late 1940s.

36. Raymond Aron, *Progress and Disillusion: The Dialectics of Modern Society* (London, 1968), 192.

37. Quoted in Pinto, "Sociology as a Cultural Phenomenon," 174–75.

38. See, for example, Fourastié's *Grand Espoir du XXe siècle*, which went through several editions; and his title in the "Que sais-je" series, *La Productivité*, which also had multiple editions. Fourastié was only slightly less optimistic in a later book: *Lettre ouverte à quatre milliard d'hommes* (1970).

39. Richard F. Kuisel, *Capitalism and the State in Modern France* (1981), 244.

40. Fourastié quoted in Gagnon, "*La Vie future*: Some French Responses," 177.

41. Jean St-Geours, *Vive la société de consommation* (1971).

42. Louis Armand, "Faut-il être anti-Américain?", *Réalités* no. 254 (1967): 38–43. Another rebuttal to anti-Americanism was Julien Teppe, *Contre l'américanophobie* (1969).

43. Jacques Maisonrouge, *Manager international* (1985). Some of the most

active proponents of an American approach to management were Jean Milhaud, Octave Gélinier, and Noël Pouderoux, all of whom were associated with CEGOS. A pioneering effort toward constructing a history of the subject is the collection of essays in a special number of the *Revue française de gestion* (no. 70 [1988]). Roger Priouret published his interviews with managers as *La France et le management* (1968).

44. Gilbert Gantier, "Une Source d'inspiration" in *Les Américains et nous*, 107–18.

45. Servan-Schreiber, *The American Challenge*, 276; further page references for this work are in the text.

46. Interview with Servan-Schreiber, "A propos du 'Défi américain,'" *Promotions* (April–June 1968): 25.

47. Servan-Schreiber, *The American Challenge*, 191–95, and "A Propos," 25.

48. *Le Progrès de Lyon*, 25 April 1968.

49. A lonely exception is Jacques Gasquel (*Perspectives*, 9 March 1968), who argued that in many respects Europe was ahead of the United States and that given the troubles in American society, Servan-Schreiber's next book ought to be titled "La Décadence américaine."

50. Valéry Giscard d'Estaing, "Solitaire Europe," *Le Figaro*, 7 December 1967. Giscard discussed the book with Mitterrand on Europe No. 1 (*Le Monde*, 23 October 1967).

51. The heads of IBM-France and Royal Dutch Shell, Jacques Maison-rouge and André Benard, respectively, saw no answer in trying to create vigorous multinationals by merging European firms that were unprofitable or technological laggards (*L'Express*, 4–10 December 1967; *Sud-Ouest*, 30 November 1967).

52. Julien's objections appear in an interview in *Combat* (29 January 1969). A spokesman for the Parti socialiste unifié observed: "There is the response of the shortsighted idiot that consists of being more American than the Americans in order to better resist them. One does not fight evil with evil or the plague with cholera. The struggle for national independence is indivisible from the struggle for social liberation and it means the substitution of socialism for capitalism, which, in essence, is no different in Europe than in the United States" (Manuel Brindier, "La Réponse socialiste au défi américain," *Le Progrès de Lyon*, 5 March 1968).

53. Mitterrand, "Seule une Europe socialiste . . . ," *Fédération Champagne*, 1 April 1968.

54. The Communist response is in *L'Humanité*, 25 November 1967; Charles Fiterman, "Pour une Europe indépendante, démocratique et pacifique," *Cahiers du communisme*, April 1968, 14–26; *Le Monde*, 17 January 1968.

55. Thierry Maulnier, "Le Modèle américaine," *Figaro*, 5 December 1967.

56. André Piettre in *Le Monde*, 23 December 1967; emphasis is in the original.

57. "Etats-Unis d'Europe ou Europe des Etats-Unis?", *Communauté européenne*, December 1967, 7–10.

Chapter 9. Vive l'Amérique

1. Alain Peyrefitte, *The Trouble with France* (1981) is a translation of *Le Mal français* (1976).

2. Surveys that chart the evolution of French views about American foreign policy from 1976 to 1986 appear in Gallup International, "France and the United States: A Study in Mutual Image" (hereafter cited as Gallup International, 1986); this survey was conducted for the French-American Foundation and *L'Express* over a ten-year period that concluded in April 1986.

3. *Le Canard Enchaîné*, 31 August 1977.

4. Denis Lacorne, "Modernists and Protectionists: The 1970s," in *The Rise and Fall of Anti-Americanism: A Century of French Perception* (1990), eds. Denis Lacorne, Jacques Rupnik, Marie-France Toinet (1990), 143–59. This anthology is an excellent guide to the recent turn to philo-Americanism (original title, *L'Amérique dans les têtes: un siècle de fascinations et d'aversions* [1986]).

5. For example, Jacques Thibau, *La France colonisée* (1980), 163–228.

6. Lacorne, "Modernists," 145.

7. Ibid., 153.

8. Ibid., 150.

9. "Réalités américaines," *L'Humanité*, 18–20, 25–28 January 1972. Also Annie Kriegel, "Consistent Misapprehension: European Views of America and their Logic," *Daedalus* 101 (Fall 1972): 87–102.

10. Denis Lacorne and Jacques Rupnik, "Introduction: France Bewitched by America," in *Rise and Fall of Anti-Americanism*, 18–19.

11. Thibau, *La France colonisée*, 267.

12. Henri Gobard, *La Guerre culturelle, logique du désastre* (1979), 83.

13. Lacorne and Rupnik, "Introduction," 19.

14. *Le Monde*, 20 May 1981.

15. Quoted by Winock, " 'US Go Home,' "19–20.

16. Wylie and Henriquez examined textbooks of the 1960s and 1970s in their article, "French Images of American Life."

17. The magazine *Le Point* sponsored a poll in 1976 cited in William Pfaff, "The French Exception," *New Yorker*, 24 January 1977, 66–75.

18. R. Aranda ("Les Etats-Unis vus par les lycéens parisiens," 1976) cited in Vincent, *Les Jeux français*, 326.

19. Pfaff, "French Exception," 69.

20. *Le Canard Enchaîné*, 31 August 1977. This newspaper ran a series entitled "L'Américain Connection, ou un Peau-rouge en France," in its issues of 10, 17, 24, 31 August and 6 September 1977.

21. For Lang's speech see the 29 and 30 July 1982 issues of *Le Monde*.

22. Chevènement, "Pour l'indépendance nationale," *Le Monde*, 11 May 1983.

23. Nora, "America and the French Intellectuals," 334.

24. Ibid.

25. Diana Pinto, "De l'Anti-Américanisme à l'Américanophilie: l'itinérarie de l'intelligentsia," *French Politics and Society* 9 (March 1985): 18–26; and her

essays: "The French Intelligentsia Rediscovers America" in *Rise and Fall of Anti-Americanism*, 97–107, and "The Left, the Intellectuals, and Culture," in *The Mitterrand Experiment*, eds. George Ross, Stanley Hoffmann, and Sylvia Malzacher (Oxford, 1987), 217–28.

26. Jean Daniel, "Les Mythes de la gauche française," in *Le Reflux américain: décadence ou renouveau des Etats-Unis* (1980), 109–15.

27. See the review essays by George Ross, "Intellectual Spaces and Places," *French Politics and Society* 6 (July 1988): 7–16; and "Where Have All the Sartres Gone? The French Intelligentsia Born Again," in *Searching for The New France*, eds. James Hollifield and George Ross (1991), 221–49. A generational approach is taken by Pascal Ory and Jean-François Sirinelli in *Les Intellectuels en France, de l'affaire Dreyfus à nos jours* (1986). An important work on leftist intellectuals after the Czech invasion is Pierre Grémion's *Paris-Prague* (1985).

28. See the issue of *Tel Quel* (nos. 71/73 [Spring 1977]) devoted to the United States.

29. Titles that represent the new passion for America are Georges Suffert, *Les nouveaux Cow-boys: essai sur l'anti-américanisme primaire* (1984); Léo Sauvage, *Les Américains: enquête sur un mythe* (1983); and the article "Pourriez-vous vivre à l'américaine?", *Nouvel Observateur*, 14 September 1984.

30. Pinto, "The Left, the Intellectuals," 221.

31. Jean-Marie Domenach, "Aider plutôt que défendre," *Le Monde*, 10 October 1981.

32. Suffert, *Les nouveaux Cow-boys*.

33. Jean Baudrillard, *Amérique* (1986); the English version is *America* (1988). Other examples of persistent critiques of America are Régis Debray, *Les Empires contre l'Europe* (1985) and Michel Jobert, *Les Américains* (1987).

34. Baudrillard, *America*, 76.

35. The manifesto is reproduced in *Le Monde*, 24 January 1985.

36. *Le Monde*, 6 November 1984.

37. According to a poll taken on the eve of the American presidential elections in 1984, the French preferred the reelection of Ronald Reagan to his opponent Walter Mondale by a margin of 38 percent to 25 percent. This was a stronger pro-Reagan vote than in either Britain or West Germany (*Le Monde*, 6 November 1984).

38. Janice Randall, "In Paris Today *à la mode* means *à l'américaine*," *France Today* (Autumn 1986): 36–39.

39. Such polls can be found in "Les Français aiment les Etats-Unis, mais . . . ", *Le Figaro*, 4 November 1988; Gallup International, 1986; *Le Monde*, 6 November 1984; Jacques Rupnik, "Anti-Americanism and the Modern: The Image of the United States in French Public Opinion," in John Gaffney, ed., *France and Modernisation* (London, 1988), 189–205; and Jacques Rupnik and Muriel Humbertjean, "Images of the United States in Public Opinion," in *Rise and Fall of Anti-Americanism*, 79–96.

40. Some 44 percent of the French said they were pro-American to 15 percent who called themselves anti-American. Comparative figures for West Germany were 35 percent and 19 percent, and for Great Britain 39 percent and 20 percent (*Le Monde*, 6 November 1984).

41. Gallup International, 1986.

42. "Les Français aiment", *Le Figaro.*

43. Gallup International, 1986.

44. "Les Français aiment," *Le Figaro.* Similar findings on American cultural influence are recorded in a 1984 SOFRES poll (*Le Monde,* 6 November 1984).

45. Certain features of this attitudinal profile seem immutable. Political affiliation continued to be the variable determining attitudes toward American foreign policy. As expected, the left remained the least enthusiastic (Gallup International, 1986).

46. Frank and Mary Ann, "France est devenue 'civilisée,'" *La Croix,* 6 May 1976.

47. Nicolas Beau, "Les Français de l'Oncle Sam," *Le Monde,* 4–5 November 1984. In the same issue Pascal Ory recounts the penetration of American popular culture in "Des 'Poilus' de Pershing aux moustaches de Mandrake."

48. Polls cited by Rupnik, "Anti-Americanism and the Modern," 195.

49. Richard Bernstein, *Fragile Glory: A Portrait of France and the French* (1990), 4.

50. Lacorne and Rupnik, "Introduction," 1.

51. *L'Amérique dans les têtes.*

52. Cited in *L'Express,* 27 March 1992, 36. For labor's response to the dress code see the *New York Times,* 25 December 1991. See the forthcoming article on Euro Disney by Martha Zuber in *French Politics and Society.*

53. Marc Fumaroli in *Le Nouvel Observateur,* 9–15 April 1992, 42.

54. *Le Monde,* 12–13 April 1992.

55. Willy Bakeroot, "Des Mythes devenus objets," *Projet,* Spring 1992, 84–92.

56. Finkielkraut, Gallo, and Julliard quoted in the *New York Times,* 13 April 1992.

57. François Reynaert, *Le Nouvel Observateur,* 9–15 April 1992, 43.

58. Lang cited in *Le Monde,* 12–13 April 1992. See also his interview in *L'Express,* 27 March 1992, 44–45.

59. Jean-François Revel in *Le Point,* 21 March 1992, 52.

60. Spokespersons cited by Todd Gitlin in the *New York Times,* 3 May 1992.

61. Fitzpatrick cited in *Le Monde,* 12–13 April 1992.

62. Citations in this paragraph are from *Le Point,* 21 March 1992, 57, 51, 53.

63. Todd Gitlin in the *New York Times,* 3 May 1992.

64. François Forestier in *L'Express,* 27 March 1992, 43.

Chapter 10. Reflections

1. In France the proportion of fast-food meals was 4 percent compared to 12 percent in Britain and 40 percent in the United States, according to the *New York Times,* 12 June 1988.

Select Bibliography

I have chosen some of the major secondary works as a guide for readers who wish to investigate further the topics presented in this discussion of France and the dilemma of Americanization. The criteria for selection, besides general importance, were breadth or scope and currency. And where possible I gave priority to studies in the English language.

Additional bibliographical data, especially discussion of archival and other primary sources like government documents as well as historiographical debates, can be found in the endnotes to each chapter. References for the question of national identity can be found in the endnotes to the first chapter, especially notes 4 and 5.

General Works

Ardagh, John. *The New French Revolution: A Social and Economic Survey of France, 1945–1967.* London: Secker and Warburg, 1968.

"L'Aventure américaine: de La Fayette à Reagan." *L'Histoire* no. 91 (1986): 1–131.

Berstein, Serge. *La République gaullienne, 1958–1969.* Vol 1 of *La France de l'expansion.* Paris: Seuil, 1989.

Costigliola, Frank. *France and the United States: The Cold Alliance since World War II.* New York: Twayne, 1992. (This work appeared too late for my use, but is mentioned here as the most complete survey of Franco-American relations.)

Duroselle, Jean-Baptiste. *France and the United States: From the Beginnings to the Present.* Chicago: University of Chicago Press, 1978.

Flanner, Janet. *Paris Journal, 1944–1971.* 2 vols. New York: Atheneum, 1965–71.

"Franco-American Studies: A Bibliography, 1948–1950." *The French American Review* 5, no. 2 (1981): 94–155.

"Franco-American Studies: A Bibliography, 1951–1953." *The French American Review* 7, no. 2 (1983): 67–178.

Henriquez, Sarella, and Laurence Wylie. "French Images of American Life." *The Tocqueville Review* 4, no. 2 (1982): 176–274.

Jeune, Simon. "Pro-American Sentiment in French Novelists since 1860." In *Two Hundred Years of Franco-American Relations: Papers of the Bicentennial Colloquium of the Society for French Historical Studies in Newport Rhode Island, September 7–10, 1978,* eds. Nancy Roelker and Charles K. Warner, 207–24. N.p., n.d.

Lacorne, Denis, Jacques Rupnik, and Marie-France Toinet, eds. *The Rise and Fall of Anti-Americanism: A Century of French Perceptions.* Trans. Gerry Turner. New York: St. Martin's Press, 1990.

Nora, Pierre. "America and the French Intellectuals." *Daedalus* 107 (Winter 1978): 325–37.

Ory, Pascal, and Jean-François Sirinelli. *Les Intellectuels en France, de l'affaire Dreyfus à nos jours.* Paris: Armand Colin, 1986.

Rioux, Jean-Pierre. *The Fourth Republic, 1944–1958.* Trans. Godfrey Rogers. New York: Cambridge University Press, 1987.

Simonin, Anne. "L'Aventure des idées. Eléments d'une chronologie, 1953–1987." *Le Débat* no. 50 (May–August 1988): 5–170.

Sirinelli, Jean-François. *Intellectuels et passions françaises: manifestes et pétitions au XXe siècle.* Paris: Fayard, 1990.

Strauss, David. *Menace in the West: The Rise of French Anti-Americanism in Modern Times.* Westport, Conn.: Greenwood Press, 1978.

Winock, Michel. " 'US Go Home': l'antiaméricanisme français." *L'Histoire* no. 50 (November 1982): 7–20.

Wylie, Laurence, *Village in the Vaucluse.* 2d ed. Cambridge, Mass.: Harvard University Press, 1964.

Background, 1890–1945

Allen, Donald Roy. *French Views of America in the 1930s.* New York: Garland Press, 1979.

Brooks, Charles W. *America in France's Hopes and Fears, 1890–1920.* 2 vols. New York: Garland Press, 1987.

Duhamel, Georges. *America the Menace: Scenes from the Life of the Future.* Trans. Charles Miner Thompson. Boston: Houghton Mifflin, 1931.

Gagnon, Paul A. "French Views of Postwar America, 1919–1932." Ph.D. diss., Harvard University, 1960.

———. "French Views of the Second American Revolution." *French Historical Studies* 2, no. 4 (1962): 430–49.

Galloux-Fournier, Bernadette. "Un Regard sur l'Amérique: voyageurs français aux Etats-Unis, 1919–1939." *Revue d'histoire moderne et contemporaine* 37 (April–June 1990): pp. 297–307.

Hurstfield, Julian G. *America and the French Nation, 1939–1945.* Chapel Hill: University of North Carolina Press, 1986.

Lacouture, Jean. *De Gaulle: The Rebel, 1890–1944.* Trans. Patrick O'Brian. New York: Norton, 1990.

Nouailhat, Yves-Henri. *France et Etats-Unis, août 1914–avril 1917.* Paris: Publications de la Sorbonne, 1979.

Portes, Jacques. *Une Fascination réticente: Les Etats-Unis dans l'opinion française 1870–1914.* Nancy: Presses universitaires de Nancy, 1990.

Siegfried, André. *America Comes of Age: A French Analysis.* New York: Harcourt Brace, 1927.

Cold War Issues

Amar, Marianne. "Instantanés américains: les Français aux Etats-Unis, 1947–1953." Mémoire de maîtrise, Institut d'études politiques, Paris, 1980.

Caute, David. *Communism and the French Intellectuals, 1914–1960.* New York: Macmillan, 1964.

Chebel d'Appollonia, Ariane. *Histoire politique des intellectuels en France, 1944–1954.* 2 vols. Brussels: Editions Complexe, 1991.

Coleman, Peter. *The Liberal Conspiracy: The Congress for Cultural Freedom and the Struggle for the Mind of Postwar Europe.* New York: Free Press, 1989.

"Les Etats-Unis, les Américains et la France, 1945–53." *Sondages* no. 2 (1953): 1–78.

Greilsamer, Laurent. *Hubert Beuve-Méry, 1902–1989.* Paris: Fayard, 1990.

Grémion, Pierre. "*Preuves* dans le Paris de guerre froide." *Vingtième Siècle* no. 13 (January–March 1987): 63–82.

Hubert-Lacombe, Patricia. "La Guerre froide et le cinéma français, 1946–1953." Thèse de 3e cycle, Institut d'études politiques, Paris, 1981.

Jarraud, François. *Les Américains à Châteauroux, 1951–1967.* Arthon: privately printed, 1981.

Jeanneney, Jean-Noël, and Jacques Julliard. *"Le Monde" de Beuve-Méry ou le métier d'Alceste.* Paris: Seuil, 1979.

Legendre, Bernard, ed. *Le Stalinisme français.* Paris: Seuil, 1980.

Milza, Pierre. "La Guerre froide à Paris: 'Ridgway la peste.' " *L'Histoire* no. 25 (1980): 38–47.

Nouailhat, Yves-Henri. "Aspects de la politique culturelle des Etats-Unis à l'égard de la France de 1945 à 1950." *Relations internationales* no. 25 (1981): 87–111.

Plantier, Jean-Pierre. "La Vision de l'Amérique à travers la presse et la littérature communistes françaises de 1945 à 1953." Mémoire de maîtrise, Institut d'études politiques, Paris, 1972.

Rose, Arnold. "Anti-Americanism in France." *Antioch Review* 13, no. 4 (1952): 468–84.

Verdès-Leroux, Jeannine. *Au service du parti: le parti communiste, les intellectuels et la culture, 1944–1956.* Paris: Fayard, 1983.

Wall, Irwin M. *The United States and the Making of Postwar France, 1945–1954.* New York: Cambridge University Press, 1991.

Winock, Michel. *Histoire politique de la revue "Esprit," 1930–1950.* Paris: Seuil, 1975.

Marshall Plan and the Productivity Drive

Badin, Pierre. *Aux sources de la productivité américaine: premier bilan des missions françaises.* Paris: SADEP, 1953.

Boltanski, Luc. "America, America . . . le Plan Marshall et l'importation du 'management.' " *Actes de la recherche en sciences sociales* no. 38 (1981): 19–41.

Bossuat, Gérard. "L'Aide américaine à la France après la seconde guerre mondiale." *Vingtième Siècle* no. 9 (January–March 1986): 17–35.

Brown, William A., and Redvers Opie. *American Foreign Assistance.* Washington, D.C.: The Brookings Institution, 1953.

Carew, Anthony. *Labour under the Marshall Plan: The Politics of Productivity and the Marketing of Management Science.* Detroit: Wayne State University Press, 1987.

Comité national de la productivité. *Actions et problèmes de productivité: premier rapport du Comité National de la Productivité, 1950–1953.* Paris: n.p., 1953.

Fourastié, Jean. *La Productivité.* Paris: Presses universitaires de France, 1952.

Foussé, Claude. *Traits caractéristiques de la prospérité américaine.* Paris: SADEP, 1953.

Hoffmann, Stanley, and Charles S. Maier, eds. *The Marshall Plan: A Retrospective.* Boulder, Colo.: Westview Press, 1984.

Hogan, Michael J. *The Marshall Plan: America, Britain, and the Reconstruction of Western Europe, 1947–1952.* New York: Cambridge University Press, 1987.

International Cooperation Administration. *European Productivity and Technical Assistance Programs, A Summing Up, 1948–1958.* Technical Cooperation Division, Regional Office. Paris: International Cooperation Administration, 1959.

Kuisel, Richard F. *Capitalism and the State in Modern France: Renovation and Economic Management in the Twentieth Century.* New York: Cambridge University Press, 1981.

———. "The Marshall Plan in Action: Politics, Labor, Industry and the Program of Technical Assistance in France." In *Le Plan Marshall et le relèvement économique de l'Europe.* Paris: Imprimerie Nationale, 1992.

Leduc, Philippe, and Pierre-Louis Mathieu. "La Politique française de productivité depuis la guerre." Mémoire de maîtrise, Institut d'études politiques, Paris, 1961.

Maier, Charles S. "The Politics of Productivity: Foundations of American International Economic Policy after World War Two." In *Between Power and Plenty*, ed. Peter J. Katzenstein, 23–49. Madison: University of Wisconsin Press, 1978.

Margairaz, Michel. "Autour des accords Blum-Byrnes: Jean Monnet entre le consensus national et le consensus atlantique." *Histoire, économie et société* no. 3 (1982): 439–70.

Milward, Alan S. *The Reconstruction of Western Europe, 1945–1951.* Berkeley: University of California Press, 1984.

Monnet, Jean. *Memoirs.* Trans. Richard Mayne. Garden City, N.Y.: Doubleday, 1978.

Organization for European Economic Cooperation. *Problems of Business Management: American Opinions, European Opinions.* Technical Assistance Mission, no. 129. Paris: OEEC, 1954.

Price, Harry B. *The Marshall Plan and Its Meaning.* Ithaca: Cornell University Press, 1955.

Productivité aux Etats-Unis, essai de synthèse: rapport de la cinquième mission française d'experts, 1 mars–20 septembre 1953. Paris: SADEP, 1953.

Wexler, Immanuel. *The Marshall Plan Revisited: The European Recovery Program in Economic Perspective.* Westport, Conn.: Greenwood Press, 1983.

America and Consumer Society, 1950s and 1960s

Alphandéry, Claude. *L'Amérique est-elle trop riche?* Paris: Calmann-Lévy, 1960.

Arnavon, Cyrille. *L'Américanisme et nous.* Paris: Del Duca, 1958.

Aron, Raymond. *Eighteen Lectures on Industrial Society.* Trans. M. K. Bottomore. London: Weidenfeld and Nicolson, 1967.

———. "From France." In *As Others See Us: The United States through Foreign Eyes,* ed. Franz M. Joseph, 57–71. Princeton: Princeton University Press, 1959.

———. *Memoirs: Fifty Years of Political Reflection.* Trans. George Holoch. New York: Holmes and Meier, 1990.

———. *Progress and Disillusion: The Dialectics of Modern Society.* London: Pall Mall Press, 1968.

"Aspects nouveaux de la société américaine." *Les Temps modernes* no. 152 (October 1958): 577–700.

Baudrillard, Jean. *La Société de consommation: ses mythes, ses structures.* Paris: Denoël, 1970.

Beauvoir, Simone de. *America Day by Day.* Trans. Patrick Dudley. London: Duckworth, 1952.

Bosquet, Alain, ed. *Les Américains.* Paris: Delpire, 1958.

———. *Les Américains sont-ils adultes?* Paris: Hachette, 1969.

Crozier, Michel. "Le Climat intellectuel." *Esprit,* January 1968, 3–14.

Domenach, Jean-Marie. "Le Modèle américain." *Esprit,* July–August 1960, 1219–32; September 1960, 1360–74; October 1960, 1520–34.

Etiemble, René. *Parlez-vous franglais?* Paris: Gallimard, 1973.

Fourastié, Jean, and André Laleuf. *Révolution à l'ouest.* Paris: Presses universitaires de France, 1957.

Gagnon, Paul. "'La Vie Future': Some French Responses to the Technological Society." *Journal of European Studies* no. 6 (1976): 172–89.

d'Haucourt, Geneviève. *La Vie américaine.* Paris: Presses universitaires de France, 1958.

Julien, Claude. *L'Empire américain.* Paris: Grasset, 1968.

———. *Le nouveau nouveau Monde.* 2 vols. Paris: Julliard, 1960.

Labro, Philippe. *The Foreign Student.* Trans. William Byron. New York: Ballantine, 1988.

Maritain, Jacques. *Reflections on America.* New York: Scribners, 1958.

Morin, Edgar. *Journal de Californie.* Paris: Seuil, 1970.

Perec, Georges. *Les Choses: A Story of the Sixties.* Trans. Helen Lane. New York: Grove Press, 1967.

Revel, Jean-François. *Without Marx or Jesus: The New American Revolution Has Begun.* Trans J. F. Bernard. Garden City, N.Y.: Doubleday, 1971.

Rioux, Jean-Pierre. "Vive la consommation." *L'Histoire* no. 102 (July–August 1987): 90–100.

Siegfried, André. *America at Mid-Century.* Trans. Margaret Ledésert. New York: Harcourt Brace, 1955.

"La Société de consommation." *La Nef* no. 37 (April–August 1969): 1–222.

UNESCO, *The Old World and the New: Their Cultural and Moral Relations, International Forums of Sao Paulo and Geneva, 1954.* Paris: UNESCO, 1956.

De Gaulle: Relations
with the United States

Alphand, Hervé. *L'Etonnement d'être: journal 1939–1973.* Paris: Fayard, 1977.

Charlot, Jean. *Les Français et de Gaulle.* Paris: Plon, 1971.

Costigliola, Frank. "The Failed Design: Kennedy, De Gaulle and the Struggle for Europe." *Diplomatic History* 8, no. 3 (1984): 227–51.

Couve de Murville, Maurice, Hervé Alphand, and Etienne Burin des Roziers. "Les Relations franco-américaines au temps du général de Gaulle: dossier." *Espoir* no. 26 (March 1979): 37–78.

De Gaulle, Charles. *Memoirs of Hope: Renewal and Endeavor.* Trans. Terence Kilmartin. New York: Simon and Schuster, 1971.

De Gaulle et le service de l'état: des collaborateurs du général témoignent. Paris: Plon, 1977.

DePorte, Anton W. "De Gaulle's Europe: Playing the Russian Card." *French Politics and Society* 8, no. 4 (1990): 25–40.

Deutsch, Karl W., Lewis J. Edinger, Roy C. Macridis, and Richard L. Merritt. *France, Germany, and the Western Alliance: A Study of Elite Attitudes on Economic Integration and World Politics.* New York: Scribners, 1967.

Ferro, Maurice. *De Gaulle et l'Amérique: une amitié tumultueuse.* Paris: Plon, 1973.

Grosser, Alfred. *Affaires extérieures: la politique de la France, 1944–1984.* Paris: Flammarion, 1984.

———. *French Foreign Policy under De Gaulle.* Trans. Lois Ames Pattison. Boston: Little Brown, 1967.

———. *The Western Alliance: European-American Relations since 1945.* Trans. Michael Shaw. New York: Vintage, 1982.

Harrison, Michael. *The Reluctant Ally: France and Atlantic Security.* Baltimore: Johns Hopkins University Press, 1981.

Hoffmann, Stanley. *Decline or Renewal? France since the 1930s.* New York: Viking, 1974.

Jouve, Edmond. *Le Général de Gaulle et la construction de l'Europe, 1940–1966.* 2 vols. Paris: Librarie générale de droit et de jurisprudence, 1967.

Kolodziej, Edward. *French International Policy under De Gaulle and Pompidou.* Ithaca: Cornell University Press, 1974.

Lacouture, Jean. *De Gaulle: The Ruler, 1945–1970.* Trans. Alan Sheridan. New York: Norton, 1992.

Monnet, Jean, Maurice Delarue, Jacques Putman, Claude Julien, Michel Mohrt, Paul-Marie de la Gorce, J. A. Fieschi, André Philip, Pierre Uri, Gilbert Gantier, Marc Alexandre, Serge Mallet, and Gaston Defferre. "Les Américains et nous." *La Nef* no. 26 (February–April 1966): 7–159.

Morse, Edward L. *Foreign Policy and Interdependence in Gaullist France.* Princeton: Princeton University Press, 1973.

De Gaulle: Foreign Investments and the Dollar

Bertin, Gilles Y. *L'Industrie française face aux multinationales.* Paris: La Documentation française, 1975.

———. *L'Investissement des firmes étrangères en France, 1945–1962.* Paris: Presses universitaires de France, 1963.

Brault, Olivier. "Indépendance nationale et investissements américains: la politique française à l'égard des investissements directs américains sous les présidences du général de Gaulle et de Georges Pompidou." Mémoire de maîtrise, Université de Lille III, 1986.

Delapierre, Michel, and Charles-Albert Michalet. *Les Implantations étrangères en France: stratégies et structures.* Paris: Calmann-Lévy, 1976.

Délégation à l'aménagement du territoire et à l'action régionale. *Investisse-ments étrangers et aménagement du territoire: livre blanc.* Paris: La Documentation française, 1974.

Dickie, Robert B. *Foreign Investment: France, A Case Study.* Dobbs Ferry, N.Y.: Oceana Publications, 1970.

Gervais, Jacques. *La France face aux investissements étrangers, analyse par secteurs.* Paris: Editions de l'Entreprise moderne, 1963.

Hellmann, Rainier. *Puissance et limites des multinationales.* Tours: MAME, 1974.

Johnstone, Allan W. *United States Direct Investment in France: An Investigation of the French Charges.* Cambridge, Mass.: MIT Press, 1965.

Kindleberger, Charles. "Origins of United States Direct Investments in France." *Business History Review* no. 48 (Fall 1974): 382–413.

Layton, Christopher. *Trans-Atlantic Investments.* Boulogne-sur-Seine: The Atlantic Institute, 1968.

Manuali, Louis. *La France face à l'implantation étrangère.* Paris: Société d'éditions économiques et financières, 1967.

Polier, Jonathan Wise. "Indépendance nationale et investissement étranger, une étude de cas: la politique française à l'égard des investissements américains, 1945–1967." Mémoire de maîtrise, Institut d'études politiques, Paris, 1967.

Prate, Alain. *Les Batailles économiques du général de Gaulle.* Paris: Plon, 1978.

Schmill, Erick. *Les Investissements étrangers en France.* Paris: Cujas, 1966.

Servan-Schreiber, Jean-Jacques. *The American Challenge.* Trans. Ronald Steel. New York: Atheneum, 1968.

Wormser, Olivier. "De Gaulle et la monnaie." *Etudes gaulliennes* 1, nos. 3 and 4 (July–December 1973): 124–51.

1970s and 1980s

Ardagh, John. *France Today.* New York: Viking, Penguin, 1988.

Baudrillard, Jean. *America.* Trans. Chris Turner. London: Verso, 1988.

Bernstein, Richard. *Fragile Glory: A Portrait of France and the French.* New York: Knopf, 1990.

Crozier, Michel. *The Trouble with America.* Trans. Peter Heinegg. Berkeley: University of California Press, 1984.

Ory, Pascal. *L'Entre-deux mai: histoire culturelle de la France mai 1968–mai 1981.* Paris: Seuil, 1983.

Peyrefitte, Alain. *The Trouble with France.* Trans. William Byron. New York: Knopf, 1981.

Pfaff, William. "The French Exception." *The New Yorker,* 24 January 1977, 66–75.

Pinto, Diana. "De l'Anti-Américanisme à l'Américanophilie: l'itinérarie de l'intelligentsia." *French Politics and Society* 9 (March 1985): 18–26.

———. "The Left, the Intellectuals, and Culture." In *The Mitterrand Experiment,* eds. George Ross, Stanley Hoffmann, and Sylvia Malzacher, 217–28. Oxford: Polity Press, 1987.

Ross, George. "Intellectual Spaces and Places." *French Politics and Society* 6 (July 1988): 7–16.

———. "Where Have All the Sartres Gone? The French Intelligentsia Born Again." In *Searching for The New France,* eds. James F. Hollifield and George Ross, 221–49. New York: Routledge, 1991.

Rupnik, Jacques. "Anti-Americanism and the Modern: The Image of the United States in French Public Opinion." In *France and Modernisation,* ed. John Gaffney, 189–205. London: Gowers, 1988.

Sauvage, Léo. *Les Américains: enquête sur un mythe.* Paris: Mazarine, 1983.

Thibau, Jacques. *La France colonisée.* Paris: Flammarion, 1980.

Yonnet, Paul. *Jeux, modes et masses. La société française et le moderne, 1945–1985.* Paris: Gallimard, 1985.

Index